Places of Inquiry

Places of Inquiry

Research and Advanced Education in Modern Universities

Burton R. Clark

UNIVERSITY OF CALIFORNIA PRESS
Berkeley · Los Angeles · London

University of California Press
Berkeley and Los Angeles, California

University of California Press
London, England

Copyright © 1995 by

The Regents of the University of California

Library of Congress Cataloging-in-Publication Data

Clark, Burton R.
    Places of inquiry : research and advanced education in modern
universities / Burton R. Clark.
        p.   cm.
    Includes bibliographical references (p.   ) and index.
    ISBN 0-520-08762-3 (alk. paper)
    1. Universities and colleges—Graduate work—Cross-cultural
studies.   2. Education, Higher—Aims and objectives—Cross-cultural
studies.   3. Research—Cross-cultural studies.   4. College teaching—
Cross-cultural studies.   I. Title.
LB2371.C56   1995
378.1′553—dc20   94-25325
                                                                        CIP

Printed in the United States of America

1   2   3   4   5   6   7   8   9

The paper used in this publication meets the minimum requirements of American
National Standard for Information Sciences—Permanence of Paper for Printed Library
Materials, ANSI Z39.48-1984 ∞

To Adrienne and Rajender—
for the treasures that prevail

Contents

Tables   xi

Acknowledgments   xiii

Introduction   1

PART ONE.   DISTINCTIVE NATIONAL CONFIG-
URATIONS OF ADVANCED EDUCATION AND
RESEARCH ORGANIZATION

1. The Federal Republic of Germany: Vicissitudes
of the Humboldtian Project   19

     Institutional Definition of the Humboldtian
         Attitude   21
     Twentieth-Century Travail   37
     The Institute University   50

2. Great Britain: Small Worlds, Collegiate Worlds   56

     The Exclusive Base   57
     Nationalization of Tradition   61
     Research Training in the British Context   78
     The Collegiate University   84

3. France: Subordination of the University   89
    Evolution of a National Service   91
    The Modern Complex of Universities and
        Research Centers   101
    The Academy University   112

4. The United States: Competitive Graduate Schools   116
    Emergence of the Vertical University   118
    Private Patrons and Government Funding   124
    Institutional Embodiment of Research   131
    Institutional Differentiation of Graduate
        Education   139
    The Graduate Department University   155

5. Japan: Displacement to Industry   159
    The Constraint of Graduate Education   159
    The Bureaucratic Funding Base   167
    Disciplinary Differences   171
    The Applied University   179

PART TWO. THE RESEARCH-TEACHING-STUDY
    NEXUS

6. Forces of Fragmentation   189
    Research Drift   193
    Teaching Drift   197
    Governmental and Industrial Interests   202
    Negation of the Nexus   209

7. Conditions of Integration   211
    Enabling Conditions in the National
        System   212
    Formative Conditions in the University   224
    Enacting Conditions in the Basic Unit   232
    Affirmation of the Nexus   237

8. Places of Inquiry   240
    Centrality of Inquiry in the University
        Complex   241

The Inevitability of Complexity and
  Contradiction   245
The Essential Compatibility of Research and
  Teaching   249

Notes   253

Bibliography   267

Index   281

Tables

1. Changes in Universities Funding Council Allocations
    to British Universities, 1991–1992 to 1993–1994   72
2. Top Twenty American Universities in Science and
    Engineering R&D Expenditures, 1987   134
3. World Share of Scientific Literature, by Country,
    1981–1985   138
4. Undergraduate and Graduate Courses in American
    Institutions, by Type of University and College, 1977 148
5. Undergraduate and Graduate Enrollment in Leading
    American Universities, 1991   151

Acknowledgments

This volume is the second in a two-volume work that has flowed from a research project begun in 1987. That study involved collaborators in five countries, entailed two years of fieldwork on their part, and led to an edited first volume entitled *The Research Foundations of Graduate Education*. The research and the earlier publication have provided the primary footing for my effort in this second volume to conceptualize anew the contemporary university from the vantage point of the research function and its relationship to teaching and training. I am deeply indebted to the colleagues who carried out the fieldwork for this study, wrote the chapters of the first comparative volume, and have continued to give me the benefit of their wisdom: Tony Becher, Richard Edelstein, Claudius Gellert, Patricia J. Gumport, Mary Henkel, Tatsuo Kawashima, Maurice Kogan, Fumihiro Maruyama, Guy Neave, and Morikazu Ushiogi. In a critical review of the penultimate draft of this book, Tony Becher and Ulrich Teichler offered insights and criticisms from which I have benefited greatly. Patricia Gumport and Fumihiro Maruyama provided additional data at critical junctures in this late effort. None of these colleagues should be held responsible for my characterization of their national systems of academic research and advanced education. The interpretive comparisons offered in this volume are entirely my own.

For financial support that made possible an extended international effort involving investigations in four countries outside the United States, I wish to thank again the Spencer Education Foundation for a generous research grant made in 1987. During the ensuing years I have also been materially assisted by the opportunity to serve as the first incumbent (1980–1991) of the Allan M. Cartter Chair in the study of higher education at the University of California, Los Angeles. I want to thank the university, the UCLA Graduate School of Education, and those outside the university who helped to fund the chair, preeminently Jill Cartter, for moral as well as financial support that has favored sustained research and reflection.

Patricia Smith, my administrative assistant at UCLA, kept the preparation of this volume on track during the course of revisions that stretched over three years. Françoise Quéval, a graduate student at the time, gathered additional needed institutional data on American universities.

Articles based on this study, already published and drawn on in the course of preparing this manuscript, appeared as follows:

"The Research Foundations of Graduate Education: A Five-Country Exploration." Keynote Address, 30th Annual Meeting (1990), and Occasional Paper. Washington, D.C.: Council of Graduate Schools, 1991.

"The Fragmentation of Research, Teaching and Study: An Exploratory Essay." In *University and Society: Essays on the Social Role of Research and Higher Education*, edited by Martin A. Trow and Thorsten Nybom, 101–111. London: Jessica Kingsley Publishers, 1991.

"Graduate Education and Research Training." In *Research and Higher Education: The United Kingdom and the United States*, edited by Thomas G. Whiston and Roger L. Geiger, 138–150. Buckingham, England: Society for Research into Higher Education and Open University Press, 1992.

Burton R. Clark
Santa Monica, California
May, 1993

Introduction

The German university reform in the early decades of the nineteenth century, to which we commonly attach the name of Wilhelm von Humboldt, established as an enduring principle the idea of a unity of research, teaching, and study. Variously voiced in later practice, in Germany and elsewhere, this academic ideology established tenets that link the production and dissemination of knowledge. Those who teach at the most advanced levels of the educational system, themselves research centered, should train students for research by involving them in research. In laboratories and seminars, students become investigators as they seek answers to research problems that professors specify or that they themselves initiate. Professors and students in effect become research colleagues, joining hands in a common search for the truth in the form of new knowledge. With research serving as the primary component, the role of the university professor blends research and teaching: research activity quite rightfully becomes a mode of instruction. The student role fuses research and learning: research activity is transformed into a mode of study. Thus, orienting both professors and students, research folds teaching and study into a seamless web of commitment to the advancement of knowledge. A close research-teaching-study nexus is forged.

Actions taken historically in the name of the Humboldtian principle led to *the* academic revolution. In the eight centuries of university life in the Western world that have stretched from twelfth-century Bologna and Paris to twentieth-century Stanford and Tokyo, no other change compares with the emergence and development of the modern research university. At the core of this new form, the effected idea of "education through science"—more broadly, education founded on inquiry—replaced the defense of dogma with an open-ended search for an evolving truth. It pushed beyond professional training to the pursuit of knowledge both for its own sake and for its practical utility. The commitment to inquiry generated a forward-looking attitude. When possessed by its dictates, the orientation of faculty and students alike shifted from past knowledge to future knowledge: those caught up in inquiry would have a distinct preference for the new. A site of advanced education would be foremost a research site.

As a transforming idea, the Humboldtian principle in various guises became deeply influential in late nineteenth- and twentieth-century development of higher education in the most advanced nations, serving as a particularly dominating concept in first German and then American universities. For well over a century, the concept has been widely and concretely expressed in organizational use of the teaching-research seminar and laboratory as primary vehicles of advanced education. It has found increasing resonance in funding that presupposes professors will spend a third to a half of their time in research. In many countries the idea of education through science is reflected in the definition of advanced students as "research students" who invest in research-based theses from the day they embark on doctoral work. Inquiry-based education has an affinity with the modern organization of universities around specialized subjects, a type of knowledge-centeredness that requires future higher education teachers to train in the theory and method of particular disciplines. A unity of research, teaching, and study may have been formally denied in such central international models of higher education as the French and Soviet systems, where much research has been deliberately concentrated in outside academies and thereby separated from university teaching and study. But even in these frameworks, many professors have engaged in research, based their teaching on their research specialty, and involved advanced students in research projects. Dominant academics in societies that define themselves as advanced in their devotion to science and scholarship have commonly, often unconsciously, assumed the cogency of the unity principle.

As an imposing case, American academics took up this idea in the late nineteenth century. The nearly ten thousand American scholars who by 1900 had made the transatlantic pilgrimage to the great centers of academic research in Europe, preeminently German universities, came home firmly committed to the idea of academic research and re-search-based instruction and learning. They then had to adapt the idea to American conditions, and, after a long struggle, they invented the graduate school as a higher tier within which research and advanced training could be comfortably located. The American higher education system then moved rapidly in a few decades from the age of the college, prominent for two and a half centuries since the early colonial days, to the age of the university—a shift that was *the* American academic revolution. The set of universities invested most heavily in research became the dominant sector, prestigious and powerful. In the late twentieth century, a greatly expanded set of much larger universities are more than ever possessed by a sturdy belief that throughout the sciences, the social sciences, and even the humanities and the arts, advanced education should be, must be, closely related to inquiry.

But in the United States and elsewhere, the relationship of research to teaching and learning has grown increasingly complex, ambiguous, and controversial. Often loose and indirect at best, it is seemingly full of contentious difficulties. The research orientation may cramp other university commitments, notably professional education and general education of undergraduates. Reciprocally, it is often constrained by the other activities in which universities and colleges are engaged. In his classic study of higher education in Britain, France, Germany, and the United States, Joseph Ben-David made the striking point that "far from being a natural match, research and teaching can be organized within a single framework only under specific conditions."[1] Broad conditions may be readily noted which appear to be distinctly hostile to a unifying framework. With each passing decade, the scientific estate and the higher education system, each larger and internally more differentiated, develop some diverging interests. The science project has its own mandates, ones readily observed in the self-elaborating activities of scientific specialties and the substantial development of research in industry, government departments, and independent research institutes. In turn, higher education institutions are driven by imperatives other than those that follow from the interests of science. When academic staff are involved in the general education of beginning students or the professional training of nonscientific experts, they are shaped by expectations and duties that have little to do with research itself or with the training of future generations of researchers.

Science and higher education have also become drawn into fuller and more complicated relationships with patrons, principally national governments, who have their own agendas and expectations. Even in those systems where the historic commitment to integration has been strongest, governmental interests may encourage a drift of research out of higher education. Hard questions are raised. Is the university really the best home for science, especially in fields that now require enormously expensive equipment and large bureaucracies? Is the most advanced level of university study, encompassing the humanities, the social sciences, numerous professional fields, and the natural sciences, best served when it trails along as handmaiden to the research imperative? Is it not best to have most professors teach a body of established knowledge and leave inquiry to separate cadres of researchers who may be located outside as well as inside the academy?

To investigate the problematic state of the Humboldtian principle near the end of the twentieth century, especially in major systems of higher education, the general problem can be stated in four broad questions:

- To what extent in varied national and institutional settings is the execution of academic research brought together with the training of future generations of scholars, researchers, and even professional practitioners?

- What are the primary conditions found in modern universities, especially in their organizational structures, that promote a sturdy research-teaching-study nexus?

- What outside institutions, if any, on their own or in conjunction with universities, provide a productive three-way relationship?

- How do changes in the organization and funding of research shape the training of advanced scholars?

A host of more specific questions follow. At the most advanced levels of higher education in other countries, what arrangements for faculty and students parallel the American graduate level? In advanced programs, do students pursue sequences of courses or plunge directly into research—or perhaps interrelate course work and research activity? Do advanced students in various national systems work on their own, isolated from professorial advisers and mentors for long periods of time, or are they in one fashion or another systematically included in seminars and laboratories that professors direct? How fare the humanities and social sciences, compared to the sciences, in maintaining research environments for students in mass universities?

In search of answers, this study compares university arrangements in the five major countries of the Western world: Germany, Britain, France, United States, and Japan. The analysis is rooted in an investigation carried out between 1987 and 1990 by allied experts in these nations.[2] The requisite research explored both the evolved macroframeworks of research and education and the microinteractions of researchers, professors, and students in departments and other base units. The results of the field research and analysis carried out by the country experts, within a common framework, were reported in a companion volume (*The Research Foundations of Graduate Education: Germany, Britain, France, United States, Japan,* edited by Burton R. Clark; hereafter referred to as *Research Foundations*). These detailed country-based papers have provided a broad empirical foundation for efforts in this volume: (a) to highlight by cross-national comparison the distinctive configurations of research and advanced education found in each country; (b) to compare conditions over time, especially from the late nineteenth century to the late twentieth century, with Germany as the base point for comparison in the earlier period and the United States in the latter; and, most important, (c) to identify generic processes and common trends. In these efforts, I have consulted a wider literature that includes both relevant work in the history and sociology of science and analyses of science policy and higher education policy that have proliferated in the decades since World War II. A comparative analysis that embraces five countries and seeks in each case to develop a rounded interpretation necessarily must make heavy use of secondary sources. Fortunately, materials written in English on the German, French, and Japanese systems have become abundant in recent years; they extend the analytical results offered in *Research Foundations* by colleagues who both examined primary source materials and carried out interviews by means of the mother tongue.

Each nation possesses an evolved overarching structure that frames the science–higher education relationship. Reflecting varied national traditions, settings, and pathways of development, these structures are very different. No one can sensibly pretend, for example, that France and the United States provide similar institutional frames for either research or advanced education. But neither are all features country-specific, unique to national context. Certain trends and tendencies are found everywhere in advanced industrial societies, although often played out in varying degree and in different ways. The transition from elite to mass higher education works its will in the personnel struc-

ture and the curriculum of the university; the specialization of knowledge and technique in nearly every academic discipline can nowhere be
ignored in its impact on the scale and scope of academic enterprises. As
outcomes, common features are found across nations in how the modern organization of research interacts with the modern organization of
advanced teaching and training: certain primary features overflow national boundaries. A host of complexities, without undue distortion,
can be reduced to a simplicity that offers systematic explanation. Partic-
ularities of each national system can then be related to generic forces
that affect all modern and modernizing systems.

Research Foundations made clear that developments in the last half
of the twentieth century have everywhere deepened the complexity of
the research-education relationship. With the scale of operations having grown enormously since World War II, each domain has become
more dependent on governmental financial patronage, producing a
complicated relationship between a research system, a system of advanced (graduate) education, and a funding system. For one thing, the
entire research system is increasingly spread across governmental laboratories, industry, and nonprofit institutes as well as a larger number of
higher education institutions. What, then, is the university share? How
is research distributed within the university complex? How does the
funding system affect the external and internal distributions? Especially
in expensive scientific fields, government research funds have increasingly loomed large in the subsidy of professors and students as well as
in the support of plant, equipment, and auxiliary research personnel.
The issue then arises of how much government will thereby steer research, leading to "mandated science," in comparison to steerage by
scientists' choice of projects and approaches, following the dictates of
"disciplinary science." Different logics of development follow, carrying
academic teaching and student training in their wake.

The comparative analysis of national systems of higher education is
complicated by the problem of comparability of levels of instruction
and learning. Especially useful is a generic distinction between preadvanced and advanced. In the United States, Britain, and Japan, this distinction translates well into undergraduate and graduate, or as the latter
is known in Britain, "postgraduate." Each system offers the bachelor's
degree to mark the end of the first phase; each portrays that first level as
a stage in which some significant part is or should be devoted to relatively broad education or the shaping of character. The second stage is
then given over to intense specialization. However, in Germany, France,

and generally elsewhere in Europe, the concepts of undergraduate and graduate have not been generally used. In some cases all students have been seen as advanced, that is, ready to pursue a specialty. The stage leading to the first major degree, now often necessitating some five to seven years or more of study, emphasizes specialization; students often terminate with a major thesis and a degree that connect closely with professional qualification. A second formal tier similar to "graduate school" has not then been deemed necessary and has had little or no organizational life. Better then to speak analytically of preadvanced and advanced and find where in the educational sequence one becomes the other.

Levels of higher education can also sometimes be specified as introductory, intermediate, and advanced, paralleling, for example, the definition in France of first, second, and third "cycles" or the well-understood distinction made in the American system between lower-division undergraduate, upper-division undergraduate, and graduate. In the country descriptions, I have used the terminology that is most appropriate to the national context, with occasional effort to draw parallels to the levels of other systems. "Graduate education" is also sometimes used as synonymous with advanced education: a common designation in the American system, it is both easily understood in Britain and Japan and increasingly familiar to officials and academics in other national systems. Whatever the terms, any search for the location of academic research and its possible close connection to teaching and learning has to place the most advanced programs, especially doctoral work, at the center of attention.

In five chapters that maintain country cohesion, Part One lays the foundation for comparative analysis. Devoted in turn to Germany, Britain, France, the United States, and Japan, these accounts depict national configurations. Paralleling the structure of *Research Foundations*, they represent a broad effort to understand distinctive features of national settings that are clarified and highlighted by international comparison. The distinctive patterns are shown to be historical products of enduring conditions within and outside the higher education system *and* to be shaped increasingly in the late twentieth century by the role of government in supporting science and higher education.

Chapter 1 establishes the nineteenth-century baseline for cross-national comparison by depicting how German universities developed and expressed a research outlook in such new organizational tools as the research-teaching laboratory and the inquiry-oriented seminar.

In generic terms, the academic research group was born—and then institutionalized in an "institute" form of basic-unit organization. A new kind of academic emerged in the form of the research disciplinarian. This new breed—empirical, pragmatic, and even utilitarian—drew on strands of Humboldtian thought to rationalize their cause. Competition among decentralized universities favored the new academics who exemplified research prowess and cast reputations based on research output and cutting-edge training of advanced students in intimate mentor-apprentice relationships. Throughout the last half of the nineteenth century and well into the twentieth, the German university was a special kind of place, a veritable magnet that drew scholars from other countries who wanted to learn the methods of systematic disciplinary inquiry.

But even as Humboldtian doctrine became Holy Writ subject to a variety of self-serving interpretations, German universities in the twentieth century moved over decades from one societal calamity to another: war, Weimar, fascism, war. Rebuilt between 1945 and 1960, and the research transition reestablished, the universities then entered the age of mass higher education at an extremely rapid rate in the 1960s and 1970s. Attempting to cling to old structures and classic traditions, hence finding out the hard way that mass higher education is not simply elite higher education written five or ten times larger, the universities have found themselves in an awkward muddle. Humboldtian doctrine remains an intellectual force that helps to keep research in the university and closely related to the selection and training of *some* advanced students, but at the same time it has become a misrepresentation of reality in badly overloaded mass universities. The German system struggles to establish a productive differentiation among and within institutions that will maintain a unity of research, teaching, and study in certain locales, even as the historic linkage is reluctantly surrendered in institutions that are not fully research based and especially at introductory and intermediate levels of university instruction. In Germany, as in many other countries, the trend is toward greater institutional concentration within the system at large of research-based teaching and learning. In the early 1990s there is growing interest in the possibilities of "graduate school." But throughout all the macroturmoil, the understructure of the German university has continued to reflect the genetic imprints of nineteenth-century development. Exercising the leverage of cross-national comparison, we may characterize it as "the institute university."

Chapter 2 depicts the evolution and current structure of British higher education in a way that highlights the strain placed on "postgraduate" education and its research underpinnings by thorough nationalization of formerly autonomous universities known historically for their intimate faculty-student relationships and high-quality undergraduate instruction. A "collegiate" tradition is deeply rooted, exemplified in the extreme in the college structure of Oxford and Cambridge and expressed across the university system until the late 1980s in such academic delights as an 8 : 1 student/teacher ratio and student tutorials. We observe small departments in small universities in a national system that, at least up to the late 1980s, lagged behind its neighbors on the European continent, and even farther behind the United States and Japan, in expansion into mass higher education. The British problem of supporting research-based advanced education has deepened and taken on a new coloration as heavy fiscal constraint exercised by an often unsympathetic, even hostile, government has intensified the constraints of an already small undergraduate-centered system. As a result, the British university complex, long deeply committed to sharp selection and high quality, is hard-pressed to keep pace internationally in scale and scope of academic research and output of scientists and engineers. Not least of the difficulties in a highly stressed system has been a brain drain, particularly to American universities, that grew worse in the 1980s and threatens to intensify whenever U.S. competitors find top talent in short supply in their own domestic academic labor market. In a comparative frame, we observe "the collegiate university."

Chapter 3 explicates research activity and training within the high exceptionalism of French higher education: the unusual pattern of a separate sector, the *grandes écoles*, that in virtually monopolizing the selection, training, and placement of elites occupies a role normally exercised elsewhere by leading universities; the unusual (in the Western world) second pattern of a massive research sector, in particular the National Center for Scientific Research (CNRS), assigned the central place in government-funded research; and the universities then operating as the party of the third part, markedly inferior to the other two sectors in status and relatively impoverished in resources. Here the research footing of advanced education has depended largely on byzantine cross-sector relations between various types of CNRS laboratories and universities that are increasingly specialized around major blocs of subjects. Laboratories operate on university grounds without falling under university control; they bring prestige to the universities, not the other way around. To gain access to research training and later to laboratory and academic posts, French university students must climb over imposing curricular and degree hurdles and battle for sponsorship, in the context of a highly centralized national system that swept into mass higher education at an exceedingly rapid rate and finds no end to expansion in sight. While much macro change may still be in the offing, especially if long-promised decentralization of control finally takes hold, the primacy of control over research exercised by the CNRS and other outside establishments leads to a characterization of the French university as "the academy university."

Chapters 1 through 3 make clear that Germany, Britain, and France—the classic European centers of learning long known for their worldwide influence—possess critical differences in the orientation and structure of higher education and in how they thereby unite research with teaching and learning. Observing their distinctive configurations, an American is hard put to say which is the most unusual. Is it the guaranteed opportunity for qualified secondary school graduates in Germany to select their fields of university study (for the most part) *and* their universities *and*, still in 1990, to wander at will among them if they so wish, leaving the universities poorly equipped to shape their own character? Or is it the donnish concentration of British academics on the already-specialized undergraduate student, with lingering visions of tutorials in cloistered settings, that marginalizes postgraduate students? Or is it the contentious centralization of control found in French higher education that causes faculty and students to react adversely to announced plans that mark the time of national politicians rotating through the education ministry? But however striking such differences, they are only the beginning of variation found in national complexes. Continua of critical differences are greatly extended when we turn to the fourth and fifth major centers of learning in the Western world, the United States and Japan.

The American higher education configuration has long been difficult for foreign observers to grasp and represents a puzzlement for homegrown experts. In comparison to all other national systems, American higher education overall is strikingly large, decentralized, diversified, competitive, and entrepreneurial. Within an unplanned system in which hundreds of universities and colleges, public and private, compete, imitate, and diverge, a level of advanced education in the shape of formal graduate schools received structural and symbolic distinction a century ago, organizationally located to stand apart from the undergraduate realm and aside from the training offered in professional schools operating at undergraduate and increasingly at graduate levels. The graduate school invention was born of American conditions that had put secondary education and first-degree higher education on an entirely different footing from that found in Europe. In a system of more structured "vertical universities," a competitive search among universities for resources and prestige has for some decades backed the growth of research-based doctoral programs: by international standards, the output of Ph.D.'s is huge. Operationally, the research imperative has been expressed in a vast array of courses, requirements, seminars, and laboratories that compose an intricate educational infrastructure for advanced study. But graduate schools are not spread throughout the length and breadth of the system: the vast majority of colleges and universities are undergraduate centered and oriented to teaching that is not closely connected to research. With open access leading toward nigh-universal participation, only massive differentiation of sectors has protected a research-oriented realm within which the graduate school has prospered. Particularly among some fifty to one hundred "research universities," we find strong research foundations for advanced education. It is within these massive institutions that the old ideal of a unity of research, teaching, and study appears in a striking modern form. Comparatively, an appropriate characterization is that of "the graduate department university."

Japan presents a highly unusual national configuration. In a nation known for both robust research and vigorous pursuit of education, an intricate chain of historical and contemporary conditions has severely constrained the universities from developing strength at an advanced level. Private universities have absorbed most of the mass demand for higher education, but, heavily dependent on tuition income, they have remained undergraduate centered and little invested in expensive graduate programs. The leading national public universities, centers of elite recruitment and placement, have eagerly sought to establish graduate schools, but funds have been meager and potential students have been lured to industry. Intensely bureaucratic funding has led more to formula-driven distribution of fair shares than to merit-based support. In addition, for a long time academics and researchers have been able to receive doctoral degrees in one way or another without serious work in a doctoral program. The universities have adapted to a pattern in which Japanese industry has become a powerhouse of applied research and related research training and increasingly of basic research. In search of the research foundations of advanced education, we find a striking case of displacement to industry. University strength lies particularly in training in engineering. An appropriate comparative characterization is "the applied university."

In Part Two, complicated country configurations give way to analytical simplification and the order of comparative concepts. The concept of a research-teaching-study nexus is established as an organizing idea that has clear advantages over old bromides about "research and teaching."[3] Professors clearly can engage in research that is distant from their teaching, and they can teach codified knowledge that is a veritable light-year away from whatever is going on in research circles. Most important, "research and teaching" generally has had little to say about the involvement of students. The element of "study" may be readily left out, simply assumed to take place in the face of a common awareness that professors may integrate their own participation in research activities and teaching activities without thereby including students to any significant degree. In contrast, the idea of a three-component nexus insists that we determine how research becomes simultaneously interfused with teaching *and* study. The "how" is bound up in numerous conditions: organizationally, a tug of war exists between forces of fragmentation that pull the nexus apart, even negate it, and forces of integration that sustain and affirm it.

Chapter 6 sets forth fragmenting forces. From among the national variations observed in Part One, two generic trends are identified. The needs of modern research dictate that an increasing share of research activities become located outside teaching departments and, further, outside universities. Such settings may or may not have their own forms of instruction and participation of research apprentices; they clearly remove research activity from the teaching units and central curricular frameworks of the universities. This general tendency is conceptualized as "research drift." In turn, the needs of modern mass higher education, with enrollments of beginning and intermediate students expanded five- and tenfold and more, set in motion the strong tides of a "teaching drift" in which teaching pulls away from research-centered departments and universities into all-teaching locales and institutions. Already far advanced in the American and Japanese systems, this tendency is an insistent phenomenon in systems that have more recently come into the age of mass higher education. For this reason alone, the nexus cannot everywhere hold. Staff and students are increasingly located formally in nonresearch settings.

Research drift and teaching drift are encouraged by certain compelling concerns of modern government and industry. As governments seek to contain the spiraling costs of expensive research and expensive advanced levels of university training, they move to concentrate the nexus in a minority of settings while removing it from the majority. As they become anxious to hasten scientific productivity for reasons of economic progress, they are also inclined to subsidize all-research institutes outside of university settings. In turn, industry is primarily interested in firm-enhancing research. In industrial "R&D," research is supposed to lead to development that is firm- and sector-specific. Under R&D dictates, research can be pulled aside in separate locales; general teaching and training can be seen as someone else's business. Together, central governmental and industrial interests have powerful roles as fragmenting forces.

Chapter 7 examines in considerable detail the opposite side of the coin. The Humboldtian ideal is hardly extinct; the research-teaching-study nexus is still strongly operative wherever universities approach modernity. Integrative conditions appear at various levels of national systems. In the system at large, broad conditions set an enabling framework: a differentiation of institutions into research and nonresearch sectors permits a limited number of institutions to concentrate intensely on research and advanced education; institutional competition based on research-gained prestige becomes a favorable motivational force; certain modes of control and funding support the research-teaching-study nexus better than do others; latter-day versions of Humboldtian ideology serve as beliefs that insist on research-grounded training. At the institutional level, specific formative conditions occur. Foremost is the separation of a graduate level, an increasingly necessary component if research is to remain in the university framework intermingled with teaching and study. This distinctive strength of the American system is increasingly pursued as a needed structural development by universities in other countries. Diversified funding that permits much university self-determination is also critical, allowing, if necessary, some cross-subsidization that bolsters research and research training.

Conditions found at these higher levels constitute a general framework for the specific settings of basic units where teachers and students are physically located and possibly immersed in a research environment. What matters most are the conditions of enactment found in such operational units as the department, the chair, and the research institute. And here there are striking findings. Academics committed to the preparation of researchers have long known that advanced students should be involved in research laboratories or in inquiry-oriented seminars that serve in the humanities and social sciences as a parallel to laboratories in the sciences. The nineteenth-century lesson still holds: the academic research group is essential. The mentor-apprentice relationship is still required, especially to transmit tacit components of knowledge, attitude, and approach. But under modern conditions more is needed: advanced students increasingly need a life of study that goes beyond the limits of what research groups can provide. That life is generated in a "departmental" provision of courses and requirements that is more in tune with the substantive breadth of broad disciplines. This second formation is needed to transmit broader arrays of theory and method, outlook and skill. In generic terms, a "teaching group" is combined with the historic research group.

The concluding chapter, normative in tone, points to the necessity of basing analysis and reform on a knowledge or inquiry model of modern systems of higher education. This conception embraces research imperatives and the processes of scientific advance as well as educational imperatives and the processes of student development.[4] It corrects the distortions that are introduced when simplistic views juxtapose teaching and research in a hostile relationship. Such views have tended to follow from fixations on a single purpose that avoid the necessary multisidedness and complexities of modern universities. In the United States, for example, the most glaring case of such fixation has been the tendency in reform to concentrate on undergraduate education and its weaknesses in providing a liberal or general education. Graduate students are ignored; professional education is brushed aside. Undergraduate education is defined as a good thing, while research and research training are portrayed in a negative light. Instead of pursuing the linkages and complementarity of research and teaching, graduate and undergraduate education, critics bemoan opposition and see only destructive competition. In contrast, a knowledge perspective that embraces discovery as well as dissemination leads toward a more balanced discussion in which the role played by research activity and research-based graduate education, once explicated as sought here, can be placed alongside professional education and the ever-problematic preadvanced education of undergraduates. Research and teaching—and student learning—have an essential compatibility that will only grow stronger in the decades that lie ahead. A society rooted in inquiry as a means of problem solving, if not already here, is just around the corner.

Near the end of the twentieth century, the Humboldtian quest of 1810 is still with us. The ideal formulation set forth almost two centuries ago has now been transmuted into the most critical question that can be posed about modern systems of higher education: How do they interrelate the production and dissemination of knowledge? It is not possible to understand modern higher education without first grasping how it is involved in the production of knowledge and then determining how that task is related to the tasks of teaching and public service. Not only basic to the preparation of future producers of knowledge, the research-training linkage pursued in this study is also central in the ongoing revision of the knowledge base that undergirds both general education and specialized professional training.

At the cutting edge of modern society, the transfer of research-generated new knowledge and technique to the minds of students may well be the most important form of knowledge transfer. Such education amounts to a fast track in the sophistication of advanced human capital. The institutional provision of that track requires advanced university programs and degree levels within which, as much as possible, research, teaching, and study still form a seamless blend. As fully embedded research activity and related training slip away from the undergraduate realm, they find their modern home in graduate education.

Approaching the twenty-first century, the intellectual moment favors even more than in the recent past the universities that best integrate research activity and research training with teaching and study. The task in the pages that follow is to show how such integration is strengthened or weakened as generic forces and common trends interact with national configurations of university organization.

Distinctive National Configurations of Advanced Education and Research Organization

CHAPTER ONE

The Federal Republic of Germany

Vicissitudes of the Humboldtian Project

It all began in early nineteenth-century Germany, for it was there that ideology and interest first came together powerfully and in a sustainable fashion to turn research into a university phenomenon. It was there that the principle of a unity of research and teaching (*Einheit von Forschung und Lehre*) was first established. In its pure Humboldtian form, the Germanic conception insisted that university teachers become investigators who use the findings of recent research in their teaching. Their students, whether future doctors, teachers, civil servants, or academicians, should also engage in research activity. Together, teacher and student would pursue the truth. Humboldt offered an original and striking formulation.

> One unique feature of higher intellectual institutions is that they conceive of science and scholarship as dealing with ultimately inexhaustible tasks: this means that they are engaged in an unceasing process of inquiry. The lower levels of education present closed and settled bodies of knowledge. The relation between teacher and pupil at the higher level is a different one from what it was at the lower levels. At the higher level, the teacher does not exist for the sake of the student; both teacher and student have their justification in the common pursuit of knowledge.[1]

Here was the formulation for all time that put the creation of new knowledge as well as the revision of old ideas first among the tasks of higher education. "An unceasing process of inquiry" was placed in the driver's seat. Seekers one and all, teachers and students were simply co-researchers.

Like much German idealism, this early nineteenth-century formulation was quite fanciful. The general attitude and larger plan of which
it was a part, suffused with high-blown rhetoric, offered comforting
but confusing ambiguity. Contradictory actions could claim its paren-
tage, and within a few decades actual practices would stray far afield
from what such ideological founding fathers as Johann Fichte, Friedrich von Schelling, and Friedrich Schleiermacher, as well as Humboldt,
had in mind. But the broad principle that stressed the primacy of
inquiry provided an ideological umbrella under which German universities increasingly became premier educational centers. From the second
decade of the nineteenth century onward, a new breed of academic
effectively learned in these universities how to put research foundations
under the house of teaching and learning. And for over fifty years the
secrets of this new framework were virtually a German monopoly.
"Until about the 1870s, the German universities were virtually the
only institutions in the world in which a student could obtain training
in how to do scientific or scholarly research."[2] Up to the turn of the
present century and beyond, some alert English scholars crossed the
channel, a much larger number of Americans made the long and difficult transatlantic voyage, and a goodly number of Japanese would-be
academic researchers came all the way from Tokyo and Kyoto to pursue the means of working at the frontiers of knowledge and, on returning home, to attempt to graft research components onto their own
system of higher education. Mighty were the German chair-holding
professors in the last half of the nineteenth century and well into the
twentieth. They stood at the pinnacle of German culture and were recognized internationally as the leaders in a new world of research-based
higher education. Their universities in Berlin, Heidelberg, Tübingen,
Munich, and other German cities were the first true "research universities," a designation that would dominate internationally in the second
half of the present century. Here the academic commitment to research
was not only born but developed into a major institutional form. A different dynamic had been turned loose.

Thus what the German academic system became in the nineteenth
century is doubly important for understanding connections among research, teaching, and study. A genetic imprint was established for the
system itself, one that would strongly persist in the twentieth century;
and the German system became a long-sustained exemplar internationally of *how* to turn research into a foundation for advanced teaching
and study. Certain operational tools were fashioned which have had

lasting import in Germany and elsewhere, organizational devices that served well under certain conditions. In the twentieth century, however, radically altered settings have put enormous pressure on a deeply entrenched framework to adapt and change. The old ways have not only been increasingly challenged at home, particularly in the post-1960 decades, but they have been outdistanced by the new tools and procedures of another nation, the United States, which, although initiated in the late nineteenth century, blossomed after World War II. Nevertheless, nineteenth-century Germany is where historical and structural explanation begins.

INSTITUTIONAL DEFINITION OF THE HUMBOLDTIAN ATTITUDE

A principle is one thing and practice quite another. Multisided from the outset and hardly a clear set of directives, Humboldtian doctrine contained ideas that lent themselves to various interpretations and pursuits. Going off in one direction were sentiments that helped to turn loose the research imperative in whatever form it might evolve. Inquiry for its own sake was foremost. Related to it was the strong assertion of *Lehrfreiheit* and *Lernfreiheit*, concepts of freedom of teaching and freedom of learning that have persisted in Germany to the present day. For a fruitful common engagement in the pursuit of truth, professors and students needed to be free not only from state supervision but also from the constraint of mundane requirements that then as now would normally dot the curriculum and narrow the pathways of academic life. The "curriculum" would be whatever professors chose to do in their own inquiries and whatever research topics the students pursued. Directly based on current research, the teaching "program" would be the opposite of the fixed classical curriculum. Students were similarly liberated, free to choose universities and subjects to the point of wandering among them, even free not to study for long periods of time. As Lehrfreiheit and Lehnfreiheit became Holy Writ, professorial options and student choices were widened even further than what took place in American higher education in the last decades of the nineteenth century under the sway of the elective principle. Decades earlier in Germany, extreme freedom was seen to go hand-in-hand with the unceasing process of inquiry. The first would maximize the second; both would serve the production of knowledge.

At the same time, the original doctrine of Humboldtianism located this new emphasis on unlimited and unfettered inquiry within a broad humanistic concern: the research commitment should enlighten and help create a rationally organized society. Education through inquiry would lead to informed, rounded personalities who would lift German culture to new heights. *Wissenschaft*, knowledge, which entails "the unfolding of mind as it comes to understand itself through study and learning," was seen as closely connected to *Bildung*, self-formulation or self-realization, "centering on the individual's efforts to achieve intellectual or spiritual perfection."[3] The humanistic side of the Humboldtian ideology could not have been stronger: the search for truth, the "unceasing process of inquiry," should combine with ambition to bring about a correct life.

Margareta Bertilsson has aptly characterized the Humboldtian ideal of the university as "extravagant," pointing to not one but four imperatives: it would not only unite research and teaching but would also "unite through philosophy the various empirical sciences," *and* "unite science and general upbringing," *and* "unite science with universal enlightenment."[4] Thus understood, rather than serve as an apologia and a directive for highly specialized research, the Berlin doctrine of 1810 in all its fullness was actually a variant of what is now called liberal education. The new form of university was even warned to be on guard against the tendency already afoot in the natural sciences toward "excessively" empirical or utilitarian research. This type of activity should be placed "under the safe control of appropriate disciplines within the philosophy faculty such as "natural philosophy,' or shunted aside in one of the professional faculties, notably medicine, or placed in separate technical universities."[5]

But it was not long before the changing realities of early nineteenth-century academic life caught up with and pushed aside many of the tenets in this fanciful package of ideas. Although, as put by William Muir, "the University of Berlin opened in October, 1810, with a faculty hand-picked by Humboldt ... it did not stick for long to the course he had plotted for it."[6] For one, most students were still found in professional pursuits.

> In point of fact, the great majority of students did not proceed toward degrees or even enroll in the seminars that taught the research procedures necessary to carry out advanced investigation. Rather, they registered in the lecture courses that prepared them for the professional examinations in which they were interested. Even the philosophy faculty became largely

quasi-professional, as it provided the instruction leading to the qualification required for teaching in the *Gymnasia*, the reformed secondary schools that Humboldt had created.[7]

Whether in Berlin or elsewhere in Germany, the university was still largely a place for utilitarian instruction. Additionally, those students who lived in "student corporations," immersed in the social forms of aristocratic Junkerdom, could avoid all contact with the ideal life that the Humboldtian doctrine portrayed. Otto von Bismarck (1815–1898), later the first chancellor of the German Empire (1871–1890), was one such student. His student experience at Göttingen, reported in his *Reflections and Reminiscences*, "may be taken as symptomatic of the cavalier life-style: much drinking and dueling interrupted by only superficial attention to studies, usually in law."[8] The enormous space for student choice created by Lernfreiheit, freedom of study, played into the hands of those students from Junker families who came to the university for its social life—"the mindless self-indulgences of the saber-wielding fraternity students"[9]—and passed final examinations after a few weeks or months of cramming. Utilitarian and social interests took the majority of students away from the pursuit of inquiry.

Most important, the interests of professors in the broadly constructed philosophy faculty from the early nineteenth century onward were shaped by that emerging vehicle of modern science, the academic discipline, "a particular field of knowledge differentiated from the rest by the research questions it asked and the technical skills that had to be learned to answer these questions."[10] Disciplinary specialization gradually developed its own dynamics: as focused research produced new findings, it created a larger and deeper body of specific cognitive material that had to be taught and learned; from that expanded and more esoteric base, professors and students pushed on in successive waves with ever more pointed inquiries that produced still more specialized knowledge. Such disciplinary self-amplification was encouraged and given room to operate by the first part of the Humboldtian doctrine, that of unity of research and teaching, essentially "education through science." The other unities identified by Bertilsson were soon ignored by hosts of German academics; new generations of natural scientists "plunged with a vengeance into nuts-and-bolts laboratory work and sneered at attempts at speculative or integrative theorizing."[11] Wrapped around the research imperative, new academic interests, not the ideals of Humboldt, became the engine driving nineteenth-century German science and scholarship.

THE OPERATIONAL TOOLS

Those interests were to find lasting embodiment and ongoing support in two gradually emerging institutional forms: the teaching-research laboratory and the teaching-research seminar. The classic case and enormously influential model of what Humboldtian doctrine was to mean in actual practice was the laboratory organized and directed by a chemist, Justus Liebig, in the small provincial university of Giessen beginning in 1826 and lasting for three decades. Detailed analyses by historians of science have shown that the orientations and practices of this "first 'large-scale' modern teaching-research laboratory" were not deduced from broad ideals and firmly conceived plans but rather emerged as practical solutions to material conditions and emergent interests. According to Frederic L. Holmes, it is implausible that Liebig could even have envisioned during the 1820s the kind of institution he would be heading in 1840; the mature form of the institute was largely the "unplanned outcome of a series of small innovative moves."[12]

This classic laboratory began and continued to operate in a very pragmatic manner. It started out as a training school for pharmacists similar to others of its type; over its lifetime under the direction of Liebig, most of its graduates, in the words of Holmes, became "physicians or pharmacists, industrialists or farmers." Indeed, "those prominent chemists of the later nineteenth century who are commonly identified with Liebig's school [in mentor-apprentice chains] make up only a small minority of the more than seven hundred persons who spent time in the laboratory at Giessen during the twenty-eight years in which Liebig presided over its operation."[13] Whatever their reasons for attending the institute, it attracted from the beginning growing numbers of applicants. With a snowballing reputation, the laboratory had within fifteen years of its opening, by the 1840s, over fifty students at a time and had become internationally famous as a school of chemistry, not the first of its kind but by far the most imposing. "Its dramatic success prompted other German universities to evaluate the training methods established at Giessen."[14]

What the Giessen laboratory did was to contribute new knowledge while teaching existing knowledge and to do so in a way that gave the director and the institution a competitive advantage over old and new rivals at other universities. But the obstacles were numerous, especially during the first decade of existence. Instead of moving into a new building promised at the outset, the laboratory opened in "existing empty barracks." More critical, when Liebig and two associates petitioned the University Senate to establish their "chemicopharmaceutical" institute within the university, they were voted down, on Humboldtian grounds. This rebuff "was a manifestation of the conflict that surfaced repeatedly in German-speaking universities in this period between the ideal of a general education to cultivate the mind (Bildung) and the goal of training specific skills." Whereas the proper role of the university was seen by the senate, within the purview of Bildung, to educate future civil servants, the proposed institute seemed to fall too much in the direction of training "apothecaries, soap makers, brewers, and other craftsmen." With Humboldtian doctrine more hindrance than help, the new institute had to be established, with the support of a provincial ministry, as a "private activity."[15] This young, aspiring professor of chemistry could control a teaching program, but his research was institutionally marginal, deemed to be outside the boundaries of a properly constituted Humboldtian university.

Year by year Liebig drew not on Humboldt but improvised from immediate experience. He learned to concentrate lectures in a summer semester, then to devote the entire winter semester to practical work in the new laboratory. As his research interests deepened and he was able to express them in setting research problems for students, the balance of students, which at the outset had been almost 90 percent in favor of pharmacy, shifted toward chemistry matriculants. He invented simpler and more reliable instruments for chemical analysis, making it possible for students of varying levels of insight and skill to routinely produce elementary analyses at a much accelerated rate. As Liebig progressed and the laboratory prospered, student investigations became standard, first centering on problems the director set around his own interests and capabilities and then going beyond them. With more than a critical mass of chemistry students in place in the laboratory in the 1840s, competitive advantage was now fully at hand: as weighed by Holmes, "Liebig's command of so large a group of advanced students to whom he could give experimental projects useful both to their training and to his interests enabled him to exploit new research openings with a swiftness that made it hard for chemists operating alone, or with only a few students, to compete with him."[16]

By midcentury, despite what Humboldt and the idealists of his day might have wished, the teaching-research laboratory, crammed full of empirical and even utilitarian research—and not at all united with the other sciences by embracing philosophy—had arrived as a fundamental part of the organizational structure that would nurture the sciences in the remaining decades of the nineteenth century and all of the twentieth. In this central piece of the mosaic that was the modern university in Germany, and later elsewhere, education through inquiry and freedom of teaching and research became linked, not to broad humanistic education and general enlightenment, but to ever-increasing specialization. Most important, in the transformation of science from "a pastime of leisured and wealthy individuals into a regular vocational pursuit" that took place in Europe during the nineteenth century, with Germany at the cutting edge, the university laboratory played a significant role. It became *the* organizational tool of the professor-scientist; within it, training procedures were developed and effected; there, specialist qualifications were established which certified scientific competence. As J. B. Morrell has pointed out, particularly in the hands of such German chemists "as Liebig at Giessen, Bunsen at Heidelberg, Kolbe at Leipzig, and Baeyer at Munich, the university laboratory provided for science an equivalent of the Renaissance artist's studio, in that it offered to apprentices induction into the scientific guild through pupilage in practical skills under a master-practitioner." The German-modeled university laboratory became "the place where students who had acquired the grammar of science from lectures learned its language from practical experience."[17]

A similar operating tool took the form of the seminar that incorporated professorial research interests and introduced students to the practice of research. The research-oriented seminar became another institution for discovering, nurturing, and training scientific talent, another setting where the education of apprentices would convey and push forward new approaches in a discipline.[18] As Kathryn M. Olesko has stressed, seminars had been in existence for about two centuries before those that concentrated on research methods appeared in German universities in the nineteenth century. In their older form, the seminars were mainly small settings for training preachers and secondary school teachers. They had evolved from informal meetings of professors and students, replacing "the monologues of lecture courses with dialogues between professors and students" and thereby "helping to transform the nature of teaching and of learning." Then, at a time when such modern disciplines as physics were emerging and professors were turning to research, some seminars began to concentrate on research methods. They now assumed, "in addition to their professional functions, a scholarly one: vigorous instruction in the academic disciplines."[19]

A pivotal mathematics-physics seminar established in Königsberg in 1834 by Franz Neumann and directed by him for over four decades, until 1876, influenced later ventures. Before Königsberg, physics instruction was largely based on lecture courses and textbooks; self-instruction was not uncommon. Now such instruction was to include practical exercises in techniques of quantification, group review of problems, and innovative design of instruments. Again, as in the Giessen laboratory, trial and error determined outcomes. The director "had not anticipated that the route to original investigations by students would be through assigned homework problems and routine measuring exercises executed in common," as they made their weekly round from roundtable discussion led by the professor to homework on problems he assigned and then to regroup in the professor's "teaching laboratory, an extension of his seminar located in his home," where they conducted measuring exercises, "sometimes with instruments of their own design," and then to move the following week back to the roundtable.[20] Meanwhile, the professor did not always practice what he preached. Publicly "he upheld idealistic notions of Wissenschaft and especially of Bildung" in which university instruction "shaped character and drew out natural talents," but in practice he was developing a program focused on "discipline"—"training the mind to follow certain rules of investigative protocol and rigorous techniques of investigation." The mental and material tools involved in the *labor* of science were primary in the Königsberg seminar. Neumann was promoting "a distinctive set of investigative techniques."[21]

The Liebig laboratory and the Neumann seminar, classic cases and influential models in the development of German science, highlight the robust *local* organization of the nineteenth-century German university system. Such laboratories and seminars spread across the German system as strong basic units for effecting a teaching-research relationship. Students were pulled into these units both as research trainees and as research performers. Strikingly, the laboratory and the seminar gave students an intimate involvement that did not and still does not obtain in the lecture hall, or in any classroom no matter how small, where the professor presents codified knowledge and students are expected to ab-

sorb the best of the past. Now, teaching was blended with research activity, study was folded into a research framework. The "unceasing
process of inquiry" had found its operational tools.

The strength of newly fashioned laboratories and seminars in this
pathbreaking setting did not derive solely from their role as fundamental units of membership. They also became funding units; as such, they
dealt directly with governmental ministries and were thereby positioned
to largely ignore the all-university and faculty levels of organization.
The seminars and institutes, as put by Charles E. McClelland, "tended
to become *Staatsanstalten* [public establishments] in themselves, legally
and financially responsible to the state, usually directly so, with the traditional corporate structure of the faculties and other university organs
being bypassed."[22] As a result, weak university organization developed
as a generic feature: neither a strong university administration nor even
a strong "faculty" or "department" structure emerged. These features
would later become structural weaknesses, first to a mild degree in the
early twentieth century and then in a major way when later expansion
into mass higher education resulted in greatly enlarged universities. But
strong all-university organization was not necessary in universities
where students commonly numbered in the hundreds or less than two
thousand: in the defining four decades of 1830–1870, total annual
enrollment for about twenty universities did not exceed 16,000, a
sum that reflected an age-group participation rate of about one-half of
1 percent.[23] Not needing to be places of cohesive administration, the
German universities could operate with only nominal integration, in
comparison to developing patterns in Britain and preeminently in the
United States in the late decades of the century. The German research
university offered an essentially guild form of organization in which
chair-holding professors, utilizing institutes and seminars to effect an
integration of research, teaching, and study, were sufficient unto themselves. Together with the minister of education, they would take care of
governance.

Thus it was not the university in general or even the major constituent faculties that guided action and drove the German system forward.
It was the chair-controlled and chair-supervised institutes, seminars,
laboratories, and even hospitals—"comparatively small and highly
autonomous self-contained units of academic production," in Wolfgang J. Mommsen's terms—on which rested, at the operational level,
the success of the German university system.[24] Offering many advantages for professors and students alike and operating as a sort of univer-

sity within the university, these operational forms gave the German higher education system "much of its world renown in the late nineteenth century."[25] Their modeling effect internationally was enormous, since it was in these small research-dedicated communities that thousands of visiting scholars participated. The lesson taken home was that small, highly autonomous and self-contained research groups gave specific meaning to doctrines of freedom in research, teaching, and study.

Again, it is helpful to note that the changes occurring in the first half and the middle of the nineteenth century were part of a longer-term flow that had begun during the previous century. The reading of canonical texts had then been replaced in part by systematic lectures, a more fluid form that accommodated new material. To accompany the lectures, following Olesko's analysis, "exercise sessions, private academic societies, reading clubs, and other small meetings of students with professors appeared as forums," a small-group form "designed for learning through practical application what had been conveyed theoretically in lectures" which thereby "helped shape and further define disciplinary knowledge by highlighting important methods and central topics." "Instigated from below, by professors and students, and not from above, by the state," these informal and quasi-formal forums, predating the broad structural reforms of the early nineteenth century, were a forerunner of seminars. Their weakness was organizational instability. In contrast, seminars and institutes offered firmer standing, a way of "gaining official state approval and financial support, and hence the means to an operational stability that would transcend staffing changes."[26]

Thus teaching and learning by means of canonical texts slowly evolved first into lectures that could change in content; then into forums, small meetings of students with professors, that were more open to critical discussion and student initiative; and then into seminars, laboratories, and institutes, often private at the outset but later regularized as state-supported university units, in which inquiry was gradually brought forward as both a mode of teaching and a mode of learning. The long-term evolution adds further weight to the argument that operational unities of research, teaching, and study in nineteenth-century German universities were not deduced from broad ideologies of Bildung and Wissenschaft, nor were they direct creatures of gross structural reforms. Rather, they were worked out at the operating level as academics sought ways to bring research and critical scholarship into the university setting, there to meld with pedagogy and training. New

grand ideologies and macroreforms arguably helped to open up intellectual and organizational space: they established what in Part Two we
call *enabling* conditions. But it was the evolution in operating units,
born of changing interests of professors and students, that established
the more immediate *enacting* conditions. There was much that was bottom-up.

SYSTEM CONDITIONS

Looming large among favoring conditions at the more macrolevels of
system and university in the German setting was a political structure
that encouraged academic competition and the proliferation of research institutions. In sharp contrast to the Napoleonic unified national state characteristic of nineteenth-century France (see chap. 3),
German government of the time was exceedingly fragmented. Before
unification under Bismarck in 1870, German territories were ruled by
nearly forty sovereign states; after unification, the new Reich still consisted of over twenty principalities, kingdoms, duchies, and free cities.
Under the new national constitution, these various polities retained control over educational, cultural, and religious matters, thereby ensuring
that throughout the rest of the nineteenth century formal government
control would remain radically decentralized. This structure had an
enormous effect in promoting competition in the developing academic
system. As the perceived capability and the reputation of universities
became based on the research prowess of professors, their laboratories
and their seminars, state education ministers sought to entice to their
own states and universities, in one discipline after another, the established and rising talent in this new business of inquiry. A multistate or
"federal" framework thereby helped to create an academic labor market in which research-oriented scholars could move from one university
to another according to comparative attractiveness; preeminent was the
chance to occupy a chair and direct an institute or seminar. Mobility
was also not particularly hindered by position in a civil service, since
the German academics were not part of a single official framework as
found elsewhere in European unitary states. In the fragmented German
setting, it was possible for a minor university such as Giessen to become
the place in an emerging discipline within the system and indeed then to
become a magnet for talent internationally. Competition among states
and universities became a primary condition of system development.[27]

McClelland has expressed well the emerging dynamics of this type of institutional field. As "the expanding private and state-financed seminars produced larger and larger numbers of dedicated scholars imbued with the scientific values and methods of men who virtually founded their disciplines on a critical basis," the research ethic "received an institutional value: its product—notable scholarship—came to be the major national criterion for appointments in the ceaseless struggle between ministries and faculties."[28] What had been "more the offspring of individual faculty members than of state planning" now acquired state and institutional motives. By the last decades of the century, states could be found developing seminars and institutes at "a feverish pace." In Prussia between 1882 and 1907, where nine universities were located, a noted (and much disliked) higher education minister, Friedrich Althoff, helped establish no fewer than seventy-seven institutes and seminars in the philosophical faculties, eighty-six medical laboratories and clinics, nine seminars in law, and four seminars in theology. Althoff was a classic case of the strong minister who wanted to directly fashion the base units of universities and proceeded to intervene. But in turn the academics whom he wanted had considerable leverage: among outstanding candidates who could bring the coin of notable scholarship, hardly one came "without demanding an institute—or without receiving it, immediately or shortly thereafter." And unspoken collusion of minister and academic was only a step away, since Althoff "could then turn to the state financial authorities with the argument that to refuse funds for an institute would lead to filling the vacancies with second-rate talent."[29] Especially as spurred by state comparison and competition, the setting developed a logic readily recognizable in twentieth-century ministries and state-funded universities, in Germany and elsewhere, as bureau chiefs and related sector personnel attempt to maximize the resources of their common domain against the counter-constraints of finance officials responsible for cost containment and an integrated state budget.

The dynamism of nineteenth-century German academic science was thus given a major boost by growing governmental interest in "notable scholarship," leading to expansion based on growth in knowledge *before* the states began to react to enlarged consumer demand. Particularly in the larger state governments, political reorganization in the early nineteenth century had given the universities some economic security: state bureaucratic fiscal administration, often later cursed, was a big improvement over "the inefficient, semifeudal, corporate management" of the eighteenth century. With Prussia taking the lead, the various state governments then increasingly committed themselves to direct support of seminars and institutes. Despite the fact that student numbers increased very little up to 1870, the states dramatically increased their funding of research. At Berlin University, in the half-century between 1820 and 1870, while the overall budget tripled and academic salaries grew by less than double, the support of seminars and institutes increased 1,000 percent. In 1826, Berlin "spent over six times as much on faculty salaries as on institutes and seminars; by 1870, the amount spent on the latter actually exceeded the total budget for professorial salaries." Other universities showed a similar pattern of change. And state governments saw to it that the funds were earmarked for specific institutes and seminars, thereby avoiding the corporate control of the university at large, within which traditional professors, suspicious of innovation, could exercise a conservative hand. The direct line between institute director and education minister, described earlier, served both parties, establishing along the way "the quasi-independent status of the major research organizations within the university" as a major and lasting peculiarity of German universities.[30] The institute-minister link became a carrying vehicle for promoting a research-based university framework.

After 1870, enlarged "consumer demand" then entered the picture as an important basis for state interest and university growth. While enrollment for all the universities had fluctuated only in the range of about 12,000 to 13,000 between the 1830s and the 1860s, it grew to 34,000 by 1900 and 61,000 by 1914; the number of students had not even kept pace during the earlier period with the growth of the general population, but the student rate of growth between 1870 and the turn of the century was twice as fast.[31] In this latter period, some universities doubled in size, and some increased four- to eightfold. Heavy increases occurred in the philosophical faculties containing the basic disciplines, as well as in the other two major faculties, law and medicine. Multiple interacting reasons for such growth were not far to seek, together establishing a pattern that was to become commonplace and enlarged in twentieth-century growth: more families were financially able to support university study; more career opportunities were opening for university graduates; the secondary school system produced more students qualified to attend the university, in the German case predominantly from the *Gymnasien* but also now from two "less noble" types of high schools, the *Realgymnasien* and *Oberrealschulen*; foreign students increased to nearly 9 percent of total enrollment by the early twentieth century, and women increased by 1914 to about 7 percent. By the standards of the mid-nineteenth century, the university of 1900–1914 had been transformed into a "heterogeneous mass."[32]

Here were the seeds in the German system of what would become known in the second half of the twentieth century as the shift from elite to mass higher education.[33] Along with this early increase in numbers and types of students came indications, written large at the time in the minds of many participants but appearing small in the hindsight of later perspective, of generic problems for university research and research training. One problem was a rise in the student/teacher ratio, from an earlier 9:1 (1840–1870) to 11:1 (1880), 12:1 (1890), and 14:1 (1905). Higher ratios spelled increased teaching and compressed research time. A second disquieting circumstance was more expansion in junior academic positions than among the full professorships: the number of students per major professor (*Ordinarien*) doubled between 1870 and 1905 from seventeen to thirty-four; two subordinate categories, *Extraordinarien* and *Dozenten*, the latter essentially "unsalaried academic freelancers licensed to teach by the regular university staff," were, by 1910, giving the majority of all lecture courses. At Berlin, by 1900, "the irregular teaching staff was doing the majority of the teaching." Or, more accurately, they were *posted* as teaching more than half the courses. Nonsalaried and completely noncivil service, they may or may not have taught their listed courses: "even if lectures were announced, there is no way of knowing if they were given; the announcement was enough to retain PD [*Privatdozent*] status."[34] "Freedom of teaching" created abundant space for instructors as well as for professors to teach or not to teach, just as freedom of study in effect supported the right of students *not* to study. In any event, in an early form of strains induced by growth, "bigness had begun to cut a trench between student and professor."[35] The senior professors could not accommodate the "overflow" of students if they were to give primacy to research and research training, tasks they had set aside in the small worlds of the institutes and the seminars to which only some of the students would be called. Lectures offered the setting to which all students had access.

With rapid industrialization under way after 1870, German industry also increasingly entered the picture as its leaders developed an appetite, particularly in chemistry, for the results of research and for well-trained scientific specialists. New major chemical firms both invested heavily in laboratories of their own and "provided limited financial and material support to selected university laboratories to encourage basic research of interest to them."[36] After unification the new national government itself also looked to universities for assistance in nation and empire building, including the applied science and technology that would help arm a powerful military establishment. State officials at national and *Land* (individual state) levels saw to it that by the end of the 1880s "various technical schools had been consolidated into nine *Technische Hochschulen* [technical universities or institutes of technology] and given the same administrative structure as the twenty-one universities."[37] Within a decade (in 1899), over the objection of the traditional universities, this alternative sector was given the right to award a general Doctor of Engineering degree. Impatient with restrictive attitudes and practices in the universities, officials were also increasingly prone to develop, in an ad hoc fashion, government-supported research centers outside the universities in not only physics and chemistry but also biology and medical research. By World War I, Germany developed what we later conceptualize as "an institute system" that beyond the traditional universities was composed of three other sectors, industrial laboratories, institutes of technology, and government research institutes, all with considerable status and offering certain advantages in research performance over the universities. Competition now had a new dimension: if the university sector itself had become more rigid and less stirred by institutional competition, intersector competition within a larger research system could stimulate responses to changing conditions, even in hidebound settings, "to move stodgy colleagues or a stingy government" with the threat of falling behind.[38]

And some of the most research-minded among the university professors were very much in the forefront of these new developments as they sought the funding and the institute structures that would enhance the pace of their investigations—and their power and prestige. Particularly promising were the possibilities of well-funded but independent research institutes formally initiated outside the universities. The most important instance was the Kaiser-Wilhelm-Gesellschaft, founded in 1911, which after World War II became the Max Planck Society for the Advancement of the Sciences.[39] The Kaiser Wilhelm Society was a national body, not a creation of one or more of the states. It was a quasi-official institution at the outset, funded more by industry than by the Imperial Treasury but understood to be under the protection of the Kaiser (Wilhelm II). It established and funded its own institutes. Eminent university chemists played a leading role in its organization and leadership: the first two research institutes of the society, opened in 1912, were devoted entirely to chemistry, and the first four, in place by the outbreak of war in 1914, involved chemistry. The new laboratories proved immediately useful: they were soon integrated into the war effort to do research in weapons and in synthetics that could replace imported goods cut off by blockade. By 1920, this new sector had grown to twenty institutes.

This development of a nonuniversity research sector found encouragement in the pull and push of quite different academic interests. Then as now, some ambitious academic scientists saw the regular university research settings as too small, too lacking in financial resources and personnel, and too pure in their pursuit of knowledge for its own sake. The opening shots of Big Science arguing for research concentration could be heard in calls for "national" laboratories. Growing enrollments in the universities also meant much more teaching, including presentations to students who lacked interest in the subject matter and were inclined to vacate their seats in the lecture hall. Even then, such academic work could be depressing; at the least, it would often not compare with the challenge of running a major institute and the rewards of pursuing new research findings. Then, too, a sizable share of the traditional professoriate—those who were in effect on the other side of the aisle—wanted to exclude "applied research" from the university and were only too happy to have it placed outside. Finally, particularly with its "chair" form of local control, the university operating level that had evolved since the 1820s had in many cases become rigid by the end of the century. Institutes that once were instruments of striking change had become restraining points of solidified power. Their controlling professors had developed "vested interests in keeping new specialties that arose in their fields as subspecialties within their own institutes rather than allowing them to become separate chairs with claims for new institutes."[40]

New nonuniversity institutes could then be a preferred power solution for all: the innovators pressing new initiatives; the old guard holding onto power and wishing the innovators would go away; and the state officials mediating between the two types of faculty and seeking ways to get new institutes under way. The nineteenth-century German university had not become a flexible enterprise that would err on the side of inclusiveness, similar to the orientation developing in the United States by the turn of the century, particularly under the public service mentality of the land grant state universities. In Germany, the sharp

limits placed around professional training (only a few fields were considered legitimate for the university) and the commitment to unfettered
pure research together spelled a restraining distrust of a technical, applied role for university research.[41]

By the turn of the century, government officials, industry leaders, and
academics who were mindful of national strength in science and technology also confronted new international comparisons that worried
them. The rapid growth of universities in the United States and the
new startling role played by philanthropy in that country led to warn-
ings of a rising behemoth that could soon overshadow European systems, including Germany, in pure and applied research. Particularly
eye-catching after the turn of the century was the establishment in
1901–1902 of the Rockefeller Institute for Medical Research of New
York, which concentrated in biomedical fields, and the Carnegie Institution of Washington, which was ready to award astonishingly large
grants to researchers in a wide range of fields. Taking immediate note,
the chief scientist of the British Royal Institution, in his 1902 presidential address to the British Association for the Advancement of Science,
computed that "the *interest* from Carnegie's endowment for one year
exceeded all that had been spent by his institution [university] in the
previous hundred." In their turn, German officials and senior scientists
could express shock in the calculation that the combined annual interest
from the Rockefeller and Carnegie endowments approximated the total
budget of a large German university, and it was all earmarked for research![42] By 1910, the Prussian Ministry of Education was ready to ac-
knowledge that perhaps the top twelve American universities were
worthy of comparison with the twenty-one in the German system. And
there was no mistaking the comparative rates of growth. The American
universities now had much larger and more rapidly increasing budgets.
While it was true that much of the American money was spent (squan-
dered?) on the general education of young untutored students, the
American universities in a wholesale fashion were also developing graduate programs firmly based on research. Moreover, the Americans were
showing that scientific work could be promoted within both public and
private universities and that private contributions from individuals and
foundations could play a significant role.[43]

In short, between the growing capability of American universities
and the resources for research support offered by new private foundations, the American challenge in scientific productivity and preeminence had begun. Influence now flowed across the Atlantic in both

directions. Part of the German response to this challenge was to use "orchestrated philanthropy" to establish *alongside* the universities the Kaiser Wilhelm framework "for the advancement of science."[44] What we later conceptualize in Part Two as the phenomenon of research drift began early in the German system, not as early as in France as we later see but earlier than in Britain, the United States, and Japan. The seeds of this movement of basic as well as applied research away from university settings of teaching and learning were sown in part by a form of university that by the end of the nineteenth century had become considerably rigid in its capacity to share power and restrictive in its willingness to allow emerging fields and ongoing outside fields to have a place at the table. University exclusiveness encouraged the growth of alternative settings, research-centered settings that could leave teaching and learning behind.

TWENTIETH-CENTURY TRAVAIL

With Humboldt suitably interpreted and research-centered units institutionalized as the prized core of the university, the German system of 1900 was without any doubt *the* place in the world where a productive research-teaching-study nexus existed in great profusion. But the system ran aground in the next half-century and thereby helped to substantially transfer preeminence in academic research and related research training to other countries, principally to the United States. World War I brought staggering losses in manpower, with the virtual physical elimination of an entire generation of young men. The deeply troubled days of the Weimar Republic (1918–1933), with its hyperinflation, unemployment, war exhaustion, and deeply divided political life, were no time for a sector dependent on the public purse to prosper. And then the Fascist period (1933–1945) became *the* watershed. On the one side, Germany, however troubled, was still internationally preeminent in scientific research and university training. On the other, its badly weakened system, physically battered by war, ideologically compromised by Fascist doctrines, and shorn by emigration of much of its outstanding talent, was now overtaken and surpassed by other national systems. Henry Turner put it aptly: "At the end of the war, the country's once proud universities and scientific institutes sat idle and discredited after twelve years of collaboration and repression, stripped of much of the talent that had won them worldwide prominence before 1933." Morally, "the country appeared bankrupt."[45]

The exodus of talent to an American system that had begun its own scientific takeoff between the two world wars was important both for the immediate war effort and for the long run. The German loss, the American gain, primarily in the sciences but not limited to those disciplines, amounted to a sea change in the international location of research and scholarly work.[46] Arguably most damaging to Germany was the loss of legitimacy wrought by the years of Fascist domination and intervention. By the summer of 1945, the surviving cadres of professors were badly scarred by the political struggles of the Weimar and Fascist years. They were unsure of support by state and national governments whose own character was often in question, and they were mistrusted by many students and outsiders who thought they had seen too many compromises with an evil state.

But the ideal of the unity of research and study was not lost. The first fifteen years of postwar academic reconstruction (1946–1960) in the new "West Germany"—the Federal Republic of Germany—were given over to the task of getting the German universities back on their feet in their earlier form. High on the agenda was the necessity of decentralizing the "domain of culture," a realm that included education. German federalism reborn assumed a moral character. "The creation of a federation of states of the Federal Republic of Germany [in 1949] was a conscious revival of the traditions of the Weimar Constitution and as such a conscious reaction to the degradation of the centralized state by the National Socialists from 1933 to 1945."[47] The control of education was returned to the individual states (*Länder*), now to number eleven. (Following the creation of two Germanies in the late 1940s, the German Democratic Republic—East Germany—treaded an opposite centralizing path under a Soviet-style structure of control.)[48] For higher education in West Germany, the main exception to a Land-centered constitutional definition was the authority given the national government to promote scientific research. This was of course no small opening, especially in a country where universities had been built considerably as loosely connected assemblies of research institutes.

The universities had to be rebuilt in all primary dimensions: personnel, buildings, equipment, student body, overall morale, and sense of purpose. During a massive reconstruction, the universities sought and were largely able to reclaim their historic autonomy. Chair-holding professors, the Ordinarien, again became dominant figures, largely unchallenged in their own domains, who were able to construct research programs of their own choosing and to select the few students who, after completing the first major degree, wished to stay on at the university in junior positions that might lead to an academic career. By the late 1950s, much of the academic world of the early 1930s had been restored: "reconstruction after 1945 exhibited a direct return to Weimar conditions."[49] The system had returned to its classic elite form. The participation rate for first-degree students remained low, approximately 4 to 5 percent of the age group,[50] with the number of people pursuing advanced degrees always a much smaller proportion, about one to seven compared with the "undergraduate" base. With such limited numbers, faculty-student relations at the most advanced levels, as in the prewar decades, could be more like those found in small guilds or crafts than in large bureaucracies or professions. Scholarly scientific work could again center on the senior professor who would assemble "at the bench" a few subordinate members of the staff and a few would-be apprentices.

Thus, as part of the restoration of the university, the old building block of the chair-institute regained its long-standing primacy. Chair holders were again the only senior professors in particular fields at the universities *and* the sole heads of institutes. In turn, the institute continued as "a self-contained teaching and research unit, containing all necessary personnel and facilities, such as laboratories, a library, and lecture and seminar rooms."[51] These self-contained units were still called seminars in the humanities and social sciences and clinics in the medical faculties; "institute" is here used as a generic term that embraces the other forms. The control of an institute again greatly enhanced the power of the individual professor, against which faculty- and university-level organs, constituted essentially as occasionally convened assemblies of barons, were relatively impotent. The institute was still a state establishment and in many critical matters did not answer to the faculty and the university of which the professor was a part. Instead, as institute director in full charge of budget, facilities, and personnel, the professor was subject only to the authority of the ministry and continued to have a direct relationship.[52] The hybrid institute-university form of organization, with its sharp hierarchy of status and power, continued.

The German institute and the American department have sometimes been viewed as functionally equivalent, serving as the lowest operating units in their respective systems. But the institute has generally been smaller in scope, usually covering what Americans would call a subfield; it is also more self-contained, right down to possession and control of its own space. When major administrative reform finally came to the German system in the 1970s, departments (*Fachbereiche*) were created not to replace the institutes but to substitute, as a substructure, for the five or six large unwieldy faculties. A larger set of departments—fifteen, twenty, twenty-five—became the second level of organization; and under the 1976 Framework Law, the departments were given greater authority over the allocation of funds and personnel than the faculties had had. Even though the departments had been inserted partly to better control the institutes, the institutes still remained intact.[53] Thus the department in Germany is not the lowest operating unit but rather a larger faculty-type assembly of a set of institutes. The institute in the main still deploys courses and examinations and functions as the unit within which doctoral training takes place. In the late 1980s, "traditional small units headed by full professors are still very much in evidence," although now somewhat subject to Fachbereiche control and tending to rest "on a more informal basis."[54] Even after smaller institutes (and seminars in the humanities) were merged into larger units in the early 1970s reform, institutes remained "the institutional units for research"[55] in a setting where research came first in long-established practices and rewards as well as in hallowed doctrine. Just as it was the guiding element in the old unity principle, research remained "the structuring element of the universities."[56]

IMPACT OF MASS HIGHER EDUCATION

But the old principle and the institute structure had hardly been restored before massive changes rendered them highly problematic. If the institute was the immovable object, mass higher education now became the irresistible force. Expansion hit the German university system with enormous force in the 1960s and continued through the next two decades with little surcease. During that thirty-year period student numbers expanded no less than fivefold. A total of no more than 250,000 students in thirty-three universities in 1960 became over 1,300,000 students in sixty-eight universities by 1990. Faculty increased from 17,000 to over 70,000. A major nonuniversity sector (*Fachhochschulen*), established and encouraged by the government to handle professional preparation in additional fields of study, grew by 1990 to over 325,000 students in over twenty institutions, one-fourth of the university enrollment, with rate of growth running in its favor. What had been a university system thereby became a binary system of postsecondary education.[57] Other major structural changes were attempted, often to be later discontinued or partly rolled back. For example, an effort in the 1970s to establish "comprehensive universities" (*Gesamthochschulen*) that would combine the more practical tasks of Fachhochschulen and teacher training colleges with the traditional tasks of the universities soon encountered considerable resistance, especially by professors in established universities. Rather than sweep the field, this major innovation became a small enclave of institutions.

Given the magnitude and rapidity of expansion, the creation of a major second sector could not save the universities from extensive massification. Their enrollment rosters bulged: in the 1980s, the largest universities (e.g., Munich, Berlin, and Hamburg) had an enrollment of up to 50,000 students. German observers noted concomitant increases in the ratio of students to staff: from $29:1$ in 1975 to $38:1$ in 1988 in the number of students per "professor"; from $10:1$ in 1975 to $15:1$ in 1985 in number of students per "academic staff."[58] And there was little or no internal university structure to channel the student flow. Now facing greater increased numbers of junior faculty as well as virtual hordes of students, the chair-holding professors who had been restored to power became more remote than ever. Politicization set in with a vengeance. The great student discontent of the late 1960s and early 1970s that stretched across many nations had a particularly sharp edge in Germany; radical students and not-so-radical junior staff were willing to portray establishment figures as reactionary, even tainted with a history of Fascist sympathy if not Nazi party involvement. Student and governmental actions during these years of bitter protest led to new formal arrangements of stronger rights and greater privileges for junior faculty, students, and nonteaching staff. These schemes burned brightly for a few years, led on by the idea that they would usher in a new day of democratic participation. But by the mid- and late 1970s, they were somewhat retrenched by adverse court decisions and new legislation *and* by the day-to-day realities of power, in which rank, seniority, expertise, and fund-raising capacity determine that some academics will have considerably more influence than others. Chairs did not disappear; neither did research institutes directed by key professors.

By the mid-1980s, in this German age of expansion, some 20 percent of the age group, having achieved the *Abitur* or other qualifying school degrees, were in higher education, with about 14 percent in universities and 6 percent attending Fachhochschulen.[59] In this setting of greatly expanded enrollment, the wild card has been the long-standing tradition of maximum student choice. For the most part, other than in the case of entry controls (*numerus clausus*) established for medicine and a few other fields, students have continued to be free to choose both the institution they will attend and the field of study in which they will specialize. As a result, individual universities have had little control over their total size or the size and balance of their departments. Having selected their university and subject, entering students embark on long programs of study that in the 1980s were taking five to seven years to complete. With some military service (for men) along the way, graduation often does not occur until about twenty-eight,[60] an advanced age for first-degree attainment; in Britain, students who go straight on can take the three-year bachelor's degree by the age of twenty-two or twenty-three, and in the United States, students can also complete the four-year undergraduate program at a relatively young age. In both Britain and the United States, entry to "graduate" programs can take place by the mid-twenties.

The German first tier of instruction and degree completion emphasizes specialization and professional qualification in all fields. Essentially no distinction is made between "academic" and "professional" offerings; that is, basic disciplines and professional schools are not linguistically and structurally distinguished as they are in the United States.[61] And all students are considered advanced. Toward the end of their first-degree work, they typically prepare a thesis, a bit of concentrated work that may be compared to master's-level work in the American system, which students can use to take a diploma or a degree. Two types of completion are essentially academic: the *Diplom* and the *Magister Artium* (M.A.), taken in the mid-1980s by 41 and 4 percent of the students, respectively. A third type, *Staatsexamen*, is a more professional (in American terminology) degree, administered predominantly in medicine, law, and teacher training, jointly supervised by academic staff and public examination officials, and awarded by the state, not the university.[62] Over one-half of the students complete in this fashion, producing a close connection between many first-tier programs and state certification that adds to the rigidity of the existing structure: change in certain university courses of study requires changes in the rules and regulations of the civil service and hence the concurrence of government officials.

Behind the centrality of the prolonged first tier of university study lies the basic condition that most university students have passed through the Gymnasium, the classic university-preparatory secondary school, where, on graduating with the Abitur at the age of eighteen or nineteen, they are defined by one and all as broadly educated young adults who now have the "maturity" to study at institutions of higher learning.[63] They are not, as in America, culturally defined as "kids" still in need of a general or liberal education to deepen the mind and gentle the soul. Rather, having been exposed to generalized knowledge and having attained "maturity," students entering the university historically have been considered ready for specialized learning. From the first year on they can concentrate on a specialty, vocational or academic. They specialize in medicine by entering a self-contained faculty of medicine, or in law in another equally bounded unit, or embark on a disciplinary specialty. With course work stretching over five or more years, leading directly to professional qualification and possibly even a master's degree, a second major tier of operations similar to the American graduate school hardly seemed necessary. Hence the German system has not until recently attempted to distinguish between "undergraduate" and "graduate" education, or to position "professional schools" at a post-first-degree level. Notably, German universities have historically not developed sequences of courses for advanced work in the basic disciplines that would constitute a de facto advanced curriculum.

Within an essentially single-tier structure, the most advanced level of education and training is constituted by a combination of the upper years of the first-degree work and noncurricular arrangements beyond the first six years. For most students the first tier has become operationally divided into an initial two- to three-year segment largely given over to lectures organized to present introductory and intermediate materials and a second two- to three-year component of seminars and lectures in which students ostensibly edge closer to the traditional "quest for truth," particularly as they prepare for and then write a thesis.[64] Beyond this point, those students—one in seven at the end of the 1980s—who wish to pursue a doctoral degree do not enroll in a department to take advanced courses or even register with the university.[65] Instead they need to find paid employment, if possible, in the form of a teaching position or a research post, the latter either inside the university or in an outside research institute. Thus "doctoral students" cultivate not a graduate student role but a junior occupational niche that directly involves them in research or that at least supports them while they independently do the research or scholarly writing that can lead to a doctoral dissertation. But posts for these research staff, or "graduate staff," are in short supply.[66]

The structure of doctoral training as of the end of the 1980s has been crisply summarized by Hans-Jürgen Block.

> Doctoral studies are not well structured in German universities. Doctoral students (*Doktoranden*) have to be accepted by a personal supervisor who ought to be a professor. They pursue research work. Most [of them] are employed by the university. They hold university posts (teaching or research assistant, often in part-time positions) or they are funded by research contracts awarded to their supervisors. In addition there is a grant system.... The doctoral degree requires 3–5 years of research work.... The necessary course work to pass the doctoral examination is negligible.[67]

Or, as summarized by Ludwig Huber, "German universities, with few exceptions to date [1986], do not offer doctoral *programmes* incorporating a minimum systematic institutional effort to qualify candidates further. It is entirely a matter of the individual master/apprentice relation between the candidate and 'his' supervisor whether he gets training and advice in his work and, if so, how much."[68] Hence, beyond the upper years of the first tier, there lies mainly a nonformal segment of activity in which direct research work or independent study provides the main vehicle of student involvement, while courses and seminars have little or no role. For many candidates in the humanities and the social sciences, the minimization of structure means that would-be advanced scholars work largely on their own at home, with only nominal contact with the professor(s) to whom a dissertation might some day be submitted.

German academics may still hope and intend to have the upper years of the first-degree work serve as a place for inquiry, but mass higher education has imposed another story.

> The conditions are anything but intimate. Lectures with several hundred students are no exception, and seminars often contain one hundred or more. The amount of written work is minimal, and the habit of not attending lectures or seminars at all is widespread. Thus the tacit institutional control and supervision which is a structural given in many other systems hardly exists in Germany.[69]

In this setting, the old seminar functions more like popular upper division courses in bachelor degree programs in American universities, where professors concentrate on specialized topics and may draw considerably on their own research. Claudius Gellert found in the late

1980s that only a few students in first-degree programs, less than 10 percent, had a close relationship with a professor by means of laboratory or seminar participation, following the pattern idealized when a much smaller number of students sought research training and disciplinary knowledge was considerably simpler. Now, "the average student at German universities is not involved in research."[70]

Among responses to the great change in student life wrought by mass higher education and expanded knowledge, disciplinary differences increasingly loom large. The sciences exhibit relatively strong conditions of student involvement and capacity to adjust in contrast to the humanities and "soft" social sciences. For example, physics and history offer sharply different settings. In the former there is much external funding, while in the latter there is very little. Physics is also strongly involved in the institute system that lies outside the universities, while history has only a token appearance. Research posts are relatively numerous for those pursuing advanced training in physics but not for those in history. Extensively in physics, and increasingly throughout the sciences, research candidates take up assigned places in research teams and projects, while in history they generally work on their own and often at a distance from academic staff and peers. Thus, while conditions have become more difficult in general for those pursuing advanced training within and beyond the first-tier programs, a much stronger support structure is available in the sciences than in the humanities; for the most part, the social sciences are positioned in between.[71] In a university system so much based on institutes as prime units, it is even more the case that the more scientific the field, the more likely it is that research training in one form or another will receive support. It is also more likely that linkage will be made between the research of the professor and that of trainees: "whether the master apprentice model is effective seems simply to depend upon whether there exists a 'workshop' where others meet regularly and work, too, in which the 'apprentice' may become fully and daily integrated. For this, organized research like that in engineering and the natural sciences with its bigger projects and research groups is apparently a necessary, though insufficient condition."[72]

Aided by their greater overall support and their greater affinity for an institute framework, the physical and biological sciences are also better positioned to fashion informal and quasi-formal pathways for bringing able research students forward, involving them in research, and even offering some supervisory attention to their progress in research training. This includes taking some of them into "outside" institutes in which the professors themselves are centrally involved.

> At the Max Planck institutes a number of advanced students are also engaged in research as part of their diploma thesis [which may take a year, serving as a mini-doctoral dissertation] or as doctoral students [holding two- to three-year part-time paid positions].... [O]ne of the professors at an institute, who usually share their time with positions at a university, takes responsibility for the overall supervision of diploma candidates as well as for doctoral students. As a physics professor in an institute near Munich pointed out, he and his colleagues had very positive experiences with diploma candidates, since most of them were highly motivated and could be intensively supervised at the institute. Each member of the institute supervises on the average between one and two diploma theses. The results, even on the diploma level, are sometimes published in international journals.[73]

Thus advanced students, before or after taking the first degree, may find a place in research-performing and research-training niches in outside institutes as well as in ones within the universities. Professors who are themselves based in the two locales of institute and university provide the bridge. Selection is relatively informal and even highly personal. And the vast majority of first-degree students, under modern conditions, cannot get close to the bridge, let alone cross it.

DIVERSIFICATION OF AN INSTITUTE SYSTEM

Built over a long period of time but with noticeable acceleration in recent decades, the German research system is quite diverse in its possession of nonuniversity instruments. At the end of the nineteenth century, as earlier noted, certain kinds of research began to ease out of traditional universities into other types of research organizations, notably the Kaiser Wilhelm institutes, which were financed by industry and state. This research domain was reconstituted and strengthened in 1948 as the Max Planck Society, a body largely financed by national government to establish and fund its own institutes. The society's institutes, numbering about sixty in the late 1980s, play a central role in German science. Relatively well funded, they are committed to basic research and have a reputation for high quality. Their researchers are mostly full-time, as compared to university teacher-researchers who can only devote part of their time to research, a part that diminishes as teaching burdens increase.[74] The institutes represent a significant diversification of the German research system.

Such diversification has been furthered since the 1950s by the extension of the idea of state-supported "independent" research institutes to applied research, notably in the form of the Fraunhofer Society, a growing set of industry-linked institutes that numbered over thirty-five by the end of the 1980s. Other distinctive research sectors have developed at a rapid rate: a set of Big Science institutes (thirteen by the close of the 1980s) funded by national government, chiefly for nuclear research; a varied array of smaller institutes, numbering over three hundred, that were supported by either national or state ministries or both. These proliferating mostly government-supported sectors exist alongside the major R&D investment German industry has made in the form of thousands of industrial laboratories and institutes that, in the late 1980s, employed as many as 90,000 researchers.[75]

The universities are thereby just one part of a state-supported research system in which other sectors offer greater concentration of attention on research on the part of researchers as well as greater concentration of resources and personnel on particular disciplines and specialties. The universities are far from having a monopoly of basic research, let alone applied research; they have to watch carefully their share of resources and personnel and the comparative attractiveness of their research conditions. In overall R&D expenditures, where the "development" component weighs heavily in costs, industry has the dominant role, both in putting up the money and spending it. In state expenditures alone, the universities have about one-half the pie, with the other half distributed among the many nonuniversity sectors. As a result, the research system is unusually dense, especially when seen in the context of a nation whose population (61 million in the late 1980s) was in the range of France and Britain (55 million and 56 million, respectively) and only one-half that of Japan (120 million) and one-fourth that of the United States (240 million). Density of research establishments is also heightened by the relatively small geographic size of West Germany, which is roughly equal to the state of Oregon and has a population density ten times that of the United States.

Adding to complexity in the distribution of the research function is the way the German federal structure of government operates in university and research funding. Similar to the United States, but notably different from Britain and France, substantial support issues from the state level, that is, from the eleven Länder—Baden-Württemberg, Bavaria, Berlin, Bremen, Hamburg, Hesse, Lower Saxony, North Rhine-Westphalia, Rhineland-Palatinate, Saarland, and Schleswig-Holstein. The states provide the main line, the "institutional line," of university support, including faculty salaries, similar to the pattern found in state universities in the United States. At the same time, the national government has become the primary player in providing an additional "research line" of support, offering the second half of what is commonly known in European countries as the dual-support system. Both state and national governments participate in capital grants, funding the construction of buildings and the availability of equipment. In comparison to a single-government framework, this state-federal duality adds variation, first by inserting state-by-state differences in culture and government, for example, northern liberal Hamburg in comparison to southern conservative Bavaria, and then by placing the institutional and research lines under different levels of government, where they are then subject to different interests and biases.

The interplay among funding sources, money streams, and research outlets in Germany has become ever more complicated as the higher education system has grown greatly in population size and many times more elaborate in knowledge specialties and operating units. Heavily affecting research and advanced research training in the university sector is the tendency for general institutional support funds distributed by the states to flow toward mass instruction at beginning and intermediate levels. With so many more students, "the financial support from the Länder has been diverted from research to education"[76]—or more precisely, from research activity and research-based training to instruction that is not blended with research but instead presents codified knowledge. This tendency puts strong pressure on academic researchers to increase the funds they obtain from the national government and other external sources through the research line. But these funds are always limited, particularly when one-half already go outside the university and the long-term flow seems adverse to the universities. The competitive struggle among university research groups and between them and the other research performers is then increased. University institutes, in particular, have become more dependent on national bodies, preeminently the national German Research Society (Deutsche Forschungsgemeinschaft, or DFG), a key national group set up in 1951 as an amalgamation of former research-funding bodies.[77] A few private foundations, notably the Volkswagen Foundation, have emerged since 1960 as supporters of research, traditionally a state function. Whether public or private, the research line distributes funds unevenly rather than by bureaucratic formula and standardized allocations. As research grants are awarded competitively by means of peer review and staff decision in national bodies, there is a lengthening continuum of supported and nonsupported research groups, successful and unsuccessful applicants, in varying degree: big winners and small winners shade off into small losers and big losers.

The plurality of strong nonuniversity sectors in the overall German research system has at least three major implications for research and research training in the universities. First, the existence and prowess of these alternative sites opens the door for much outward research drift; research can clearly find other homes, even more attractive ones. Second, competition for research funds *and* for research personnel is intensified, serving simultaneously as a drain on the universities and a spur to their research efforts. Third, formal advanced training in the universities is more than ever seen as a secondary activity, even a quite minor and perhaps not necessary one, compared to the actual doing of research that is so immediately attractive. If the many research institutes individually and collectively seem to get the job done, then perhaps advanced university training is not a problem after all—a view easy to adopt in an outside institute eager to get on with its research and able to acquire the young supportive personnel *it* needs over the bridges it has built to the universities. Then, too, much research training can take place on the job, as it always must to some degree; so, arguably, it can all be done here with "us" rather than over there in the large impersonal university swamped with students and first-degree teaching.

However, the "overloading" of first-degree programs in both student numbers and years of study had come together by the 1980s with an evident understructuring of doctoral studies to produce widespread concern that would not diminish, no matter how successful the overall research system. Why not shorten and simplify first-degree programs, limiting their upward reach, while putting more structured and more concentrated "graduate" research-based programs in place? By 1986, Germany's leading national scientific body, the Wissenschaftrat, was ready to argue publicly that "the concept of 'unity of research and teaching,' a traditional claim of the German university, has now to be dropped from undergraduate education and reserved for postgraduate work alone."[78] The most able doctoral candidates should attend *Graduiertenkollegs* (graduate colleges), which might be established in particular fields at particular universities, thereby simultaneously serving selectivity, concentration, differentiation, and competition.[79] As of 1990, after a few years of experimentation, about seventy organized

graduate courses were under way, approved and funded on a competitive basis by a national research association. But all was tentative and
against the long-standing mold. "The courses are not meant to substitute [for] the traditional paths of gaining a doctoral degree through
part-time teaching and research positions at the university or through
scholarships. Rather, they are meant to supplement these forms."[80]
The old combination of belief and interest in which close linkage of research, teaching, and learning is taken to apply to all academic staff and
students, in all fields at all universities, still exhibits a powerful hold on
academic thought.

Then, in 1990, all debate and reform on the issue of graduate education had to stand aside, overshadowed by the huge problems of integrating two systems of higher education and two systems of research
organization that stemmed from the unification of the Federal Republic
of Germany and the German Democratic Republic. The future direction
of structural reform that would institutionally relocate, focus, and concentrate the unity principle might be clear, but it would have to wait on
solution of unification problems as well as on greater recognition by the
professoriate that the gap between idea and reality was growing steadily
wider.

THE INSTITUTE UNIVERSITY: A SUMMATION

The Humboldtian formulation of 1810 is without doubt the most influential academic ideology of the last two centuries. Truly liberating, this
doctrine opened an extremely broad conceptual space that stretched
from inquiry as a basis for teaching and learning to idealist formulations of broad self-development and general enlightenment. Academics
who wanted to concentrate on research and thereby have it serve as the
foundation of university life found elements in the doctrine that were
congenial to their emerging interests: for them, Humboldtian thought
became foremost a research ethic comfortable with scientific specialization. Their new interests set the tracks; the Humboldtian idea, specified
in a helpful form, rationalized a move into disciplinary science.[81]

The new disciplinarians who seized this conceptual opening gradually developed supportive tools in the form of seminars, laboratories,
and institutes that could operationally integrate research, teaching, and
study. Not created to meet increased student demand or to answer cries
for more and better people for the civil service and the outside labor
force, these instruments served a growing interest in creating knowl-

edge and teaching new specialized bodies of theory and method. During the second half of the nineteenth century, these forms became deeply institutionalized in the German university, especially in the omnibus philosophical faculties that formally housed the basic disciplines. Institute-type settings became academic locations that set research-intentioned students apart from those pursuing degrees to enter the civil service and the professions and from those who sought the dueling scar as the mark left by university life. Critically, these new tools became tied to the immense local power of the men who possessed university chairs and simultaneously served as directors of institutes. These chair-directors developed a direct relationship to funding government officials that generally bypassed both university and faculty levels of organization.

However, the chair-institute organizational form was subject to hardening of the arteries. By the period 1900–1920, the German system experienced the rigidities and sheer arbitrariness that flow in time from baronial powers, leading to problems of control and change that would surface in a major way in the last half of the twentieth century. But within that local structure, a fundamental process was established: the "research university" that was to flower internationally in the twentieth century learned in nineteenth-century Germany to differentiate programs and methods of teacher-student interaction in such a way that small enclaves could pursue research-based teaching and study while large instruments for transmitting established knowledge, especially the lecture hall and the professional curriculum, processed the much larger number of students who primarily sought practical training or university social life.

By the early twentieth century, other modern features of academic differentiation had also been born. A second sector composed of technological schools and more applied universities became a significant element, thereby giving engineering, for example, an academic home even if legal, medical, and philosophical faculties wanted little, if anything, to do with it. Especially important were the beginnings of a nonprofit research sector separate from the university, supported by industry and government, a development spurred in part by academic scientists who wanted concentrations of attention, resources, and talent for research purposes beyond what the individual universities could seemingly offer and who were impatient with the "diversion" of time to teaching and other university duties. Full-time research settings that might well leave teaching and learning aside were already proving attractive to some university scientists who wanted to maximize the pursuit of research productivity.

Fully mature by 1900, this historic system experienced enormous turbulence throughout the first half of the twentieth century which led not to significant adaptive change but first to coping with continuing disasters and then to effecting a return to the status quo ante. After 1945, virtually heroic action was needed simply to return German higher education to what it had been several decades earlier. In moving away from Fascist controls and practices, old ideas of freedom of research and freedom of teaching were given new meaning, deemed so important that they were written into the new constitution, the Basic Law of 1949, in the form of an article that simply read, "Art and science, research and teaching, are free."[82] As the autonomy of universities was vigorously stressed anew, primary emphasis was placed on individual scholars who, as researchers, should be free to choose research subjects, methods of investigation, and modes of dissemination of results and, as teachers, should be completely free in what and how they taught. To bring universities back to what they had been before the Fascist regime meant to stress again the operative tools crafted in the nineteenth century. The institute retained its primacy as the atom and molecule of German university organization—the place for inquiry and the place for linking research to teaching. Following the formula "one chair–one institute," the institute continued to be *the* means by which to organize research, base teaching on research, and involve students in research.

After 1960, the system entered an entirely new phase of development in which student expansion and knowledge expansion interacted to produce a furious pace of change. The old instruments of institute, laboratory, and seminar were placed in the context of the "mass university," with its overwhelming loads of introductory and intermediate teaching and its deepening requirements for systematized instruction and standardized pathways of study. In need of still more protective enclaves for the research-teaching-study nexus, professors devised largely informal ways deep within the formal system to separate and bring together research-minded students. As more research moved outside the university, more professors also entered into a bridging role that spanned the formal gap between university and external institute. Only a small minority of students were then chosen to cross that bridge, to become deeply involved in research—another vehicle for the natural elitism of "best science." In the linking of research to teaching and study, context and content have moved far in Germany by the 1980s from both the original Humboldtian formulation and its nineteenth-century expression in practice.

In the mass university, research activity needs the aid of much institutional differentiation. On this score the contemporary German problem runs deep. While the system has changed from elite to mass in student numbers and has become much more complex in scale of operations, its structure remained relatively undifferentiated among and within universities. Across a set of universities that number nearly seventy in 1990, little differentiation has been formally introduced or informally evolved. Hence neither resources nor personnel nor research work itself could be readily concentrated. Much applauded as a means of maintaining formal institutional equity, such nondifferentiation inflates costs: any greatly expanded system that formally treats all academic staff as if they are equally involved in research will become a high-cost system. Costs are then contained by increasing student-teacher ratios and otherwise reducing per capita support across the board. Also, as teaching occupies more time, research capacity is diminished. Further, lack of university control over student access severely retards differentation: when students are deemed fully qualified on exit from the secondary system and then left free to choose both their institutions and their fields of study, the universities "are subjected to a continuous leveling-out process."[83] When the equalization effect is so strong, universities are weakly positioned to develop their own configurations of strength, their own integrative identity.

Within the universities, as we have seen, study beyond the first major degree has had little formal definition and support, even as the function of research training tends to be pushed up and out from the first level. The differentation of a true doctoral level is increasingly, if reluctantly, seen as a step that will have to come about one way or another. If not, the temptation to let research move out of the universities to alternative sites becomes stronger. Officials and academics come to believe that better results can be gained by investing more in outside concentrations of equipment and personnel.

At the end of the twentieth century, the German system has become subjected to a vicious circle of effects. The incantation of Humboldtian doctrine across the system as a uniform principle for all serves as a serious obstacle to the development of a limited set of institutions where research and study could be productively integrated at an advanced level. Viewed from the perspective of the American system, where an

elaborately developed graduate level is the key element in the science–
higher education relationship, the contemporary lack in the German
system of a strong graduate tier is a major stumbling block. At the
same time, the commitment to research is widely and powerfully institutionalized in a plethora of major organizational instruments—many
nonprofit institutes, state and national institutes, and industrial laboratories as well as the universities. Whatever the structural deficiencies in
the universities, the willingness and capacity to fund and enable scientific research has remained world-class.

The deep and persistent problem in the German system is whether
strong research settings can be and will be maintained in key locales in
the universities, institutions where advanced teaching and study take
place across the increasingly far-flung and varied array of fields that
make up the physical sciences, biological and medical sciences, social
sciences, humanities, and many professional fields. Experiments with
"graduate colleges" under way in the early 1990s exemplify the search
for new organizational and curricular patterns that could reverse what
we can call the retreat of the research enclaves in the universities. New
forms are sought that could systematically offer thousands of microset-
tings that can closely link research, teaching, and study.

In their monumental work on the development of physics in nine-
teenth- and early twentieth-century Germany, Christa Jungnickel and
Russell McCormmach noted that three things are presently needed for
a university discipline: research by established scientists; advanced
training for students by means of involvement in research; and a comprehensive course of study.[84] Bringing these three elements into alignment in modern universities is not easy: imbalances in emphasis result
when historically determined settings push one element to the fore.
The German setting has put much weight on the research activity of
established staff. In the numerous nonuniversity sectors, with the Max
Planck institutes as foremost examples, staff research is at the forefront.
Student research is a subsidiary activity; a comprehensive course of
study is not even a part of the agenda. In the universities, staff research
again comes first, with student research somewhat emphasized but increasingly limited by the diversion of staff time and resources to "mass
studies." Critically, the element of "a comprehensive course of study" is
in short supply. Traditional patterns have long given short shrift to organized courses of study, for all students and especially for doctoral
students. A historically "thin" curricular structure has been made even
thinner by the student expansion and knowledge expansion of recent

decades. Advanced study, in a phrase, is curriculum-poor. In the inter-relating of research, teaching, and study, the basic weakness of an "institute university" is that it leaves the study component relatively unsystematized.

An observed in Germany, mass higher education and expanded disciplinary knowledge together tend to overwhelm the old tools of small-group interaction based on research when those instruments remain lodged within first-degree programs. As the organizational ground shifts, efforts to maintain appropriate settings seemingly have but three lines of change to pursue: to set aside special enclaves within the first-degree realm to which only a few students have access; to fashion inter-sector bridges that link university programs to outside institutes; and, finally, to move the integration of research, teaching, and study to a higher university tier, there to devise a teaching program and a curriculum that fuse with research activity. The latter direction of change is perhaps the one that is the most difficult to bring about. It is also the most essential.

CHAPTER TWO

Great Britain

Small Worlds, Collegiate Worlds

Studies of higher education in Britain have typically overlooked education beyond the bachelor's degree. Comprehensive volumes of thoughtful analysis have commented at best for only a page or two on "postgraduate study" or "postgraduate courses," British terms referring to graduate education and programs.[1] At the same time, throughout the twentieth century Britain has had its share of brilliant scholars and scientists and world-famous laboratories located on and off university campuses. Talented researchers have obviously been identified, brought up to a high level of capability, given resources, and offered supportive careers. Some preparation beyond the bachelor's degree surely must be a significant segment of university work. Why then has so little been said? Is the most advanced level of university work so unproblematic that it does not need to be described, let alone assessed? Is there perhaps not much that warrants comment?

The typical neglect in Britain of graduate education and its place in research activity and training testifies to certain fixations in that country in the thought and practice of higher education. As in Germany, ideas, structures, and procedures developed before the present century established a virtual genetic imprint whose features have persisted even after great change in the late twentieth century. That imprint is one of an exclusive base of operations that combines the elements of undergraduate commitment and small-scale organization, modeled historically by the highly selective residential college. Oxford and Cambridge, each operating as a conglomerate of such colleges, fathered a systemwide emphasis on intensive, high-quality undergraduate instruction that until quite recently was operationalized throughout the university sector in a generous ratio of one teacher for every eight students. This commitment has long involved sharply limited access, more than in the Continental systems, let alone the American and the Japanese; and, as a corollary, it has entailed high unit costs, a feature that in recent years has come home to roost with a vengeance. In the late twentieth century, this historic pattern has become thoroughly nationalized, its ideas and practices in many respects even officially standardized.

At the same time, an English research system has developed both within and outside the academy. British academics have found their way to disciplinary specialization in the form of academic departments overlaid with the expectation that research is part of the role of all university academic staff. Special lines of research funding developed; students were brought forward beyond the first degree as "research students." But the place of research training has continued to be powerfully shaped by the general university framework. If in the forming of a research-teaching-study nexus the German system has offered an "institute university," the English system presents distinctively the setting of a "collegiate" or "undergraduate university." In this setting, resource constraint under single-source governmental funding became in the 1970s and 1980s a major obstacle to the development of a robust, competitive postgraduate tier in which systematic study could be fused with the research activities of professors.

THE EXCLUSIVE BASE

The history of British higher education is a history of high institutional concentration, since just two universities, Oxford and Cambridge, monopolized the higher learning in England for six centuries, from the twelfth and early thirteenth until the founding of the Universities of London and Durham in the second quarter of the nineteenth. In the centuries leading up to the Reformation, Oxford and Cambridge were mainly "clerical institutions concerned with educating clergy for the two national churches"; after the mid-sixteenth century, they "ceased to be merely the education organs of the Church" and slipped sideways to educate, alongside the secular clergy, a new lay clientele, the sons of landed gentry.[2] Despite the lack of alternative institutions, student numbers were never large, with annual intakes at each university ranging between 300 and 500; when the intakes fell away in the mid-eighteenth

century to 200 to 250, the universities remained barely alive. During a
sustained period of decline, they slipped badly in tone and practice.
Continuing well into the eighteenth century, the academic staff—
"dons"—had a reputation for a mindless combination of dullness, de-
bauchery, and rebellion. At the beginning of the nineteenth century,
when Humboldt was organizing the University of Berlin under new
principles and Napoleon was casting the unitary national university in
France, the two (and the only) institutions of higher education in England and Wales were in a deep slumber. In thought and practice, these
were institutions antithetical to scientific research.

What Oxbridge long cultivated was the useful tool of the undergraduate residential college, the operational unit that is the essence of their
distinctiveness internationally among major forms of university organization. Here the university did not become a set of four or more major
faculties organized around such fields as law and medicine, as on the
Continent, nor was it primarily to take the shape of an extended array
of letters and science departments and separate professional schools, as
in the case of the American university that emerged in the late nineteenth century. Instead the university essentially took the shape of a federation of colleges, with each college operating as a self-contained unit,
with its own staff, students, buildings, grounds, financial resources, and
identity; for example, Balliol at Oxford and King's College at Cambridge. For staff as well as for students, the colleges were as fully residential as they could be. Notably, the staff were not "professors" but
"fellows," "tutors," and "dons," academics intensely interested in the
forming of student character, for which a liberal education, one decidedly not professional and certainly not disciplinary, was the proper
medicine. The "classroom" ideally was a tutoring session, a face-to-
face and hence highly personal encounter between a tutor and a student. Since a system of this type depends on a low ratio of students to
faculty, it was intrinsically a high-cost system. When each tutor had "to
teach the whole syllabus to a handful of students,"[3] there was no way
to do it cheaply, especially when the syllabus was just part of an expensive larger but tightly knit educational community—the residential college as a whole—staffed with servants and equipped with fireplaces and
"dreaming spires." In spirit and organization, the Oxbridge form of
university was the antithesis of the emerging German pattern in which
research came to the fore as the foundation of much teaching and study.

But a second historic imprint also developed in the higher education
of Britain in the eighteenth and nineteenth centuries: Scotland was a

subsystem in its own right and had four ancient universities that went a different route. St. Andrew's, Aberdeen, Glasgow, and Edinburgh, all founded in the fifteenth and sixteenth centuries, had by the eighteenth century given up the expensive tutorial system and "adopted the much cheaper system of using professors expert in a single subject as lecturers to large classes."[4] Based on such specialization, a few professors became advanced thinkers and researchers, for example, Colin Maclaurin in advanced mathematics, David Hume in philosophy, Adam Smith in philosophy and economics, and hence were forerunners internationally of the research ethic that was to flower in the nineteenth century. Critically, when new institutions were finally created in England, beginning with the University of London in 1826 and the University of Durham in 1834 and extending on after midcentury with such civic "redbrick" universities as Manchester, Leeds, Birmingham, and Bristol, they followed the Scottish professorial system as the basis of teaching and organization and moved into a departmental rather than a fully collegiate structure. In turn, Oxford and Cambridge, under heavy criticism, went through meaningful reform in the third quarter of the century to introduce modern teaching of modern subjects and to strengthen "the university and the professoriate against the colleges and the tutorial fellows."[5] This revolution "accepted just enough of the alternative tradition to keep Oxford and Cambridge in front in social prestige and intellectual eminence," while "the college fellows continued to dominate the education of the undergraduates."[6]

Thus an extended research orientation grounded in departmental structure came into the English system in the late nineteenth century in both new and old universities, arguably more from the influence of the indigenous Scottish model of disciplinary specialization than from the foreign German example that many advocates of reform, the new men of science, watched closely and whose growing strength was used to argue for change at home.[7] The English did not borrow the German research institute, they did not turn professors into civil servants appointed and paid by the state, and they did not turn students loose to wander from university to university. Critically, the chair did not become a base unit, with its incumbent dominating all in sight, nor did junior faculty labor as unpaid assistants, like Dozent in Germany. Instead, both in the interdisciplinary residential college and in the disciplinary department, members of the academic staff were colleagues, with a common stake in development of their unit.[8]

The Oxbridge heritage was particularly powerful in establishing small size as a reigning characteristic of individual universities and the system as a whole. At the turn of the twentieth century, when less than 1 percent of the age group, compared to 4 percent in the United States, were entering higher education as a whole, Oxford and Cambridge together totaled less than 9,000 students, a small number divided among many residential colleges.[9] The civic universities, even if located in industrial cities and somewhat more attuned to practical affairs, were also inclined to be small, stressing selectivity and high quality as well as institutional autonomy. In 1914, on the eve of World War I, the five existing redbrick universities, together with the University of London, did not total more than 20,000 students.[10] The characteristic of smallness was to endure as an almost permanent feature, setting British universities apart from Continental and American ones right down to the present time. In the late 1930s, *average* size of the then-existing twenty-four British universities was 2,000 students; in the early 1980s, the average across forty-seven institutions was 6,400 students. In both instances, the average was pulled up by the uncommonly large size of the University of London, a federation of colleges that in the 1980s totaled nearly 50,000 full- and part-time students. More revealing, the *modal* or most frequent university size in the late 1930s was under 1,000 students; in the early 1960s, only 1,000 to 2,000; and in the early 1980s, only 3,000 to 5,000.[11] Hence the size of the English university, when compared to American institutions, has been closer to that of a large private liberal arts college with an enrollment of 2,000 to 3,000 than to that of a major university with an enrollment in most cases of over 15,000 and in many cases, private and public, 30,000 to 50,000. Institutional size has been nowhere near the massive scale of many German, French, and Italian universities.

Additionally, the nineteenth-century universities were essentially private. The Oxford and Cambridge colleges had long accumulated their own resources, living as much as possible off of endowments, gifts, and student fees. Not dependent on either church or state, they became addicted to the habit of rugged independence, offering to the world a model of institutional autonomy. The new universities also raised funds from private benefactors, less than Oxford and Cambridge were able to do but still enough to place the system as a whole as "largely a matter of private enterprise."[12] As late as 1920, when an evolution toward state funding was well under way, about as much university income came from fees, endowments, and private donations as from parliamentary grants and allotments from local authorities.[13] The contrast with such centralized systems as the French was sharp: a financial base existed for autonomy from the state.

To sum up the historic pattern: at the end of the nineteenth century an imprint was firmly embedded. British higher education had been first priestly, then aristocratic. Closed and always sharply selective, it was intensely elite in its numerical and social intake. The students were fully supported in the sense that they were persons of independent means, an early form of "entitlement" that was later taken over by the state. The universities were small and their subcolleges and departments intimate: student life was residential; faculty concentrated on close face-to-face relations with undergraduates. Some professors had clearly begun to incorporate research in their own activity, but in contrast to late nineteenth-century Germany, research was an add-on to teaching duties rather than the basis of university organization and professorial orientation. Notably, systematic research training of students was not much in evidence. The Ph.D. had not yet been introduced. The bachelor's degree was the degree that counted, and the degree of overwhelming importance was a bachelor's from a college at one of two leading institutions. A basis was well established for the marginalization of postgraduate work. "University" meant "college."

NATIONALIZATION OF TRADITION

In significant part, the twentieth-century story of British higher education is one of erosion of the fiscal base of university autonomy, with the universities financially converted into state dependencies. As a percentage of total university income, grants from the national government—"parliamentary grants"—rose from 33 percent in 1920 to 80 percent in 1946.[14] Thus, in its financial foundations, the British system has been basically nationalized for almost a half-century, a simple fact long masked by the intermediary role played by the well-known University Grants Committee (UGC). In a golden age that stretched from 1920 to the mid-1960s, this committee composed of senior academics showed the world how a set of universities could be dependent financially on one public source, the national treasury department, and at the same time remain administratively and academically independent. But there was nothing in the structure of the relationship to ensure that the committee would indefinitely co-opt the government rather than the reverse. The decline of the UGC began when a direct, privileged relationship to the Treasury became transformed in the mid-

1960s into a subordinate relationship to the education department of
the national government. Decline became demise in 1988, when the
UGC gave way to a new funding body, the Universities Funding Council (UFC).

What is certain in retrospect is that steadily but surely there accumulated a national approach, a sentiment and a willingness to conceive of
all universities in the country as part of a national system, one in which
it was appropriate, even in the face of the towering distinctiveness of
Oxford and Cambridge, to administer fairly and uniformly across a national set of institutions. The habit had obtained since at least the mid-
nineteenth century to think of standards setting as a quasi-national responsibility, one that in the first instance was handled by a supervising
institutional parent. Rowland Eustace and Graeme Moodie have noted
that when a new body established in the 1960s (the Council for National Academic Awards [CNAA]) took up the task of authenticating
and guaranteeing the standards of a new nonuniversity sector composed of polytechnics and colleges of higher education, it was essentially following the classic pattern laid down by the University of London "from the 1860s for the new sector constituted by the English
provincial and civic universities," in which the new institutions had
their work examined and certified by a parenting central institution.[15]
The supervision exercised by the University of London was essentially
private or nongovernmental in nature, while that of the much later
CNAA was considerably closer to governmental rule, but both were
cases of "central quality assurance."

Then, in the twentieth century, beyond the system-integrating pro-
pensities of fiscal dependency on national government, early specific
steps toward nationalization were taken which seemed at the time to
be minor adjustments. For example, as early as 1946, long before the
days of heavy-handed governmental encroachment, the British universities moved to a national pay scale for their sector.[16] Salaries were
henceforth to be negotiated nationally, not locally, essentially among a
department of the national government, a national committee of university heads, and a national union. Hence, among other effects and in
sharp contrast to German and particularly American counterparts, university administrators and faculties could no longer use monetary rewards competitively as a way to attract talented academics to their
own institutions. And such salary scales have a developmental logic of
their own. By the early 1980s, a British observer has noted, this academic scale had become "one of the longest single scales in the whole

of public employment. It is largely age-related, with extensive use being made of an age tie point at 26. [It is] unimaginative, plodding and designed to discourage creativity and eliminate incentives. Once appointed an employee creeps toward the maximum with only minor variations in speed."[17] As cogently argued by Harold Perkin, this nationally unified salary structure has had "a deleterious effect on professional mobility," since it has reduced greatly the incentives for staff movement among British universities and thereby has provided "little opportunity for the almost automatic shake-up for both individuals and institutions that comes from migration."[18]

Other nationwide uniformities were gradually introduced, if not as specific prescriptions then as "important general constraints." By the 1960s, staffing ratios were "indicated"; that is, universities received their funds "on the assumption that" not more than a stipulated share of the staff would be in the top grades of senior lecturers, readers, and professors.[19] The UGC not only came to stand for "the national interest" but took on the responsibility to define plans for the development of the universities "as may from time to time be required to ensure that they are fully adequate to national needs."[20] Long before block grants to the universities were completely abolished, the grants were in actuality an addition of costs for component departments of each university, and those sums were known to UGC members. Scholarly experts on the evolution of the UGC, notably Lord Ashby and Robert Berdahl, characterized the state of affairs existing as early as the 1950s as "crypto-dirigisme"—hidden, unavowed state planning and control.[21]

The "crypto" could soon be deleted: the real thing, the overt form, developed between 1963 and 1982. With each passing year, the beat of central direction picked up. Shortly after the UGC was placed under the Department of Education and Science (DES), the comptroller of the national government, in 1968, took up the right to audit the records of the universities and the UGC. Additionally, the UGC "was persuaded to take a much more positive line on productivity, specialization, concentration of subjects, and control of building through cost limits."[22] The UGC's system of expert advisory subcommittees steadily expanded, with each subcommittee responsible for the "rationalization" of a subject field. What had been gentle "general guidance given orally in meetings between the UGC and the individual vice-chancellor" (the campus chief officer) became a written Memorandum of General Guidance that sketched the thinking of the committee in such crucial areas as "total student numbers, postgraduate numbers, unit costs, collaboration with industry, inter-university and inter-sector collaboration, fields covered by earmarked grants, and the various subject areas in which the Committee was taking a particular interest."[23] By 1970, the committee was even issuing a *preliminary* Memorandum of General Guidance, to help channel university quinquennial planning in "realistic" directions. The UGC steadily became more quantitative and specific. By the end of the 1960s, it self-consciously reported that it had necessarily abandoned "the neutral buffer principle." Henceforth it, together with the DES, would be centrally steering the university sector.

Britain's budget crisis of the 1970s then produced a virtual quantum leap in top-down control. All public sectors were placed under tight reins. For higher education this meant, in 1974–1975 for example, no more money despite 20 percent inflation. Capital expenditures were severely cut. By 1976–1977, the governmental outlay was announced as a "cash limit," with no additional funds available for any reason. Critically, the government felt obliged to end its quinquennial pattern of finance, which had traditionally been a major source of stability and capacity for self-development in the universities. For the 1977–1982 period, only a grant for the first year could be stated firmly, with provisional estimates made for the second and third year—a "rolling triennium." By the end of the 1970s, the universities were struggling to keep afloat financially.

The year 1979 saw the Thatcher Conservative government come to power, with even tougher medicine in mind. The government immediately instituted "level funding," a freeze. It then insisted, among other changes, that fees charged foreign students be raised to full cost, intruding in a major way on the universities' right to set fees. As of 1980 the UGC had become so much the enforcer of centrally determined governmental restrictions and impositions that full-bodied dirigisme was at hand. Said the chairman of the UGC to the universities that crucial year,

We want you to concentrate on your strengths, and not support pallid growths which are now never likely to reach maturity. The excision of these feeble limbs is something where the committee can help, even [if] it is only to lend you a financial pruning knife.... There is going to be in the future a somewhat greater degree of direct intervention by the UGC in the affairs of individual universities than has been customary or necessary in the past.... The fact remains that the reconciling of what is desired *locally* with what is desirable *nationally* can be done almost covertly in an expanding system, where all the signs are positive, and the committee maintains steerage by selective addition, but in a system where some of the signs are going to be negative, where resources are going to be taken away as well as added, steerage necessarily becomes more overt.[24]

Here was the open admission that the UGC had for some years been engaged in covert guidance. And here was the open promise that overt steerage would now be national policy.

The crisis of the early 1980s centered on an overall budget cut between 1981–1982 and 1983–1984 of approximately 13 to 15 percent.[25] As the group that had to wield the knife, the UGC chose selective pruning rather than cutting by equal shares. To make certain fateful decisions, the committee, through its numerous subject area subcommittees, judged the strengths and weaknesses of university departments. Bypassing the institutional level of university control, this process produced overall effects on institutions that followed from centrally aggregating the assessments of individual departments. In the resulting actions, two institutions received cuts in the neighborhood of 6 percent, while three received reductions that ranged between 30 and 44 percent. Among subject areas, engineering and technology received small increases, while the social sciences, the arts, the biological sciences, and medicine received cuts.

In the early and mid-1980s, it had become patently clear that the old cozy relationship among the universities, the UGC, and the government was gone forever. Links that a half-century, even a quarter-century, before had been personal and informal, in a context of "clubby benevolence,"[26] were now bureaucratic and formal, in a context of adversarial relations. What had evolved was "an official system."[27] But, ironically, this grand systemization took place without Britain ever truly entering the age of mass higher education. By the early 1980s, when systems in continental Europe had expanded to 20 to 30 percent of the age group or higher, the British system remained in the 12 to 14 percent range overall, with only 6 to 7 percent gaining access to the universities. With a low rate of access, expansion remained a steady item on the policy agenda: the famous Robbins Report of 1963 took the lead in advocating increased access.[28] But the strong commitment to quality, defined on a systemwide basis for all to see in such forms as the low student-teacher ratio, insisted on funded expansion that would not dilute the "unit of resource." For many devoted academics this meant that if costs had to be contained, then there should be no more students; if costs had to be reduced, then better to have fewer students than seemingly to diminish quality. But the maintenance of high quality on this basis could best stall for a few more years, in the 1980s, the inevitability of expansion on a reduced cost basis. The government wanted both expansion and lower per-person costs, and it had the means to achieve its wishes.

The university part of British higher education thus came to possess the logic of a homogenizing system, one at once relatively tidy and non-innovative. The convergence of institutions on a single university model was as much brought about by UGC guidance as by emulative drift. Michael Shattock has identified well the contents of this logic.

> Throughout its history, the UGC, while strongly upholding the universities' autonomy, had tended to emphasize the homogeneity of the system. It is perhaps inevitable that a central bureaucracy, armed with the power of the purse, should unconsciously guide individual institutions down a common path.... [T]he system of resource allocation, both capital and recurrent, the use of full-time student equivalents as the "currency" for recurrent grant, the categorization of student targets into Arts, Science and Medical ... and the use of norms to control the proportion of senior to junior academic staff or the allocation of capital grant, have all had the effect of providing a university model that is easier for universities to fit into than to depart from.... [T]he system suffers from a tidyness and a homogeneity which has discouraged innovation outside the conventional university model.[29]

In effect, British universities could be autonomous provided they marched to the same drummer. As of the 1980s, they were by international standards decidedly unfree. Higher financing and supervising bodies, if they wished, could simply ignore the evolved organic character of whole institutions as they assessed the comparative strengths of departments and funded accordingly. In more than one aspect of centralization, British academic life had become more Napoleonic than present-day practices in France.

Alongside the universities, a second major sector of British higher education was created in the mid-1960s with a decision to establish thirty polytechnics and to introduce a binary principle. On one side of an officially established line, there would be an "autonomous" sector made up of universities, including ten former colleges of advanced technology (CATs) "upgraded" to the status of universities; on the other, the government defined a "public sector" of higher education that consisted largely of polytechnics and teacher colleges. The polytechnics were financed out of local taxes and come under the oversight of the local education authorities (LEAs) that administer primary and secondary education.[30] They were not given the privilege, possessed by the universities, of validating their own degrees. Instead, in some detail, their curricula had to be reviewed and approved by the Council for National Academic Awards, an official national validating body that answered to the Department of Education and Science.

When the central government redefined its relationship to higher education in the 1970s, assuming an ever more powerful interventionist posture, the teacher-training segment of this second sector was extremely hard hit. Operating under the control of the DES, with none of the protection that university status might give, the teacher colleges were vulnerable to edicts that forced many of them to close their doors entirely and others to give up their identities as they amalgamated with other institutions. The number of student teachers under training was reduced from 45,000 in 1977 to 18,000 in 1981.[31] Here was top-down manpower planning with a vengeance, as dirigiste as anything in France or Sweden or elsewhere in centralized systems of the Continent. The polytechnics, in turn, remained for a time under local government control and were relatively free to expand, especially as students were diverted to them by enrollment caps placed on the universities. But the "polys" were not long to escape central hands. In 1982, the national government established the National Advisory Board for Local Authority Higher Education (NAB) to provide central oversight. Reporting directly to the Department of Education and Science, NAB examined individual institutions on such dimensions as cost-effectiveness and subject balance and managed to embroil itself in the minutiae of approving courses and allocating students. In a few years' time, NAB became for the second sector what the UGC was for the first—an intermediary agency acting in an executive capacity at the national level. In both sectors, responsibilities previously located at the grass-roots level, institutional or governmental, had moved upward to national departments of government and to "academic" agencies that operate directly under them.[32]

In the space of two decades then, between the mid-1960s and the mid-1980s, the control of higher education across the board moved away from a policy style of "bottom up, hands off" and toward one of "top-down, hands on" that is generally characteristic of formally nationalized systems.[33] The system came under active government intervention to specify student enrollment, to close institutions or to force their amalgamation, to allocate additional resources to certain fields of study while reducing funds for others, and, even, to affect institutional personnel policies by means of earmarked allocations for subjects and by the use of broad early retirement and new-blood policies that could hardly take into account local variation and need. Twenty years after the government began gently to increase its systemwide interventions, the British system had embarked on "an unprecedented exercise in dirigisme."[34] At the end of the 1980s, when the minister spoke, everyone listened; an official system was indeed in place. As central bodies concerned themselves with systemwide patterns of subjects and looked to the sums of institutional outputs, system replaced institution as the foremost unit for consideration.[35] The idea of a unitary state, dominant in British political life, had become in higher education the idea of a unitary system. The idea of the university, so much talked about since at least the mid-nineteenth century, was now formally encapsulated in a governmental framework.

But no matter whose hand was on the tiller of the system at large, what did not change drastically up through the 1980s was the twin commitment to undergraduate education and small universities. A key indicator was the nature of a new set of institutions developed during the 1950s and 1960s. At a time of major expansion, when enrollment increased from 83,000 in 1951 to more than 200,000 in 1968, eight so-called plateglass universities were established, all residential, all in small towns, all in the range of 2,000 to 8,000 students.[36] The most noted of this new set of institutions, the University of Sussex, was planned and funded to have a faculty of 350 to 400 for a student body of 3,000, based on the traditional staff-student ratio of 1:8. Undergraduate students in their first two years were to have tutorials, then move on to third-year seminars. The plateglass university ideal, expressed in *The Idea of a New University*, a collection of essays written by the new Sussex faculty, was a match for the traditional ideal in its focus on intense, high-quality undergraduate instruction in an intimate residential setting.[37]

Despite the large, wrenching changes at the macrolevel of creeping governmental control, other significant, ingrained practices were continued at the operating levels of the system. Central was the continuation of the practice of "external examiners" in which students are examined by academics from universities other than their own.[38] As they test the quality of students, visiting examiners naturally cast their eyes over quality of curriculum and quality of staff. Broad quality control over teaching and the conditions of undergraduate learning is thereby effected by academic professionals rather than by state bureaucratic staff or market interactions. This uncommon practice fits hand-in-glove with the finely tuned grading of English undergraduates at the end of the three-year program in categories of first-class, second-class, and third-class honors and pass. Further discriminations have been made by using such categories as "upper second class," followed by efforts to subdivide that band of approval. These graduation markings retain great importance: for those hoping to go on to postgraduate work to become "research students," achievement of first-class, or at least upper-second-class, honors becomes a virtual necessity to attain financial support from a national council in the form, in the 1980s, of a three-year studentship.[39] Thus, relative to operational patterns observed in Germany, France, the United States, and Japan, British academics as a matter of traditional style watch one another closely across institutions and the university system at large. And they evaluate first-degree graduating students closely in categories that have intense systemwide meaning. In short, external examination and common degree ranking have been central elements in a systemwide pursuit of "a pure, thin stream of excellence."

From all sides, the preservation of quality wins high praise, even placed front and center. In the early 1990s, the incumbent minister for higher education, from the Conservative party, spoke of "existing traditions of high quality teaching and research" as "a massive strength." The out-of-power Labour party asserted in a policy document that "quality has been the touchstone" in a "well-deserved international reputation." The Committee of Vice-Chancellors and Principals (CVCP), arguing against "expansion on the cheap," maintained that "throughout the 1980's UK universities have resisted pressures which would have led to loss of quality and standing. In the face of Governmental exhortation ... they have expanded only where they could still be sure of offering students a high quality education."[40] Specific actions went beyond the torrent of words in praise of quality. In the late 1980s, for example, the CVCP, on behalf of the universities, established their own "academic audit unit" to provide systematic external review of courses and teaching, going beyond the less systematic external examining system, now thought somewhat inbred and lacking sufficient reassurance. This second self-imposed homogenizing device, to be effected by ostensible peers turned auditors, was invented to attempt to head off more governmental intervention by means of externally based instruments of quality control, for example, "an alien corps of full-time HMI-style inquisitors."[41] Long entitled to visit the elementary and secondary schools of the realm, Her Majesty's Inspectors were now at the university gates.

With a seemingly inexorable drift to state-framed coordination and direction, creeping nationalization had led by the end of the 1980s to much standardization of resources, programs, personnel policies, and institutional assessments. To bring all institutions under one tent, even the binary distinction was erased in 1990, establishing officially a single system, with funding bodies and central committees overlaid with super bodies and even higher committees, or consolidated in single units, to narrow to a peak in a pyramid of control. At the same time, the universities and their academic departments have attempted to cling to their traditional orientation and curricular organization. "The English idea of a university" has continued to be voiced in unconscious assumption and unspoken attitude as well as in spirited rhetoric: when the academics themselves paid homage to high quality, they still meant honors programs and finely graded undergraduate degrees, small-scale settings and personal interaction in the tutorial session and the undergraduate seminar. New universities and colleges have steadily taken on long-approved patterns designed to ensure quality undergraduate teaching and study. Both informally and formally, the idea has a national embrace. The tools of unity are multifaceted. As summed up aptly by Eustace,

> The key to British higher education remains its academic unity, held together by a rigorous system of degrees policed directly by central validating bodies; indirectly by the interlocking system of external examiners; and by the emulation and ambition of teachers, institutions, and students. To this is added the aversion of government and its agencies to spending money on anything which does not appear to be of high standard.[42]

Proceeding within a thoroughly nationalized mode of control that it had obtained, the British government, by the end of the 1980s, was also strongly pushing the universities into a whole new set of relationships that were lumped in a confusing way under the idea of "the market." One direction of change under this general mandate is reduction in the share of university costs provided by governmental subsidy. As government deliberately reduces its share, the price of institutional viability is to increase income from such other sources as student fees, private donations, and contracts with industrial firms. No longer is the national purse to pick up 80 percent of costs: by 1990, some universities in the forefront of this change, for example, Warwick and Bristol, were down to 40 percent; according to claims of the committee of vice-chancellors, the university sector as a whole was down to less than 50 percent in dependency on government funding in the form of core support provided by recurrent institutional funds (47% in 1990 compared to 63% in 1980). Another 20 percent flowed through a research line of grants and contracts largely provided by the government through research councils; 14 percent came from tuition fees; and the remaining 20 percent or so came from services, endowments, and miscellaneous sources.[43] During a decade that was more fateful for British higher education than any other in the twentieth century, institutional entrepreneurship and diversified finance entered the picture, but all under the close scrutiny and detailed monitoring of central funding bodies.

A second major move has taken the form of increasing effort to separate funding for teaching from funding for research, and in a way that would differentiate the universities. The "market" in this case consists of institutions competing for governmental outlays based on performance in teaching and, separately, performance in research, as each is assessed by government. Some of the flavor of this state-and-market combination in a solidified unitary system is exhibited in a single table offered in 1992, reproduced as table 1, that depicts fifty-one universities of England, Wales, Scotland, and Northern Ireland according to percentage changes in a three-year period in allocations made by the Universities Funding Council. In this fascinating and rapidly evolving scenario, the council funds each university for a predetermined number of students; the universities are free to add students who pay their way ("fees-only" students), with no money from the council for their support. The UFC then compares the universities on their prior "success" in recruiting the no-cost students and rewards institutions that score above average: institutions that expand faster than others on the backs of such students can garner more resources by increasing allocated funds for teaching. In turn, having assessed university departments on their research productivity in an elaborate and highly mechanical exercise, the funding council also sets financial rewards for above average research rankings; institutions with favorable ratings could then "top up" their overall allocations with more funds earmarked for research, a clear case of "the more, the more." The universities were also directed not to spend money intended for research on teaching and vice versa: blending and cross-subsidization were somehow to be ruled out.

Thus universities already well positioned to become part of a small group of "research-dominated" institutions can keep down student ex-

TABLE ONE CHANGES IN UNIVERSITIES FUNDING COUNCIL ALLOCATIONS TO BRITISH UNIVERSITIES, 1991–1992 TO 1993–1994

	Percentage Change in:				
	Funded Students	*Fees-only Students*	*Teaching Funds*	*Research Funds*	*Total Resources*
Aston	−0.5	2.1	2.5	2.0	2.4
Bath	0.0	7.5	3.0	8.8	4.8
Birmingham	1.9	16.4	5.1	9.2	6.5
Bradford	3.6	16.5	6.9	3.0	5.8
Bristol	0.3	11.4	4.0	15.4	8.0
Brunel	12.0	22.7	13.8	−3.0	9.3
Cambridge	−0.8	2.7	2.7	18.9	9.6
City	14.1	36.8	14.6	12.5	14.0
Durham	8.5	19.5	11.5	11.6	11.5
East Anglia	0.6	9.9	3.9	14.5	7.5
Essex	23.7	26.9	25.6	16.8	22.4
Exeter	3.8	16.5	6.9	11.7	8.2
Hull	4.3	20.3	8.9	4.3	7.6
Keele	29.8	48.0	32.2	2.5	23.4
Kent	3.5	23.7	8.0	8.1	8.0
Lancaster	1.5	18.0	5.3	10.9	7.1
Leeds	10.6	25.2	12.2	8.7	11.1
Leicester	9.2	33.7	12.4	13.1	12.6
Liverpool	12.2	32.2	13.1	9.4	11.9
London Business School	0.3	5.6	3.3	27.6	13.7
London	4.0	17.4	6.1	13.7	9.1
(Imperial)	0.1	6.4	3.2	19.9	11.0
Loughborough	9.9	24.9	12.1	3.5	9.5
Manchester	2.5	13.9	4.8	9.5	6.4
(Business School)	−5.8	−3.3	−2.5	13.4	2.2
Manchester Institute S&T	4.6	14.9	7.8	10.6	8.9
Newcastle	10.8	23.8	12.3	12.4	12.3
Nottingham	4.6	19.5	8.5	11.6	9.6
Oxford	0.4	4.6	3.8	18.2	10.2
Reading	2.2	18.2	6.0	6.8	6.3

	Percentage Change in:				
	Funded Students	*Fees-only Students*	*Teaching Funds*	*Research Funds*	*Total Resources*
Salford	11.8	22.4	15.3	0.8	11.4
Sheffield	0.5	17.4	3.6	10.5	5.8
Southampton	0.2	9.3	3.2	10.2	5.6
Surrey	2.9	12.4	5.2	9.7	6.7
Sussex	9.6	23.1	14.0	9.7	12.4
Warwick	0.5	14.1	3.5	17.0	8.2
York	−0.2	9.7	2.9	13.7	6.5
ENGLAND	4.7	17.2	7.4	12.1	9.0
Aberystwyth	1.2	9.2	4.3	8.8	5.6
Bangor	15.7	27.3	19.2	3.8	14.5
Cardiff	12.3	30.9	13.7	1.9	10.2
St. David's	20.4	31.5	23.2	1.1	18.2
Swansea	28.6	40.6	28.6	4.7	21.5
University of Wales, Medicine	−4.8	−17.5	0.8	8.9	3.4
WALES	13.8	27.9	15.1	4.6	12.0
Aberdeen	9.6	23.3	11.9	8.1	10.8
Dundee	21.7	40.7	20.6	12.1	18.0
Edinburgh	2.6	17.9	5.9	17.0	9.8
Glasgow	7.3	17.7	10.1	13.9	11.4
Heriot-Watt	12.8	25.3	14.4	6.4	11.7
St. Andrew's	2.6	15.4	5.1	10.0	6.6
Stirling	16.1	35.2	19.7	9.0	16.7
Strathclyde	15.0	25.6	16.8	6.0	13.4
SCOTLAND	9.3	22.6	11.6	12.0	11.7
Belfast	6.8	18.0	10.6	−0.3	7.8
Ulster	6.3	14.9	10.4	−12.1	5.1
NORTHERN IRELAND	6.6	16.2	10.5	−6.2	6.3

SOURCE: *Times Higher Education Supplement*, February 28, 1992, 3.

pansion while they engage in research expansion: institutions headed in this direction, shown in table 1 by a large increase in research funds in a three-year period, include Cambridge, Oxford, Bristol, Warwick, Imperial College, and York. Institutions headed toward "teaching dominated," as shown by large increases in teaching funds, include Keele, Salford, and Swansea. But this route is less desirable because for academics it spells second-class status. The only way to reverse direction is to improve the institution's research rating in the next "selectivity round," a time set for new ratings.

However, even in Britain not all universities can be above average. There have to be relatively low scorers on research who are then ostensibly driven toward funding based largely, if not wholly, on teaching; others in a middle range are financed to have modest research capability; and a dozen or so are blessed with more research money. Strong steerage is effected by means of a "market" of choices framed by government-defined rewards and punishments. And effects can reach deep inside the universities. In a close and exacting early review in 1990 of the "effects on university research of the new funding policy announced by the UGC in 1985," Bruce Williams noted, first, that "in the sciences and technologies the low research ratings of small departments have provided strong incentives to review their continued existence"; second, that "the traditional dominance of the needs of teaching ... has been called in question"; and third, institutions with low and medium ratings have sought in scientific fields "to provide research teams of sufficient size and number to qualify for high research ratings, at the expense of a range of specially designed courses for undergraduates." Overall, "in all but universities with very high research ratings the new funding policy had a considerable effect on the extent, nature and organization of research."[44] Unanticipated and undesired consequences have reverberated throughout the system, as when the assessment and rating exercise encourages more commitment to research in relatively research-poor settings that are supposed to settle into a posture of "teaching dominated."

THE INTEGRATION OF AN ACADEMIC RESEARCH SYSTEM

In a comprehensive analysis of macrofeatures of graduate education and research training in Britain, Mary Henkel and Maurice Kogan have stressed that the British government does not have a graduate education policy, that, in particular, relatively little thought has been given to the doctoral level and its viability in various disciplines.[45] Reflected in major divisions for higher education and science in its own structure, the British DES has had, in effect, a dual responsibility for graduate studies. On the education side, it has laid down a broad framework within which the national coordinating bodies for the university and public sector institutions, among their many other actions, specify the distribution of student places among subjects and between undergraduate and graduate levels. In the case of graduate students, however, allocated places have not been funded places. On the science or research side, the department has allocated funds to national research councils to which universities, departments, and students turn for research support. For that assistance, the funds of the councils have become the principal money stream.

The research councils have been a product of growing national interests in the promotion of science and technology. Like governments in other advanced nations, the British government has hardly needed through the years to give much practical thought to the teaching of sociology or literature, or indeed even to the teaching of physics. But virtually throughout the twentieth century, as in the case of Germany, the attention of government officials has been drawn to scientific research and its potential contribution to national welfare. As early as the turn of the century, the British government moved out of the passive stage of supporting the likes of the Geological Survey and the Ordnance Survey, plus giving a few grants to individual scientists, to the active stage of supporting state-owned laboratories. The National Physical Laboratory (1899), a facility intended "to bring scientific knowledge to bear upon everyday industrial and commercial practice," opened the door to substantial state involvement in the form of laboratories, supported by ministries, that were to number fifteen soon after World War I.[46] Their rapid growth elicited concern that decisions about research might become overwhelmingly located in the hands of ministers, leading by 1920 to "the Haldane principle" that the government should fund research by means of lump-sum allocations to autonomous research councils. The council mechanism gradually took center stage in the allocation, planning, and coordination of British research. The Medical Research Council, established in 1920, was followed a decade later by a council for agriculture and still later by others for nature and the environment (1949), the sciences (1964), as a transfer of support from an earlier department of scientific and industrial research, and the social sciences (1965).[47]

In the 1980s, the universities received their core funding from the DES via the University Grants Committee (after 1989, the Universities Funding Council); and the polytechnics received theirs in a parallel fashion through the National Advisory Board (replaced in 1989 by the Polytechnics and Colleges Funding Council). This "institutional line" of support for the universities assumed that professors spend about a third of their time on research (for the polytechnics, little if any of the core support was imputed in this fashion, giving them lower unit costs). Hence some support for research was provided in the form of general subsidy of faculty time. But other monies have had to come mainly via the second stream, the research council line, including financial support for graduate students. The five councils distribute studentships as well as research funds that go directly to faculty.

As key players on the institutional stage, the councils have had multiple ways to spend their money. They can allocate to institutes directly under their own supervision and to institutes at the universities (the three councils in medicine, agriculture, and environment have used institutes heavily), as well as offer research grants and make graduate student awards. The governmental science budget in the late 1980s, comprising four-fifths of the funds of the councils, was distributed about one-third for the support of institutes, one-fourth for research grants, and one-eight (13%) for student awards, with the balance of funds going to administration, capital, and international involvements, such as participation in the Centre Européen pour Recherche Nucléare (CERN) in Switzerland.[48]

From their beginning in 1920 through the 1960s, paralleling the golden age of the University Grants Committee, the research councils were field led: they answered primarily to the demands of academics. But as in the case of the UGC, they came under increasingly heavy pressure from government to steer and be steered: the 1980s saw vigorous efforts by government to construct a pyramid of central research bodies with power concentrated at the top. In 1987, the five councils—and their already-existing coordinating body, the Advisory Board for Research Councils (ABRC)—were formally put under the new super Advisory Council on Science and Technology (ACOST), which was placed close to the prime minister and chaired by an industrialist. In the late 1980s, discussion was under way concerning whether the five councils should be consolidated in a single omnibus research council, the better ostensibly to steer and coordinate science policy. Whatever the zigs and zags in council and governmental reorganization, "the transfer of power over research and science policy from leading academics ... to government" has been the overriding trend, with the government determined to place "greater emphasis on the role of industry and employment in the determination" of those policies.[49]

As part of the "determined rationalisation" of the system, as mentioned briefly above, efforts have been made to formally assess universities and differentially distribute university research funds among them. Beginning in 1986, the UGC engaged in selective efforts to concentrate graduate teaching and research. The UFC has continued down this track, assessing individual departments and thereby ignoring the overall fabric of a university, whether well constructed or not. The research councils moved to put more money into Interdisciplinary Research Centres (IRCs) and less into existing disciplinary-focused research centers. The concept of "strategic research" came into play, allowing the councils to edge away from the seeming purity of "basic research" without going all the way to "applied research." Amid the confusion of many year-by-year changes, little doubt was left by the end of the 1980s that the government was moving to a form of support in which the funding of research and teaching would become more separated.

Basic to this effort, and cutting even more deeply than the relative ranking of institutional capability in teaching and in research, was a strategy that we have cause to note in other countries in this study and to offer in Part Two as a general trend: shift monies for research from the institutional line where core support is based on such common criteria as number of students in different disciplines to the research line where funds are obtained by means of research grants and contracts that are awarded after peer review in central councils and committees.[50] The research line offers a competitive process that differentiates individuals and institutions into winners and losers and thereby tends over time to differentiate, as much discussed in Britain, a range of institutions that contains full-bodied research universities, "middle-range" institutions that have some departments with sturdy research foundations, and then still others that become virtually "teaching only." In British terms the differentiation of institutions, when dichotomized, consists of "research-dominated" and "teaching-dominated" universities.

Behind all such major efforts to delimit the research foundations of the universities has been growing governmental impatience with the

high per-unit cost of the universities. The government wants more
done—and done more cheaply. The ratio of students to staff in the universities has slowly increased, from 9.5:1 in 1981 to 11.5:1 in 1989,
and in the early 1990s the trend apparently accelerated.[51] The humanities exhibit relatively high numbers: English departments showed an
increase from 12.8:1 in 1987–1988 to 15.7:1 in 1989–1990, with departments reporting greater dependence on graduate students and temporary lecturers to meet teaching commitments. With departments
"making much more use of hourly paid casual staff."[52] the staffing elements of the mass university more than had a foot in the door. Reduced
resources in proportion to student numbers meant that "the prized tutorial component" of British higher education was gradually attenuat-
ing.[53] And the hits of selectivity were everywhere to be seen; for example, a deliberate downsizing of social science was evidenced in a sharp
fall in studentships offered by the Economic and Social Research Council (ESRC) from about 1,000 to 250 in a five-year period in the mid-
1980s.[54] Seen on an international scale, the latter small number for all
of Britain was less than the number of financial support packages assembled in the social sciences by just two or three of the major American universities, for example, Stanford, Berkeley, and UCLA together.

Such are the joys for academic staff of having their financial eggs
largely placed in one basket, particularly in a nationalized system that
evolved from a highly exclusionary base and remained committed to
high-quality education for all who were allowed to enter. Little or no
alternative or compensatory sources of support to that of the national
research councils were available in these disciplines in Britain. The unitary nature of the national system had become a virtually classic case of
the "all-eggs-in-one-basket" approach, offering beyond the crippling effects of single-channel downsizing the huge threat that if you should get
it wrong, you will get it very wrong. Direct state steerage and steerage
by state-specified markets had become key system features that condition the whole nature of university research and research training.

RESEARCH TRAINING IN THE BRITISH CONTEXT

British universities made a delayed and essentially secondary commitment to the graduate level. The modern Ph.D. was not put in place until 1918, virtually half a century after its introduction and takeoff, in the
1870s and 1880s, in the United States.[55] Before that time, beginning in
the mid-nineteenth century, only a few "higher" doctoral degrees were

awarded for original research that stretched over five years or more. A modern research-based doctorate in the form of the Ph.D. was taken on somewhat reluctantly as a response to pressure from institutions and academic associations in the United States and Canada on behalf of students who wanted to come to Britain for advanced work and to receive appropriate certification. Otherwise, they would continue to go to Germany!

Adopted in the form of a three-year program, the doctorate was almost completely given over to actual engagement in research, a practice that has continued to dominate. A British academic observer writing in the early 1980s on the training of researchers noted that "at present we assume that the need for researchers is best met by selecting some of our academically most able graduates and giving them three years in which to carry out one major research project and write a thesis."[56] Future researchers did not need more course work in the American sense of courses; instead they needed "a B.A. plus some research time."[57] Graduate students were to be "research students." Although a formal line was drawn which distinguished postgraduate work from undergraduate status, there would be nothing like the American graduate school with its overarching panoply of rules and regulations for admissions, course credits, written and oral examinations, and dissertations.

The approach of "a B.A. plus some research time" has followed directly on the high degree of subject specialization and hence ostensibly of subject mastery that is characteristic of English undergraduate education and indeed its secondary education. In the concluding volume of the extensive Leverhulme Study of British higher education that was conducted in the early 1980s, Gareth Williams and Tessa Blackstone portrayed "excessive and premature specialization" as "the curse of English upper secondary and higher education," a veritable "English disease." They noted that "in preparing themselves to qualify for entry to higher education very few [upper secondary] English students take more than three subjects, and fewer than one-fourth take a range of subjects beyond the age of sixteen which includes both a 'science' and an 'arts' or 'social science' subject." Lord Robbins, they pointed out, had returned to this fact repeatedly since the time of the famous expansion-minded Robbins Report of 1963, remarking as late as 1980 that "as regards specialisation at the later stages of schooling we are completely out of step with the rest of free societies," possessed by the "iniquitous habit of ultra specialization at tender ages." But his criticism was to no avail: English upper secondary education remained uncommonly specialized. Then, in higher education, students are admitted by department, not the university as a whole, and "departments seek to recruit those who appear to have the greatest chance of success in the department's area of specialization." As a result, after they squeeze through the eye of the needle in the secondary school-leaving specialized A-level examinations, "three-quarters of the students entering British universities register for a specialized degree in a single subject."[58]

In short, contrary to the common American perception of U.K. education, the British emphasis on subject specialization is the virtual opposite of the orientation toward subject breadth found in American high schools *and* in the spread of courses considered appropriate in undergraduate programs in the name of liberal or general education. But against the large disadvantage that "narrow specialization from the age of sixteen onwards" leads to university graduates with "an over-narrow intellectual world view,"[59] such specialization "does have intrinsic merits; it is centered on the idea of an academic discipline: a coherent body of knowledge or range of subject matter that 'holds together' in proven ways as well as providing recognized methods of analysis. If successful, it trains the student in a particular way of thinking.... It discourages superficiality and produces graduates with considerable knowledge and depth of understanding in their chosen fields," all at the undergraduate level and in three years of full-time study.[60] Hence, with bachelor's degree in hand, the student is ready to leave instruction behind and become an apprentice researcher who concentrates on a project and a dissertation.

With British advanced education largely innocent of formal foundations in the form of lectures, seminars, or even systematically provided tutorials, Ph.D. training has depended heavily on student-supervisor relationships that are in turn variously shaped by the style of research work and the mode of funding found in different disciplines.[61] As elsewhere, as we have already seen in the case of Germany, students in the sciences are likely to be caught up in team research, hence to be close to supervisors and several levels of peers, while students in the humanities work on their own projects in a much more isolated fashion. In the sciences, compared to the humanities, progress to the degree is systematic and short: with knowledge more integrated and sequential, work toward the Ph.D. can be more structured. Again as elsewhere, the social sciences tend to fall between the sciences and the humanities in the possibilities of systematic, integrative study. But across the disciplines a general lack of structure follows from the definition of the Ph.D. program as essentially a period of time to do a project and write a related dissertation.

This British definition has been encouraged by the generally small scale of the local postgraduate setting. As put by Tony Becher, "Except in a few of the largest departments, there is not a sufficient critical mass of doctoral students in any one subject area to allow for a suitable range of viable taught courses to be mounted."[62] The opportunity to mount "broader elements" such as research training courses and graduate seminars and workshops depends considerably on the size of the doctoral population at hand; and, generally, "the population of doctoral students is too widely scattered to allow for convenient clustering along such lines."[63] As a result, "what seems quite clear is that no possibility currently exists in Britain [as of 1990] to move toward a pattern comparable with that of the large American graduate schools, many of them providing a substantial element of organized coursework as part of the overall doctoral program."[64] The limitations of such smallness are exhibited in departments of ten to twenty faculty, or less, faced with the problem of covering a growing array of important subspecialties, and where only a handful of advanced students are present, not infrequently narrowing to as few as one or two postgraduate students newly enrolled each year. Even if inclined, such departments cannot create structured programs; there are not enough bodies to compose an instructional class.

Small academic units have the opportunity of intimacy in the form of close supervision of the individual student by one or more mentors. Such supervision is central to British doctoral programs, a defining characteristic stemming from a system that overall is relatively specialized, selective, and small, one much influenced by the long-established tradition of tutorial teaching at Oxford and Cambridge. The legacy is a craftsmen guild, "an apprenticeship model" in which "students, rather than being trained through standardized procedures, learn what their discipline is about by being attached to a master craftsman and seeing him or her at work."[65] The notion of apprenticeship and the role of personal supervision take center stage even more at the doctoral level than in the specialized undergraduate program, since it is there that the element of systematic collective training is most limited, restrained as it is "by the absence in most cases of a substantial number of students in the same or closely related fields."[66]

The personalism of British practices at advanced levels has a system-wide thrust in the extension of the external examiner system from the undergraduate realm to master's and doctoral programs. Doctoral candidates normally have two examiners on the work of the dissertation, one external to the institution and one internal (the supervisor cannot be the internal examiner). Even more intimately than in the case of undergraduates, the external examiner has "a key role in ensuring that the same considerations should as far as possible apply in evaluating student performance across the system as a whole."[67] The examination is a relatively quiet, virtually personal event, not a public spectacle in the Continental mode, generally attended by just the student and the two examiners, and perhaps the supervisor. It is understood by all that the examiner brought in from the outside represents not the local institution but the system at large. In his or her person, the visitor ostensibly brings the system to the specific event of dissertation defense and approval and hence to the otherwise completely "local" student and supporting faculty.

But the apprenticeship model, suffused with personalism, is costly: students are not batched to achieve even small economies of scale. Even small budget cuts can hit hard, threatening to drive graduate work below viable levels of subsidy. From intensive department interviews conducted in the late 1980s, Becher noted that small high-cost physics departments, despite the status and importance of their discipline, were turned into a depressed state by the budgetary constraints of the 1970s and especially the 1980s.[68] Four departments (among fifty-odd) were entirely wiped out, and as of 1990, another dozen or so were on the verge of disappearing by closure or merger with neighboring subject groups. To hold and increase enrollment, nearly all have found it prudent to turn to more applied work and master's programs. In turn, economics departments had seen a drastic fall in British doctoral students: the market here "has been destroyed." Economics has become heavily dependent on overseas students who pay full cost, and this field, too, has turned more to master's programs. Across the nation, doctoral students in all the social sciences combined who were supported by a research council studentship fell from the already low number of 168 in 1981 to 69 in 1987.[69] The supporting council (the Economic and Social Research Council), reflecting government and central agency interests in practical training and concerns about the high cost of doctoral work, was offering by the end of the 1980s twice as many awards for master's as for doctoral students. History, if anything, had been even harder hit; declining staffs and declining doctoral enrollments led to the virtual elimination of the Ph.D. in many smaller departments.

There, too, a turn to "taught master's courses" was strongly in evidence.

Thus British doctoral programs, already lacking critical size in many cases, have undergone in many fields a decrease in size as national funding has stagnated. Even the long-prized external examiner form of evaluation has become problematic. Costly in budget and especially in use of faculty time, it has become poorly paid labor. Faculty are increasingly inclined not to participate, refusing to take on " 'onerous, disgracefully low-paid and thankless' tasks."[70] The effect of an essentially qualitative form of quality control, always ambiguous, can also seem more symbolic than real when viewed from the new management style in high councils that ask for quantified proof of effective assessment. A marginal budgetary item then slides further to the margin in its financial justification.

For British postgraduate students, the downside of their operational location can be summoned in two features: lack of programmatic structure and organizational marginality. After intensive interviewing of such students as well as faculty members in the three representative disciplines of physics, economic, and history at the end of the 1980s, Becher concluded that "the commonest concern was with a lack of structure rather than a lack of attention."[71] Considerable attention continued to flow from the emphasis on personal supervision that is embedded in the mentor-apprentice relationship. At the same time, that relationship was not situated in a larger department framework of course work taken in common with a cohort of other students. Absent a curricular structure, and despite the attention offered by personal supervision in a small-scale setting, the loneliness that inheres in much advanced study, especially in the humanities and social sciences, was exacerbated. And an overall sense of marginality was in the air as the postgraduate person remembered the student life that he or she had now left behind and observed the provisions made for contemporary undergraduates in the same department and university.

> The overall level of the facilities provided by universities specifically for graduate students reflects the marginality of those students in the system. Housing arrangements, common rooms, food services, and opportunities for social and recreational activities tend to be less adequate than those available for undergraduates, where such facilities and services are separately provided.... [Additionally] many graduate students consider themselves to be only rather loosely affiliated to their parent institution—and indeed to their own department. Many have good reasons for working away from their

base in their second year, and where university regulations do not require more than a single year of residence, a significant number of them do not subsequently return.[72]

The overall lack of structure for graduate *studies* has put a heavy burden on the traditionally strong element of the British microsetting, the student-supervisor relationship. Much is left to ad hoc processes of independent individual study.

THE COLLEGIATE UNIVERSITY: A SUMMATION

The long development of universities in Britain from the twelfth to the twentieth century produced an intensely elite system of higher education. An early genetic imprint of small-scale organization was laid down which in the twentieth century continued to mean small universities in a small national system. Linked to this persisting condition has been the pattern of student life powerfully modeled by the country's two leading universities in the form of sets of residential colleges. The overwhelming influence of Oxford and Cambridge led to the spread of an essentially donnish orientation in the new institutions of the late nineteenth and twentieth century in which British academics developed a deep, lasting commitment to personal teacher-student relationships, a feature summed up in the concept of "tutor," even "personal tutor." In the last half of the twentieth century, this orientation became a fixation on honors students—full-time, three-year undergraduates who concentrated their studies in closely specified areas and then were closely graded in achievement when they took their bachelor's degree. Remarkable in cross-national perspective, this commitment did not come cheap; by international standards, staffing ratios were generous.

As a nineteenth-century phenomenon, this combination of small universities, residential life, and close teacher-student relations stood in 1900 in sharp contrast to both the large impersonal lecture halls of the European continental universities and the research enclaves, discussed in chapter 1, that expressed the research ethos in the German system. It also stood in sharp contrast to the emerging American universities that even in 1900 were organized on a much larger scale, already generous to a fault in admitting professional fields of study beyond law and medicine and already fashioning Ph.D. programs and graduate schools. The British imprint had overtones of "college," rather than "institute" or "department" or "graduate school."

Nationalization of this university system in the twentieth century, especially at an accelerating rate in the quarter-century of 1965–1990, served to unify finance, personnel policies, and student support. The system became a closely guarded official system, changing its control structure radically from essentially bottom-up decision making to top-down steerage and regulation. This nationalization extended and deepened the application of the "English idea of a university": new universities were cast as small residential universities centered on the undergraduate honors student; a new polytechnic sector established officially in the mid-1960s became a world-class case of academic drift in the yearnings of its institutions to take on the ways of the universities, to the point where the binary policy was officially reversed at the end of the 1980s, a formal unified system proclaimed, and the door to research, ostensibly applied research, opened for the polys. Viewed in a cross-national framework in the late twentieth century, Britain has come close to having one right way to organize the academic life. Homogenizing tendencies have been strong.

Thus, during the nineteenth century and throughout much of the twentieth, the British approach to university organization did not, as in Germany, eagerly seize on research as a prime university activity that should underpin teaching and study. At the time in the mid- and late nineteenth century when German universities were institutionalizing the institute and the research-oriented seminar, Oxford and Cambridge still strongly exhibited the power of the undergraduate residential college, and the newer universities, even if organized in departments, were decidedly tutorial minded. A research orientation came relatively late and haltingly, much as a reaction to scientific progress in other countries and the advent of research training programs and degrees elsewhere. The Ph.D. was not introduced until some four to five decades after its introduction in the United States, and it was to remain problematic for decades to come: a conceit developed that the possession of a higher certificate was of minor importance compared to apparent quality of mind and character. As research interests grew in British society, the initial tendency was to place research work outside the universities. But donnish inclinations could not forever restrain disciplinary science. By the interwar period, more than a few important academic laboratories were in place, especially in the Oxford and Cambridge conglomerates; research then developed gradually into a standard expectation for all faculty and became a subsidized component of faculty time. Critically, at the microlevel research developed in academic departments, there to be related to teaching and student learning, rather than, as in Germany, in academic research institutes. By the mid-twentieth century, research had become an integral part of the English university but always in the context, set by history, of emphasis on first-degree programs and residential life. Thus *the* operational unit for the integration of research, teaching, and study became the small department with a decidedly undergraduate orientation.

The British department proved to have some distinct advantages over the chair-institute units that composed the German universities. Less dependent on a single person to orient research and teaching programs, the department in England could adjust more fully to the substantive growth experienced by modern academic disciplines. As Ben-David has stressed, structural rigidity was thereby lessened.[73] The academic staffs of departments, as in the American system, distinguished undergraduate and graduate levels but also spanned them. In this embrace, and in contrast to America, the graduate component remained relatively underemphasized, even marginalized. It developed as a level where a few carefully chosen students could plunge directly into research, often, especially in the sciences, in a close relationship to mentors. Postgraduate students simply became "research students" working on a dissertation. Their programs have had little or no curricular provision and have lacked a critical size that would make course work possible. And with the undergraduate commitment heavily the primary one, postgraduate work has been vulnerable to cost-cutting efforts, especially since costs are relatively high.

For the integration of research, teaching, and study, the British system has produced its own distinctive set of strengths and weaknesses. Its supporting conditions have resided in its small size, sharp selectivity, and high quality, leading to personal relations between teacher and student that at the most advanced level could entail a close mentor-apprentice relationship. The apprenticeship, one-to-one model has operationally been central to the capacity of British science to win its way throughout much of the twentieth century on "a thin stream of excellence." But the postgraduate level has exhibited little of the curricular strength possessed by first-degree programs: the research-teaching-study nexus is not organizationally supported at the doctoral level. High cost, as perceived and defined by the government, has deepened the difficulty of building sturdy foundations for both academic research and advanced research training. Increasingly, the university complex has come under heavy pressure to differentiate itself in order to concentrate resources, researchers, and students and thereby to fashion more units that achieve a postgraduate critical mass.

Internationally, and against the grain of the British system, both science and higher education have moved rapidly in the late twentieth century in directions that make smallness more a curse than a blessing. Caught up in the inexorable sophistication of knowledge, disciplines swell in size and complexity. Small departments are then hard-pressed not to enter into a vicious circle of comparative and growing weakness in research and research training. Large departments cover more of the disciplinary waterfront; they hire more specialists, even in batches; they compete better for research grants and student support; they build slack in their resource base that gives them more leeway to take on new initiatives. In contrast, particularly in high-cost scientific fields but also outside of them, small departments risk becoming backwaters in their capacity to do research and engage in research training. While ostensibly intimate and friendly, they are also short on graduate comradeship: peers are few and far between. Graduate students lack a community of other students undergoing similar experiences at a similar pace within a common structure. The mentor-apprentice relationship cannot fill in for missing peers. Thus, while a department structure befitting modern science, one oriented to research as well as teaching and study, is well in place in Britain, a department system broadly supportive of advanced research training is waiting to be developed, dependent on the arrival of larger departments in larger universities, with an accompanying growth of subsidiary and connected institutes. The system is in search of more settings in which the historic close mentor-apprentice relationship is combined with systematic instruction provided by a larger and more diversified staff.

By the early 1990s, some British academics and observers were pounding home the point "that the enormous growth of science and engineering puts the attainment of high-level, internationally competitive expertise in these subjects beyond the scope of undergraduate courses. Postgraduate studies are therefore essential."[74] Change in mindsets and structures is needed, for, after all, as Peter Scott has brilliantly captured, "Britain's elite universities—Oxford, Cambridge, and London—are also odd universities." They succeed academically "despite, not because of, their administrative structures and … many of their archaic traditions." Oxford, for example, attracts first-class talent to its faculty and turns them into "overworked tutors," in American terms, "professors ministering to the needs of a liberal arts college."

With "an anachronistic definition of academic excellence, our instinct is to trust "first-class minds rather than scientific and professional expertise." If these elite institutions "wish to compete with the Harvards and Stanfords into the next century—and with increasingly better organised and better funded rivals in Europe as well," they need "to tilt the intellectual balance of the university towards research—by, among other things, teaching undergraduates less intensively and creating more specialized graduate colleges on the pattern of Nuffield or St. Anthony's." The 1990s "are likely to see often violent shifts in institutions' centres of academic gravity," not only among the universities destined to be "teaching only" but also among the chosen few who will fill the status of "research dominated." The latter have to find a way "to concentrate on postgraduate training and research."[75]

Thus, by the early 1990s, the time had come in Britain for active consideration of the idea of graduate schools. In 1991, the University of Warwick established a graduate school "to promote high quality graduate education across the entire institution ... [and] to support the University's central strategic aim of enhancing its research base and maintaining its research reputation." Between 1985 and 1990, the university had already doubled its number of graduate students and more such recruitment was intended "to complement the research-led strategy." In a similar vein, University College London began a graduate school in 1992 and similar efforts were under consideration at Manchester, Essex, and Glasgow.[76] By 1992, the chairman of the ABRC could say that the idea of British graduate schools represented "a strand of thinking which is now becoming quite common."[77] The search was on for new organizational arrangements that could help give research activity itself and related research training of advanced students a home over and above what the established system had traditionally provided. The structural insufficiencies of the collegiate university, a place fixated on elite training of undergraduates, had become all too apparent. A new center of gravity would have to be found which gave a greater role to the research mentality. Leading universities would increasingly need to be places that thought of themselves as producers of research and as centers of systematic research training instead of, as under the old idea of a British university, as places that happen to do some research and research training alongside their undergraduate teaching.

CHAPTER THREE

France

Subordination of the University

All national systems of higher education are exceptional, but some are more exceptional than others. French higher education exhibits world-class particularism, not the least in how it attempts to order universities and to bring research activity into the locales of advanced teaching and the highest learning. If the Humboldtian principle is found at all in France, in modern dress, it is hidden somewhere in intricate features of an unusual structure of higher education and research. Throughout the nineteenth and twentieth centuries, specialized advanced schools known as grandes écoles have taken over the selection, training, and placement of elites that is normally exercised in other systems by leading universities. Even more important for our purposes, research has long found a government-funded home outside the universities in such organized domains as the large and complex National Center for Scientific Research. The universities have been only the party of the third part, markedly inferior to the other two sectors in status and resources and with low financial support compared to universities in other advanced nations. Thus French uniqueness that sets a large frame for the relation of research to teaching and study centers in the existence of a major separate domain for research activity alongside the education and training domains of the elite-focused grandes écoles, some recently added institutes of technology (IUTs) that, like the grandes écoles, have become more focused and selective than the universities, and, finally, a set of universities that with relatively open admission have become the shock absorbers of the system as a whole in a late transition from elite to mass higher education.

In addition, all these research and training sectors fall under the support and supervision of a formally centralized, unitary state that has long been unabashedly dirigiste. In France, when the minister of education speaks, people have to listen: another Big Plan may be afoot, to be implemented through a grand hierarchy of controls. Rare is the minister who does not feel it is his or her duty to reform the research system, improve the universities, and otherwise leave a lasting mark on French culture. But in France, as elsewhere, the best-laid plans may go astray more often than not, especially in higher education where numerous lower bodies and the academic corps at large have powerful means of defending their own interests as they see them and to exercise significant countervailing power. Listening is one thing, obeying is quite something else. But whatever the reactions of academics and ministers to one another, there is no doubting that the tradition of a centralized state that has sought exacting control over public sectors is a defining feature of the historical context of the contemporary capability of the French university to engage in research and research training. All higher education systems exhibit historical constraints, since they never start clean, even after a revolution. But some are more bounded than others, and in modern times, formally centralized state control has become the principal vehicle of elaborate constraint. In the Western world, France stands as the leading case in point. Any accounting of present-day tendencies in this system must begin with the nineteenth-century establishment of a genetic imprint that can be called the construction of a national service. That service is at once centralized, concentrated, and deeply segmented along lines largely determined by the central state.

But in France, too, as in the case of Germany and Britain, modern forces of expansion and sophistication of knowledge have pressed hard on long-established patterns; reform efforts in the last quarter-century have led to a succession of efforts to effect a host of changes. One central outcome has been the deepening of a particularly French way of differentiating and integrating research organization with advanced education. In sharp contrast to Germany, the Humboldtian university-based ideal has continued to be minimized. Instead, relations between research and teaching and between research and advanced study depend on local official relations between outside laboratories and the universities *and* on informal and quasi-formal ties that help bridge this institutional divide. A second outcome that bears directly on state control is the way that the growing complexity of university operations increasingly distances local action from close top-down direction, thereby heightening the import of decentralization. French higher education seems headed into its own version of pluralism and muddling-through that has profound effects on research and research training.

EVOLUTION OF A NATIONAL SERVICE

The French university has deep historical roots. The University of Paris dates from the twelfth century and rivals the University of Bologna as the earliest of the lasting European universities. Some twenty universities, a number similar to that found in Germany at the time, were in place by the end of the ancien régime that was deposed in the Revolution of 1789. The universities were also overthrown. The French revolutionaries, especially the Jacobin extremists, were determined to destroy all the old statuses and corporate monopolies that seemed eternal sources of privilege. They saw established institutions that mediated between the state and the individual as entailing special rights for the few and hence evil in the extreme. Better then in the new democracy to construct an embracing polity that would tower over all other forms of social organization.[1] The existing universities were clearly in the way, one more roadblock to the ideals and purposes of the Revolution that centered on a direct relationship between state and citizen. "Off with their heads" had an institutional parallel. To make sure that the old universities were radically submerged, they were all closed.

But even in a new, raw democracy, as far back as the late eighteenth century, the state needed experts, especially if it were to span all of society. What was carried over from the higher education of the ancien régime were a few specialized professional schools, notably the École de ponts et chaussées (1747), the École de génie militaire de mézières (1748), and the École de mines (1783).[2] Others of this type were newly founded, particularly the now-venerable École polytechnique in 1794 and the École normale supériéure shortly thereafter, giving early pride of place to "grandes écoles" as a special set of institutions that were to outdistance the later reborn universities in elite recruitment and placement. The important écoles became direct arms of the central government, specific parts of the national service instructed to provide small cadres of needed administrators and professionals.

But not even the new France could make out indefinitely without universities; a smattering of specialized schools would not be enough. It was left to Napoleon Bonaparte to produce the answer for a nationally unified approach. If France were to have universities, it would have one. The Imperial University was created in 1808 as a single, unified organization for the whole of the country, one that was to operate regionally by means of centrally directed administrative units called academies.[3] Faculties, rather than universities, became the organic operating units, four of which—medicine, law, letters, and science—gradually became standardized in a mold that was to last until the late 1960s, with one original type of faculty, theology, abolished along the way and another, pharmacy, added. During the course of the nineteenth century, the faculties became the entrenched units, relating to the Ministry of Public Instruction in Paris directly or through the prefectorial arms of the ministry in the regional academies.

The single embracing Université was also designed to link higher education closely to secondary education in a fashion strikingly different from other countries. As aptly described by Roger Geiger,

> By 1860 each educational district outside of Paris possessed a *lycée* for secondary education, accompanied by faculties of letters and science. These latter bodies were integral parts of the Université, but they bore little relation to higher education as it was known elsewhere in the world. Their chief function was to conduct baccalaureate examinations for students who had completed secondary school. That function largely determined their form; and that form was consequently ill-suited for anything else. The faculties of letters and science had no real students to teach, and could not even supply the requisite number of qualified secondary schoolteachers needed in the state schools. Their total preoccupation with the culture of the baccalaureate left them quite remote from higher learning as it was cultivated elsewhere. At a time when the scholarly prowess of German universities was receiving worldwide acclaim, only a handful of scholars in Paris was keeping France from becoming a backwater in the world of modern science.[4]

Here was a most unusual university system whose genetic imprint, although later much modified, was to have lasting consequences. All faculties were rolled up in a single national university. That "university" contained secondary schools, the lycées. While faculties of law and medicine could operate at an advanced level, much like counterparts elsewhere, the faculties of letters and science served mainly as governors of the secondary level. They were to guarantee superior secondary school standards, guarding the diploma (the *baccalauréat*) "which allowed the students access to the legal and medical faculties, and, more important, to the highly esteemed and powerful national *grandes écoles*."[5] Teaching at the university level was inconsequential. "Since the undergraduate certificate, the *licence*, called for a mere 15-minute oral examination beyond what was required for the *baccalaur-*

éat, systematic and serious instruction designed for conscientious and committed students was inappropriate, and was indeed often regarded by the Parisian educational administration as undesirable."[6] Only a trickle of students appeared.

With the letters and science faculties centered on the testing of those leaving secondary school and essentially lacking a student body of their own, both teaching and research received short shrift. Officially, teaching duties became defined as three hours a week, largely in the form of public lectures tailored for "an audience consisting of urban notables and their wives.... Those in attendance were mainly in search of entertainment, or at best were seeking what the French refer to as *la culture générale*."[7] Research was deemed even less important. Disapproved by state officials, it was tolerated "only when it did not interfere with the awarding of the *baccalauréat* or teaching, and when it did not challenge government policy for the recruitment of professors. This policy had long sought to grant posts in the faculties as rewards to elderly *lycée* teachers and court favourites."[8] Money was also extremely hard to come by. "Loath to pay for the work of the faculties," the government insisted that funds come from student fees. With few students, the letters and science faculties frequently found not only that there was no money for research but also that "there was none for teaching, for books or even for basic administrative and secretarial services."[9] Finally, for almost seven decades, until late nineteenth-century reform, any coordination of the faculties in a single place was impossible, with the central ministry refusing to allow the different faculties in the same city or town to have any connections with each other. From ministry to individual faculty, vertical bureaucratic lines were to be in full control, not challenged by local coordination. The French university system was thereby not only extremely centralized but also highly fragmented at operating levels.

The French nineteenth-century imprint for the modern university thus stood in the sharpest possible contrast to the Humboldtian ideal and especially to the emerging German universities oriented around research and engaged in a competitive race for scientific and technological excellence. Research was downplayed and even university-level teaching poorly supported. Elite training for governmental cadres was placed out of the hands of university faculty, and so it was to remain. In short, there was far less than what comes to mind in other countries when the term "university" is used. The contemporary weakness of the French university has deep historical roots.

By the 1860s and 1870s, especially with one eye on developments elsewhere, there was so much about this archaic arrangement that needed reform that reformers hardly knew where to start. Meaningful reform began as a movement in the mid-1860s and extended through the late 1890s, a period, we might note for comparative purposes, during which research-oriented universities were introduced in the American context and the first universities in Japan were born. Zealous reformers, Victor Duray and especially Louis Liard, occupied the top post in the central ministry for most of these years. The faculties were considerably enlarged, and research became a primary criterion in the appointment of professors. More full-time students were enrolled, producing a genuine student body. The new faculty scorned the traditional public lectures, which then soon disappeared. Municipalities, industrialists, and individuals were permitted to give money directly to faculties, particularly helping the sciences with chairs, laboratory equipment, and buildings. And in the 1890s, the grand pretense of a single university spanning the nation finally gave way. The traditional entity was officially dismantled and higher education formally differentiated from secondary instruction. The faculties located in a particular city or region were now to compose a university, finally bringing the French concept officially in line with what the term meant elsewhere.[10]

But the new type of university was a largely nominal form, one that would endure in the twentieth century.[11] It was given little coordinating power. As before, important matters continued to be settled in the offices of central government or within the continuing local faculties in which a few senior professors chaired their individual realms of teaching and research and occasionally sat together to govern the larger body. Even after three decades of late nineteenth-century reform, what came out of the French preference for the unified state and the Napoleonic effort to construct a centralized system of education was a particularly strong top-bottom combination of bureaucratic and guild authority in which lines of funding and linkage run from the center to operating levels, like vertical stakes driven into the ground, largely bypassing what in Britain and especially the United States was and is a meaningful university level of identity and administration.[12] As expressed by a leading French expert as late as 1985, "The *université* was and still is very largely a legal fiction.... Each faculty protects its own interests, arranges its budget, and insofar as the Ministry will allow, sets its own curriculum.... *Université* is a term which is simply lacking in substance. Today, as at the turn of the century, it is the individual faculty which has a real social existence."[13]

Thus, even after the single university was abolished, the French university system was cast as an inclusive system of control in which central officials were responsible for an all-system point of view and were expected to achieve a certain amount of unifying dominance. If there was to be differentiation, it would be governmentally sponsored and centrally steered. The individual university would be a federation, even a confederation, of faculties, each individually tied into the national system. And faculty members would be individually and collectively a part of the state. They were all members of a single official corps, a *corps enseignant*, or teaching body, a permanent segment of the civil service.[14] Within the unified system in which they held their basic positions and by which they were directly paid (and *not* by their universities), they were equal across the nation, equal, that is, within seriated ranks bureaucratically defined and centrally administered.

THE OPERATIONAL LINES OF CENTRALIZATION

With centralization serving evermore as the benchmark of the French structure of control, its operational meanings became worked out in a host of bureaucratic lines that connected the center to the field. Financial patterns have been central. The universities have derived the great bulk of their money, roughly 90 percent, from the national treasury: there has been little or no income to be had from provinces, cities, individuals, private bodies, or student fees. Then, within the central government, those responsible for the overall state budget dominate the ministry responsible for higher education.

> In budget matters it is the government, and especially the Ministry of Finance, that monopolizes the preparation of the draft Finance Law every year. During this phase the Secretariat of State for the Universities, like most of the so-called "social" ministries, has almost no influence. Unwanted at the technical level, it is also suspected by the Ministry of Finance officials of being a mouthpiece for higher-education interest groups rather than the champion of the state's superior interest. Furthermore, the actual drafting of the budget is done in a rather mechanical way, leaving no room for broad policy options.[15]

The finance officials relied on quantitative criteria in which the budget for next year is this year's budget adjusted by increases or decreases based on changes in the general price index and other indicators provided by a central bureau of economists and statisticians. Changes were hedged about by rules laid down in agreements between the central government and unions of government employees. Marginal changes needed to be equitable, if they were to be seen as neutral, objective, and fair. With such formula funding, old norms were perpetuated, adjusted a few points one way or the other across the system or within its major segments.

Centrally allocated funds in the French university system have also been highly categorical. National staffing ratios were applied in each of six designated basic areas of study. Overhead allocations for heating, lighting, furniture, and maintenance are separate from provisions for teaching, which in turn are isolated from allocations for research. For overhead allocations, universities have been classified in an elaborate formula that includes the surface area of the premises, a standard teacher ratio, and a standard staffing ratio for administrative personnel. University libraries are governed by a special service of the Secretariat of State for the Universities, receive their grants directly, and administer them according to special rules and methods.[16] In "a set of watertight compartments," allocation relies exclusively on quantitative criteria.[17] In short, the financial pattern has been the opposite of block grants. The universities have had little leeway for exercising initiative in internal distribution of funds, especially since the largest item of all, faculty salaries, is completely out of their reach. As P. Cazenave has computed, three-fourths of a university's resources typically have not been in its budget.[18]

Beyond budget, a second major set of bureaucratic lines has existed in personnel matters. As employees of the national state, teachers and researchers have their salary categories, rights, and privileges spelled out in official codes of the national civil service. National committees administer hirings and promotions according to formal rules; the central ministry can transfer posts within the university system at will. But once faculty members are tenured, they are firmly sited in the civil service. They have strong job protection in the form of "acquired rights" (*droits acquis*). As a result, the individual universities have little control over their own teaching staffs. As noted earlier, power is distributed between a bureaucratic top and a guild bottom, with the members of the guild also occupying governmental posts and able to use the civil service to protect individual and group statuses and privileges. The marriage of the individual scholar to the state has brooked little interference by the corporate entity known as the university. After all, faculty positions have been posts in the budget of the state, not the university.

Beyond finance and personnel, a third crucial line of centralization has been curricular in nature, found in the specification of fields of study, courses, credits, and the awarding of degrees. Since the days of Napoleon Bonaparte, degrees have been awarded by the national system as a whole, not by the individual university, with the state thereby certifying that the graduate is qualified to enter government service or one of the professions. Following the great 1968 crisis in French higher education, there were efforts to do away with the national diplomas entirely and to replace them with ones granted by individual universities. This form of decentralization was very unpopular. Students continued to believe that the national degree was more valuable to them for postuniversity placement, and when both types of degrees were made available, they continued to choose the national one. Despite a throwing open of the system in the years immediately after 1968 to much local regrouping of staffs and subjects, the central ministry retained the right to approve subjects in which national degrees would be offered and to concern itself with adequate preparation of students in those subjects. Otherwise the national degree would become an empty pretense that the state guarantees, field by field, the competence of graduates. When degrees are nationalized, ministry officials cannot leave subjects and courses entirely to local determination.

THE STRAITJACKET OF CENTRALIZED ADMINISTRATION

The French experience in reform since 1968 has shown just how hard it is to decentralize a deeply centralized system, one that has taken the form of a "national service." Authority seems to snap back to central officials like a stretched rubber band returning to its normal shape. Individual citizens and major interest groups have generally wanted it this way. "The individual looks to the central government for protection of his acquired rights (*droits acquis*). Each group calls on the bureaucratic sector responsible for its realm of activity to preserve the interests of its members.... [T]he reluctance of individuals (and institutions) to cooperate at lower levels and the habit of resorting to higher levels of government for the settlement of controversies and the regulation of policies buttresses centralization."[19]

The systematic administrative centralism found in French education has increasingly had the effect of deeply politicizing the context of decision making in higher education. In the relationship of officials and academics, Alain Bienaymé has stressed that

between the representatives of the government and the elected representatives of the faculty, students, and administrative personnel, the relationship
is neither primarily hierarchical nor primarily professional. It is extremely
political and inasmuch as the opinions of the common program of the Left
and leftists are better represented among the university teachers than in the
rest of the nation, the relationship between the government and the university community is by nature fraught with conflict.[20]

What the central administration proposes is always suspect: it is "the
establishment" several times over. As new proposals and edicts come
raining down from on high, the relationship between center and field
generally becomes a standoff: the many factions of the academic
world, organized in blocs by rank *and* by subject *and* by general political persuasion, fight politically against central proposals and make
clear that the implementation of most changes finally lies in their hands.

Much has happened in France since the student revolt of 1968 by
way of attempted reforms in higher education. The huge University of
Paris, the Sorbonne, was decomposed into what, with some additions,
became thirteen universities. Old faculties were disbanded and some six
hundred new units of teaching and research (*unites d'enseignement et
de recherche* [UERs]) were created. Much regrouping was encouraged,
and a great deal of thrashing around occurred, especially in the early
1970s. Votes in deliberative bodies were given to junior faculty, students, support staff, and lay persons. Central campus administration
was strengthened by introducing a presidential system and providing
more adminisrative staff. New national councils replaced old ones.

How much did all the reform change the system? Arguments have
raged for two decades between those who see a changed system, one
more differentiated and responsive, and those who see more of the
same, a system that remains heavily centralized in its general control
and blocked from significant change by the stubbornly defended "acquired rights" of national academic strata and the rigidities of across-
the-board governmental attempts to steer major segments of the system. The now-famous Orientation Act of 1968 ostensibly favored decentralization; but since "the text of the act is couched in general
terms," it was left to "the ministry to prepare a long series of decrees,
regulations, and circulars to interpret and apply it." Officials issued
model statutes, "because of the alleged necessity 'for the constituent
assemblies to be able to proceed on the basis of texts juridically acceptable from the point of view of the central administration.'"[21] And the
last half of the 1970s saw one major action after another by central
officials in the name of rationalizing the system which were seen in the

universities as heavy-handed, top-down commands, producing resistance by faculty and students in the form of prolonged demonstrations, campaigns, and strikes. The power of the purse remained centralized, with the ministry making "substantial new allocations of funds only in areas that it wished actively to promote."[22]

Modern ministers in charge of education in France feel obliged to attempt major changes. Broad policy is their responsibility, the public expects actions, and political careers ride in the balance. Writing in 1983, Guy Neave noted this phenomenon.

> During the past twenty-five years or so, scarcely any Minister of Education has passed up the opportunity to associate his name with various educational reforms of equally varying degrees of radicalism and success. Berthoin (1959), Fouchet (1963), Fontanet (1974), Haby (1975), and Beullac (1978)—such is the litany of secondary education. To this war memorial of past reforms, one might add the names of Edgar Faure (1968), father of the Higher Education Guideline Law of that year (current revisions of which have given rise to much parading and shouting between the Bastille and the Gare d'Austerlitz), Mme. Alice Saunier Seité (1976), and finally, the present incumbent, M. Alain Savary. The unhappy M. Savary faces a coincidence of reforms at all levels of the education system: the internal structures of lower secondary education (the Legrand Commission Report); changes in the relationship between the private—more accurately termed, "the non-state"— sector of both primary and secondary schooling; the redefinition of the structures and objectives of undergraduate study; and last but not least, changes to the balance of power in the internal governance of universities.[23]

Neave pointed out that no matter how comprehensive the purpose of these reforms, all detoured around the parts of the system that trained the country's administrative, economic, and political elites.

> Without exception, both in secondary and higher education, reform applied to nonelite institutions. In secondary education, for example, the key institution, the *classes preparatoires des grandes écoles*, have remained untouched.... Their position across that golden road to posts of higher preferment is as commanding as ever it was. The same may be said for the *grandes écoles*, that truly elite sector of French higher education.... The uproar and protestation that accompanied the overhaul of French higher education left them an oasis of tranquility, unmentioned in the Higher Education Guideline Law of 1968.[24]

The years since 1968 have seen the elite status of the grandes écoles only increased, especially in comparison to the vastly expanded, messy, and deeply troubled university sector.

The rigidity and institutionalized capacity of the elite sectors of education and government to resist change have given much credence to

Michel Crozier's characterization of his country as a "blocked" or "stalled" society. Subjecting the French model of centralized authority to withering criticism in a succession of books,[25] Crozier asserted that change is restricted particularly by a "straitjacket of centralized administration" and a "rigid style of education and models of thinking that are completely hostile to any form of experiment."[26] It is not that the French are unwilling to change, he claimed, indeed they are "feverishly active" in this regard, aware that the very complexity of modern societies increases the opportunities for individual and group action while it renders old hierarchies inefficient. But they are trapped more than ever in vicious circles in which they end up preserving their traditional forms of government and administration. "Whatever their intentions, the logic of the system distorts their activities and forces them to collaborate in preserving the model."[27]

In this view, there is "an instinctive tendency toward the monopoly of power."[28] And the centerpieces of the rigid framework around which the rest of French society is built are education, public administration, and elite recruitment. These "blocked" subsystems are closely linked. The leading grandes écoles select severely, recruiting the cream of the cream of the secondary school students through special preparatory channels. Those few schools then dominate placement into top posts, especially in government. It is "a hallmark of the French public administration system.... that most of its executive positions are, to all intents and purposes, restricted to graduates of two elite training schools: the Polytechnic School and the National School of Administration."[29] The superelite status of just a few special schools gives a more pinched peak to the institutional hierarchy of French higher education than is found anywhere else among the major democratic nations, approached in lesser degree only by the special status of the much larger Universities of Tokyo and Kyoto in Japan and the place of Oxford and Cambridge in the British system.

Ezra N. Suleiman has highlighted the degree to which the French administrative elite "has succeeded in placing itself in what amounts to an indispensable position."[30] The modern highly centralized state is an ever-enlarged government that must be manned by dozens upon dozens of cadres of highly trained administrators and technical experts. Since they are absolutely essential, the first task of higher education, for reasons of merit and efficiency, is to provide them in a steady, reliable stream. In turn, they staff the offices that are formally responsible for the control of higher education: in that capacity, they are well positioned to protect the elite tracks in secondary and higher education that selected and trained them and are responsible for shaping a very thin stream of superior talent. Governmental control of higher education thereby becomes considerably involuted and closed.

Higher education thus becomes in the first place an instrument for producing and maintaining state-created elites in a self-propelling cycle of interaction between elite schools and elite segments of governments. Additionally, virtually irresistible compulsions of unified personnel management are at work. In an analysis of the French professoriate, Erhard Friedberg and Christine Musselin concluded that "conditions of access, statutory rules, salaries, and all other aspects of personnel management are run centrally by the state bureaucracy in bilateral ne-gotiations with national unions. Such a unified personnel management system and its corollary, a united corps of civil servants, is probably the most accepted and thus the most resistant dimension of centralization in French universities."[31] In the French structure, vested interests occupy national bureaucratic and political channels that are the backbone and sinew of monopolization.

But, as we later see, the stalled society thesis can be carried too far, distorting interpretation of the elaborate and changing settings of both research and advanced education in France. Much change took place during the 1970s and 1980s: at operating levels, local adjustments were made; local government and private industry have sought to play a greater role. As elsewhere, the sheer complexity of greatly enlarged higher education has increased the dysfunctions of old unified control. The determination of what will be done, especially in the opaque do-mains of esoteric research and advanced disciplinary instruction, may indeed be shifting significantly from central ministries to regional and local governments and to universities and their constituent units.

THE MODERN COMPLEX OF UNIVERSITIES AND RESEARCH CENTERS

As in Germany, France moved into the modern age of mass higher edu-cation at an extremely rapid rate that could not help but cause much institutional dislocation. Here, too, expansion was in the magnitude of threefold in a decade, virtually sixfold in three decades: student num-bers rose from somewhat over 250,000 in 1960–1961 to roughly 750,000 a decade later and then to 1,500,000 by the end of the 1980s. Age-group participation rates, variously calculated to run between 20 and 30 percent, were generally taken to approximate the higher figure by 1990.[32] With a high rate of expansion that would be difficult to handle administratively under the best of circumstances, and with the traditional grandes écoles sector and the new IUT sector both operating selectively and on a relatively small scale, the universities together have indeed been the relatively open, mass-demand sector that would undergo severe overload and aggravation of problems of student anonymity. Student-teacher ratios have been as high as 30:1 and more in the humanities and social sciences,[33] with three times as many students per instructor as in English universities and with student loads for the purposes of first-degree teaching that are more like those to be found in struggling public and private "comprehensive colleges and universities" in the American system than in its leading research universities, especially private ones.

With the universities even in "the good old days" serving as a relatively low-cost operation, expansion produced striking deterioration of an already low-grade physical plant. Some campuses in Paris became recognized nationally and internationally as virtual academic slums, located in undesirable industrial neighborhoods, poorly constructed, and hard to maintain at even a minimal level of cleanliness and attractive appearance. And old universities sometimes took on the physical conditions of poor cousins now asked to do five times as much work. An experienced American journalist, Richard Bernstein, in a friendly portrait of French institutions, could not contain his dismay over "the shabby, ramshackle collection of buildings, laboratories, amphitheaters, and classrooms that constitute the vast French university system."

> The Sorbonne, the oldest and most highly reputed, is an example. Outside, it has a certain splendor, its domed building occupying a commanding position in the Latin Quarter, its entryway containing touches of earlier grandeur, an inner courtyard of cobblestones and arcades, ancient mosaics and sculpted columns. Then shabby reality takes over—yellowed, peeling walls, dingy corridors, exposed wires hanging around doorframes, naked light-bulbs dangling from ceilings, overcrowded, badly lit classrooms, neglect, decay, atrophy, despair. Elsewhere, the twelve universities in the Paris area and the fifty-nine in the provinces are often sprawling, tarnished arrays of the worst in shopping center architecture, signs of great quantities of money spent without adequate planning or forethought.[34]

The universities, "arguably among the least brilliant, the most unkempt of any in the Western world, despite the prestige many of them enjoy," are very different from the leading grandes écoles, such as the École national d'administration (Éna) and the École polytechnique. Not only do these premier écoles take in very small numbers of carefully screened students but they also receive resources at a level many times higher than that of the universities. At Éna, for example, students receive a state salary right away, in "a place whose sole and only function is to draw in bright young men and women, generally in their twenties, and to ready them for careers in state service that will last over the next forty years."[35] The exceedingly special nature of Éna, as against the diffuse character of the universities, comes through clearly in the fixation on selection and training of top government cadres. As a corollary, "the most prestigious institution of higher learning in the country, the one most difficult to get into, does no scientific research, produces no Nobel laureates, invents no new theories about literature or art, publishes no books, and is certainly not a center of political unrest."[36]

With so many more students destined for a more varied occupational structure freely entering the university, after attaining the baccalaureate at the end of their secondary education, one major response of the French system has been extensive structuring of degree levels and types of degrees. The French curricular structure traditionally did not offer a clear distinction between undergraduate and graduate levels, or pre-advanced and advanced. An elongated first tier of instruction led to a major degree, the *Maîtrise*, that approximated the master's rather than the bachelor's degree in the American system and was, as in Germany, closely connected to professional certification and qualification for public employment. Only a few students interested in academic careers, for whom separate systematic instruction hardly seemed necessary, stayed on beyond that point. After the advent of mass higher education, however, officially defined new levels of study and a plethora of types of degrees have issued in a bewildering and complex fashion. The vertical sequence of years of study was first broken into three successive "cycles" of two years duration. Then, in the 1980s, those cycles became in effect five or more degree levels: a "DEUG" (Diplôme d'etudes universitaires générales) after two years, the end of the first cycle; a "Licence" one year later; a "Maîtrise" after four years, the end of the second cycle and the end of "preadvanced" in the terminology of this study; a "DEA" (Diplôme d'etudes approfondies) after five years for research-minded students and a counterpart "DESS" (Diplôme d'etudes supérieures spécialisées) for those headed for the professions; a Ph.D., a single doctorate (Doctorat unique) that replaced four abolished doctorates in a 1984 reform, to take another three to five years; and a much later Habilitation, which few had taken by 1990, that, like the German counterpart, should put the research scholar on an exalted plane. In particular, more vocational tracks were inserted from the second cycle onward, with selection admission, such as one in management. If this were not enough, a Magistère degree was created in the 1980s as a fast-track alternative to the taking of the Licence and Maîtrise degrees for outstanding students coming forward to research, with selective admissions at the start of year three. In short, within the French mass university, as Neave has emphasized, reforms of the 1970s and 1980s reinforced selection, multiplied selective programs, and established particular paths to research.[37]

Amid all the change of the 1970s and 1980s, efforts to enhance research training promoted special entry points and programs that would help select talent for research and distinguish research students from professional students. Students enter a "zone of research" about five years after the secondary school "bac," on admission to the program for the DEA, with the possibility as of 1990 that a new Magistère degree will move this zone down to year three for selected students in selected programs. The DEA level of instruction that is explicitly designed to separate research students from all others also now encourages universities and faculties to admit students to this level from other institutions and not simply to select from within the local second-cycle cohort. In short, while the French system has undergone enormous expansion that has produced mass universities, considerable internal structural adjustment has been under way to bring forth an advanced level of university study, nationally competitive, that is research oriented and research based.

While all this elaborate curricular restructuring was taking place inside the universities, the universities were also undergoing, chiefly in an unplanned fashion, a grand restructuring around narrower bands of disciplines and professional fields. Traditionally, each university was comprehensive in coverage of medicine, law, sciences, and the humanities. In the 1968 grand response to historic rigidities, disciplines were suddenly given the opportunity to compose new university clusters, from the bottom up, with, of course, ministerial approval. The various fields took the opportunity both to find congenial partners and to distance themselves from unloved cousins. As a result of this major breakup, by 1980, only sixteen out of sixty-seven universities could be judged as truly multidisciplinary; another ten were "partially multidisciplinary"; and forty-one were composed of just one or two faculties.[38] The University of Paris became thirteen largely specialized universities; the city and region of Grenoble saw the creation of Grenoble I for the sciences and medicine, Grenoble II for the social sciences, and Grenoble III for the humanities and languages.[39] Thus official attempts to liberate the universities and to allow for locally chosen recombinations led to organizational distancing of disciplinary differences. When size and geography are factored in, the universities fall into three major clusters; Parisian, specialized and large; provincial, specialized and smaller; and provincial, comprehensive and medium size.[40]

The disciplinary breaking apart of the French university is extended by the tendency of students to stay on in the faculty to which they were originally admitted. Student mobility has always been relatively low in France, compared, for example, to the German tradition of the wandering student or the vast interinstitutional transferring of American students during their undergraduate years and then especially at the point of transition from undergraduate to graduate study. With disciplinary specialization looming ever larger in the French university framework, together with the need of students as they proceed up the years of study to obtain the attention and sponsorship of faculty members, students have been all the more impelled to remain in one academic groove— knowing all the time that the same national degree is available to all in a given field regardless of university location.

From the 1970s on, another major structural adjustment has taken the form of greater differentiation of faculty roles. As elsewhere, expansion in enrollment, especially when occurring at an extremely rapid rate, has tended to produce an "instructor class." This process was given a great leap forward in France when hasty recruitment in the 1970s—after the great shaking of the university and the state in the 1968 turmoil—led to the hiring of teachers with little or no research training and experience. Such hiring was deemed to be temporary, but it soon led to permanent employment under the conception, endemic in the politics of French administration, that those who are employed for more than a year or two have acquired significant job rights and should be regularized in a civil service category. Many of the new instructors were neither equipped to do research nor interested in it. Rising teaching loads, particularly in first- and second-cycle teaching, also diminished overall staff time for research. By the end of the 1980s, the government took note of a "research deficit" in university output, relating it to the heavy burdens of instruction in a system that had moved into mass higher education.[41] Under expansion, the problem of enhancing research and research training in the universities had deepened considerably.

THE RESEARCH SYSTEM: PRIMACY OF THE CNRS

Everything noted thus far about the organization of the French university system must be placed in the context of the universities' relationship to an externally organized, state-supported research establishment. In effect, France has two major publicly supported research systems: a highly structured, high-prestige professional research sector centered on the National Center for Scientific Research; and a much less well structured, lower-prestige and part-time university research system responsible for research training through the DES and the doctoral degree. The outside system comes first in all respects. Its current high standing and entrenched power have deep historical roots born of central initiative within which central ministries have sought to further particular state interests by their own sponsorship of schools and institutes. Neave speaks of a "native pattern of organization" for such state-sponsored inquiry that may be traced as far back as the establishment of the Collège de France in 1529 as a veritable institute for advanced study.[42] We earlier noted that while universities were closed up by the revolutionaries of 1789, then brought back and swallowed up in the all-embracing Napoleonic national university, and then relegated in the arts and science faculties to a supervisory role for secondary schools during much of the nineteenth century, the central ministries of the French government were free to establish specialized bodies outside the universities to serve their own needs for selection and training of future personnel. Research also gradually drifted into this pattern: "The École Pratique des Hautes Etudes (1868) and the Institut Pasteur (1887) both fulfilled a research training and a research function, but outside the purlieu of the university."[43] By the time the CNRS was formed in the late 1930s as a consolidation of previous research funding bodies, precisely to sponsor research institutes largely within its own framework, the tendency was well ingrained to leave the universities officially off the commanding heights of research.

In the form of the CNRS, the Republic of Science was in effect given a substantial mansion of its own in France, with many wings, most located in Paris, a realm that became culturally as well as bureaucratically separated from the training of administrative and technical cadres in the grandes écoles and the training of professionals, especially lawyers and doctors, in the university faculties. In the 1950s and 1960s, the French government also went beyond the CNRS to establish other independent public-financed research centers in such specific fields as atomic energy, oceanography, and space. Various ministries established large, powerful research establishments of their own that centralize research, as in the case of the Institut national de la santé et de la recherche médicale (INSERM) for medical research and the Office national d'etudes et de recherche aerospatiales (ONEDA) for aerospace research. Through direct support of the CNRS network and such additional centers, the central government ostensibly can relate directly to specific scientific fields and change funding priorities according to national need without entering into the difficult business of altering university faculties. By the early 1980s, this realm of concentrated research contained approximately 17,000 scientists, a number equal to about 40 percent of university teachers.[44] Its research establishments had highly selective entry for researchers, offered full-time research work, and possessed well-defined steps for career advancement, with the possibility of virtually lifelong tenure.

Serving as the heart of the French research system, CNRS is an elaborate research bureaucracy intensively organized in disciplinary sections—approximately fifty in 1990—supplemented by interdisciplinary programs. The many sections fund a multitude of research units, all termed laboratories, that are retained within, or affiliated with, the CNRS framework. The laboratories vary greatly by discipline, geographic location, and, notably, by officially defined status that offers clear ranking and priority. There are Laboratoires propres and Laboratoires associés; the first are more central, and both are known as "B1" units. Recent elaborations have produced two more types: "B1*" or Laboratoires recommandés, and "B2," a catchall category of "poor cousins in the family of research."[45] Since these major categories are sharply stratified in status and funding, it pays and pays well to have one's laboratory reclassified from B2 to B1* and then to full B1 status. The competitive struggle of subunits within this mammoth research bureaucracy is often fierce.

Crucial for our purposes are the controlling connections that the CNRS system has with the universities. First, the majority of CNRS laboratories are physically based at universities: over a third of them are in the Paris region; a sixth of them are found just at two Paris locations, the universities known as Paris VI and Paris VII.[46] With 70 percent of all CNRS workers in the 1980s physically located in university-sited laboratories, the relationship clearly inserted CNRS full-time researchers, their projects and equipment, into the university setting. The influence of this formally external body is thereby made pervasive at the base unit level of universities where we find professors and advanced students. Second, since the laboratories bring prestige and funding to the universities and not the other way around, the CNRS units are in the driver's seat. They are the foremost base for university research competence and reputation. Their bargaining power is considerable, especially since leading university researchers are brought on board and assimilated into the CNRS structure. The better the laboratory and the higher its standing, the more it is able to remain organizationally and financially aloof from the university. As a result, key university-located research groups are not funded by the university system or controlled by their host universities.

To other than French eyes, especially in the Western world, this arrangement could hardly be more curious. But it is a major way of organizing a research system and a higher education system in order to have the one focused on research activity and the other centered on the instructional tasks of education, including the preliminary training of students for research. The question remains: Do research, teaching, and study come together somewhere in this dual structure, under modern conditions, to produce a French version of a strong nexus?

DOCTORAL STUDIES

The answer to the question is yes for a minority of the most advanced students and no for an increasing majority. The CNRS–university linkage is to a great extent oriented, in standard French style, "to identify and assist a highly performing elite."[47] As in Germany, the doctoral level of university work has traditionally not involved formal courses; students do not have a supporting university framework as in the all-encompassing American graduate schools. When students attempt to move on from the DEA level (approximately bac + 5 years) with the intention of becoming involved in research and gaining a doctoral degree, they must competitively seek sponsorship by professors and entry into limited spaces in laboratories. Grants for student support as well as for research programs and projects are made to laboratories and their directors, not to students: in a two-layer competition, laboratories compete for grants and then students compete for laboratory involvement and support. Despite the historic centralization, no uniform subsidy for advanced students is available; students who do not win the favor of a laboratory director or research team are on their own for completing a doctorate. Thus, when after a long struggle everything comes out right for students, they are positioned to relate to both professor-researchers and full-time CNRS researchers. But many students will get to enter neither relationship, or just a little of the first, in a situation where there is a dearth of formal courses within which students relate to teachers.

The CNRS–university linkage varies greatly by discipline; it operates much better for scientific fields than for the social sciences and especially the humanities. Physics is the paradigmatic field for how the linkage ought to work. In physics, there is a high degree of institutional concentration: one-half of all CNRS researchers in this field were located in 1990 at just four universities, with resources thereby similarly concentrated. A very clear hierarchy of excellence results. Relative to other disciplines, a high level of financial support for doctoral study also exists. And in the physics laboratories, there is an interfusing of university-based researchers and full-time researchers: the laboratory setting makes for "groups of organic cohesiveness."[48] But it does so to a much lower degree in the social sciences and hardly at all in the humanities. In history, for example, there is little or no research money, little or no concentration of CNRS-supported "labs," and little by way of a full-time research corps to insert into the university setting. Then students have to battle all the more for entry into charmed circles of leading historians—in the pattern of the famous "patrons and clusters" of French higher education[49]—with little or no support available from CNRS or university funds.

At the doctoral level, the grandes écoles also come back into the picture in the form of graduates who seek research training and wish to enter the leading laboratories. Here, status begets status, excellence begets excellence, in a round-robin of interaction. Already defined as high flyers, the grandes écoles graduates are deemed to be outstanding applicants who add to the luster of laboratories they choose to join. In turn, for their own benefit, such elite applicants want to go to leading laboratories that are already known for a relatively high number of grandes écoles selected, trained, and certified people. A grandes écoles engineering pathway is one of the three main flows to the doctorate, along with a university science track and a university medicine track.

For high flyers in the sciences, then, from both the grandes écoles and the universities, the fact that the universities do not significantly incorporate basic research in their own organization and finance, compared to universities in other Western countries, need not perhaps make much difference. Elaborately constructed institutional ties and student pathways bring them forward and put them into premier research groups. The structure takes care of a highly performing elite, with the reservation, we must add, that systematic course work is in short supply. But for all other students, especially outside the sciences, the unusual French structure leaves them considerably deprived of both advanced training *for* research in the universities and training *in* research by means of involvement in funded research groups. Indeed, a new Comité national d'evaluation (CNE) found in a 1986 report on research in the universities that half of the academics with teacher/research posts were themselves not engaged in research at all.[50] The pulling apart of teaching and research—by means of demands and responses conceptualized late in chapter 6 as teaching drift and research drift—was far advanced.

With such assessments at hand, recognition was growing in France by the early 1990s that perhaps the research training system had a deeply rooted structural insufficiency. The government had on its mind a desire to double doctorate recipients within five years. Yet for even the existing number of students in the training pipeline, supervision seemed inadequate; notably, formal seminars and other tools of advanced systematic instruction were lacking. What was possibly needed then were "*écoles doctorales,*" a limited number of doctoral schools fashioned in the structures of given universities or as a collaboration among physically proximate institutions.[51] Much discussion was soon afoot, under ministerial prodding and offers of special funding, on such issues as whether such "schools" should be discipline-specific, within or across universities, or should group multiple specialties and groups within a university, the latter pattern moving in the direction of the multidiscipline reach of the American graduate school. In a first round of experimentation, some thirty-two such écoles doctorales, with special ministerial approval and funding, were founded in the Paris region. The graduate school phenomenon seemed firmly on the French agenda for the 1990s and beyond. The thought was abroad in the land, in France as well as elsewhere on the European continent, that "new structures for research training within the universities, functionally and administratively *differentiated from faculties providing mass teaching,* might seem to provide the opportunity of (re)establishing elite structures on a secure basis."[52] Mass-elite tensions required new structural solutions.

Also on the agenda was the possibility of serious decentralization of control that would give universities more autonomy to make their own adaptations and fashion their own packages of constituent faculties and departments, preadvanced and advanced programs, teaching emphases and research specialties. Since centralized government has long loomed so large, meaningful decentralization would be a major change. It has been much discussed before, and as in the 1968 reform even promised before, only to come to little. Its occurrence is bound up with a larger breakup of "the administrative state," the elaborate and top-heavy administrative system laid down in the Napoleonic period that has extended from national codes and laws covering nearly every topic to territorial subdivisions under the charge of provincial governors, prefects, selected by the central government and referred to by Napoleon at the outset as "mes petits empereurs." Over a century and a half of development, this intense administrative state grew ever more complex and deeply entrenched: one administrative *grand corps* after another became virtually untouchable, almost impossible to reform. Even in France, however, it seems that the national center cannot now hold, that the sheer complexity of the business of modern government necessitates some loosening of the reins.

Efforts to decentralize government control made serious headway beginning in the early 1980s in a series of related steps: much weakening of prefect-type local control; direct election of regional and departmental councils; and even the possibility of localizing the civil service. Coming to the fore, the many levels of "local" government—regions, departments, and communes—have begun to provide "a substitute for nationally institutionalized politics."[53] And as these strengthening local polities have found self-interest in their own competitive development within France, and Europe at large, they have turned attention to the utility of their "own" universities and to exercising more local voice in university affairs. Such germane external interest converges with growing concern in the universities over their ability to engage in research and development and to train students for research at internationally competitive levels.

The large ambitions of the national state to expand the universities also has exceeded its financial grasp, leading to "the major innovation of making the central government ... turn to the local authorities to

obtain substantial financial contributions for the task."[54] The time for
more cost sharing had come, since "local authorities now clearly are
able to mobilise the resources that higher education needs so desper-
ately and that central government has so far not shown itself inclined
to provide."[55] Following the point of view expressed by the mayor of
Lyon—"Whether one likes it or not, higher education has got to be decentralized. The laws of history and of efficiency will dictate it."—the
national ministry of education agreed, as of 1990, that developmental
plans for the universities are to be drawn up, not in Paris, but in each
region.[56] And swirling in and around those plans are the issues of
"insufficient numbers of trained researchers emerging from the French
university or [of] those who have been trained in research based
techniques" and of attitudes toward research that no longer regard it
as a "species of state service" but instead take a more expansive approach that includes contract research for industry and new regional
partners.[57]

THE ACADEMY UNIVERSITY: A SUMMATION

In themselves, French universities are hardly favorable settings for
abundant research activity and in-depth research training of advanced
students. Rooted in the historic loss of prestigious functions to other
institutions, the generic weaknesses of the universities are huge. Much
elite professional preparation has been out of their hands for virtually
two centuries, with elite training of this type possessed instead by a set
of publicly supported écoles closely integrated with the grand corps of
the many powerful national ministries. Thus, in linkage to public office,
the leading French universities have none of the placement capacity of
leading universities in Germany and the United States, let alone the
enormous clout exercised by Oxford and Cambridge in Britain and the
Universities of Tokyo and Kyoto in Japan. In this important regard, the
French universities are subordinated. In turn, primary research activity
has also been outside the control of the universities for over half a century, possessed instead by a separately funded research enterprise organized first of all in the form of a huge national center for scientific research, the CNRS, but going beyond it as other major research
subsectors have been added under the sponsorship of national ministries. In their own funded and organized engagement in research activity, the French universities are no match for universities in Germany,
Britain, the United States, and Japan. Here, too, the universities are a

subordinated sector. They have a research insufficiency that deepens their prestige deficiency.

Expansion from elite to mass higher education deepened this subordination. The universities became the mass-demand sector—the shock absorber of the system—not protected by less selective nonuniversity sectors commonly found in other national systems. The universities remained relatively open to all who flowed out of the upper secondary schools in ever larger waves, while the IUTs that populated a new vocationally oriented sector became more selective as well as more focused, taking the road to status and valued function modeled by the various écoles. Overall, the IUTs may still stand below the universities in popular esteem and academic status, but they clearly have not evolved into the posture of a less selective sector that would soak up demand and thereby relieve access pressures on the universities. Meanwhile, access to leading grandes écoles became all the more desirable and valuable and, numerically, more difficult to obtain.

But within this adverse university setting, institutional responses that protect and enhance research and research training have been evolving over several decades. CNRS-university linkages have continued to develop which place most laboratories at the universities, there to open their doors to university teachers and some advanced students and in return to involve some full-time CNRS researchers in research training. CNRS units and the universities have become "interdependent." Much differentiation of university programs has also taken place in the form of cycles and degrees that separate highly selective participation at advanced levels from mass involvement in the early years and separate as well research-centered pathways from vocational tracks, albeit in a confusing maze that apparently disorients and discourages many students. A post-1968 breakup of universities into limited disciplinary groupings also has provided relatively favorable conditions for the sciences by separating on an all-university basis their funding, work conditions, CNRS relationships, and status from that of the social sciences and especially the humanities. While lower levels of university study exhibit large enrollments in the humanities and social sciences, advanced levels, where CNRS linkage is most relevant, are science dominated. With physics serving as the paradigmatic field, the CNRS connection clearly works to the advantage of the sciences.

Thus, in the large, we find in France mass universities already deprived of prestigious functions and poorly funded facing more overload as the national government plunges ahead in the 1990s toward another round of considerable expansion. But within the system, research functions are selectively underpinned and thereby made resilient. In lieu of the external differentiation of many sectors that divide up student demand and variously assume preparatory functions, often evident in other countries, the French university system operates by means of extensive internal differentiation. The resulting jerry-built complex of operational arrangements is truly byzantine. It is also difficult for students to negotiate, particularly as they attempt to move through the years of study to a fourth- or fifth-year degree and beyond, a progression that requires students to bring themselves forward to obtain sponsorship. Student pathways have their weakest link at the point where students are emerging from the introductory mass teaching of the first cycle and seeking to find programs and personal connections somewhere between their third and fifth years of study that will move them forward into third-cycle doctoral work and settings, largely CNRS defined, where they may finally find themselves "at the bench."

Without doubt, the feature of the French system that stands out in comparative perspective as primary in the relation of research to teaching and learning is the towering presence of CNRS. Given this feature, strong research foundations for advanced teaching and advanced study must then involve an elaborate set of CNRS-university relationships that can be readily termed "interdependent" but which in operation have generally entailed considerable dependency of the weaker party on the stronger. CNRS determines, in effect, which French universities will be research universities and which will not, on a sliding scale from research intensive to teaching dominated.

If for comparative purposes the German system can be characterized as "the institute university," in which connections between research, teaching, and study are situated primarily in institutes internal to universities, and the English system as "the collegiate university," in which connections have been located historically within an undergraduate orientation, the French system can be distinguished as "the academy university," an institutional form in which an outside set of research institutes provide the main research base and university research-oriented programs are brought into alignment with it. In both broad macropatterns of institutional ties and highly specific micropatterns of person-to-person interaction, we find that the linking of research to teaching and learning is CNRS dependent.

The long-term problem for French universities in developing research capability as the foundation for advanced teaching and study is whether the research function can be strengthened internally and thereby made less dependent on the orientations, interests, and actions of a separate set of research academies. In the 1990s and beyond, governmental decentralization and possible related gains in university resources and autonomy may provide a sturdier institutional footing for both greater research activity under university control and more structured advanced instructional programs that are research linked. But there is a long way to go.

CHAPTER FOUR

The United States

Competitive Graduate Schools

International comparisons at the end of the twentieth century strongly support the impression that American education is weak, even highly defective, at the elementary and secondary levels and strong, even highly effective, at the tertiary level, with the highest program, "graduate education," appearing as a tower of strength. This advanced tier has made American higher education the world's leading magnet system, drawing advanced students from around the world who seek high-quality training and attracting faculty who want to work at the forefront of their fields. Strongly supported by interlocking conditions, structures, and procedures that became firmly rooted in the last quarter of the nineteenth century, when "the age of the university" took over from "the age of the college,"[1] a research-centered postbachelor level found its springs of action in the academic disciplines. In a largely unplanned fashion, the American graduate school became a lasting place of inquiry that not only accommodates research but compellingly seeks it; that not only offers the highest degrees, the master's and the doctorate, but supports those degrees with an elaborate system of admission, course work, and evaluation that is separate and decidedly different from that of the undergraduate realm. By 1900, a protective and cohesive framework was in place which sustained a succession of intellectual moments in the twentieth century. The laboratory and the seminar, the advanced degree program and the requisite course work, fleshed out a format that operationally defined instruction "higher than that of the ordinary college course and yet different from that of the law, medical, and theological schools."[2] The culture of this third type of instruction incorporated the idea of research and the methods of science. It thereby acquired a forwarding thrust of its own.

To explain the development of the American graduate school and its foundations in research is to help answer some large questions that are raised around the world in higher education policy. How did it come to pass that the Americans developed so much strength at the graduate level, especially when they manage by international standards to do poorly in elementary and secondary education and are notoriously ambiguous about standards in undergraduate education? How did an unplanned, chaotic system of higher education produce the world's most structured Ph.D. programs in which considerable integration of teaching and research, study and research training, still takes place, even on a massive scale? Is it just the large size and economic wealth of the nation that led by the 1990s to an output of 35,000 Ph.D.'s a year? Or did something special happen historically to create productive settings and forms? Did university organization itself become a spring of action, liberating energies that elsewhere have been more constrained? While full answers are inordinately complex, historically and organizationally, explanation centers on the initiative exercised by a plurality of institutions in a uniquely competitive arena. Processes of competition that never developed in American elementary and secondary education, nor to anywhere near the same degree in higher education elsewhere, operated intensively in American higher education, preeminently to the advantage of the most advanced tier. It was out of competitive interaction of institutions that there developed a lasting combination of the graduate school married to specialized departments, a form that has produced elite results in a context of mass higher education. In any comparative account of the connection between research and education, it is this combination, in the American case, that must be understood and explained.

In looking backward, the metaphor of revolution serves to simplify a complex history. Even though change throughout was evolutionary, historians and sociologists alike have used the idea of revolution to point to periods in history, stretching over several decades, when rapid change in American higher education produced a qualitatively different framework for teaching and learning. In the construction of research foundations, the first and most dramatic revolution clearly occurred in the late nineteenth century when the university finally came to America. Academic work then became professionalized to the extent that disciplines and vocational specialties became individual professions in themselves.[3] The graduate school took form and became a major force, the place where William James's "Ph.D. octopus" could be found as early as 1900 and where the research imperative had begun to work its will.[4]

The second major change took place in the period between the two world wars.[5] Agencies external to the universities developed an interest in research and training for research and made funds available accordingly. Those agencies were private foundations, leading to habits of giving and receiving that avoided dependence on government. Professors learned that special monies for their own research and for the support and training of graduate students could be obtained from outside their own institutions in the form of grants, contracts, fellowships, and scholarships. Competition then developed a new dimension in the capacity of professors and institutions to relate effectively to external sponsors in an emerging research system. And it turned out that while private universities were favored in this game, state universities could also play. During the 1920s and 1930s, such flagship public campuses as Wisconsin, Michigan, and California showed they could compete with the best. But by modern standards, science was still small science.

In a third academic revolution, in the several decades following World War II, a qualitative change in the scale and intensity of academic research occurred. With a huge growth in research funds, Big Science made its appearance. Funding shifted from private to public sources, with "the federal interest" now a permanent part of the landscape.[6] University departments became large and exceedingly research centered. While intensifying in the top universities, research was also dispersed to more institutions, greatly enlarging the array of universities that would exercise initiative in an increasingly competitive and ever more complex research system. This third intellectual moment in the life of the American university has produced the intense academic department–graduate school marriage that is so prominent at the end of the twentieth century.

EMERGENCE OF THE VERTICAL UNIVERSITY

It is easy in the late twentieth century to forget that the hegemony of the small freestanding college lasted in America for two and a half centuries, from the establishment of Harvard College in 1636 to at least the 1880s. An abundance of these scattered places, all tiny by modern standards, established deep in the American consciousness a "college" conception of higher education. Beyond the nine colonial institutions in place by the time of the revolutionary war, competitive denominational fervor added hundreds of others in the first half of the nineteenth century in an uncontrolled binge of college founding that, among the more successful outcomes, left the remains of failed institutions strewn all over the expanding countryside. No universities existed in this westward-moving crowd of colleges, not even back in long-settled Boston, New York, and Philadelphia. The college form concentrated on four years of common classical instruction culminating in the bachelor's degree. Fixed around a curriculum that resembled "a closed box,"[7] the scattered colleges were hardly congenial settings for research and intense specialization. Early and mid-nineteenth-century faculty members and would-be academics who turned to research in the new scientific disciplines then developing internationally were left largely to take themselves off to Europe, Germany in particular, to become trained in research in the emerging fields. By the end of the century, about ten thousand had done so.[8] There they became acquainted with the new ways of scientific inquiry, sometimes acquired a doctorate along the way, and returned home in generational waves, committed to research specialization, full of praise for the European university, and disdainful of the many small colleges that one leading academic likened to a swarm of mosquitoes.[9] For them the time had come for the university, in the form of new institutions or enlarged colleges, to replace mosquitoes with eagles that could soar with the best that Europe offered. Out of their struggle the university in America came to take the shape of a two-layer enterprise in which an organized higher level of study would reside on top of the historic college: the latter would become the *undergraduate* level of the new system.

This form, the "vertical university," emerged from more than a half-century of debate and experimentation that was frustrating in the extreme for research-minded faculty and college presidents. Their dreams of what could be were voiced in public discussions at least as far back as the 1830s. Leading scholars and change-minded presidents kept asking, Where is the American university? A university format, different from the traditional college, they insisted, had to be worked out, to make room for inquiry, to raise the status of American culture, to eliminate the cultural colonialism embodied in the act of young Americans going to Germany to acquire advanced knowledge and technique.[10] But the birth of supportive organization was another matter. Whether in the setting of New York, the country's largest city, or in that of Harvard and Yale, the leading colleges, or at such varied institutions as Michigan, Columbia, Pennsylvania, Union College, and the new University of the South, reformers found themselves frustrated in coming up with a feasible new form.[11] Many colleges tried to fashion a "horizontal university": they added new scientific subjects to please research-minded academics; they subdivided the college into departments that represented specialties. But the box was too closed. Advanced research could hardly be put alongside tutoring in Greek and Latin. A four-year bachelor's degree, American style, could not serve as the equal of a European university degree. If horizontal add-ons would not work, then an intellectual thrust upward was required.

A higher tier required resources in the form of funds for laboratories and seminars, stipends for advanced students, and salaries for research-productive professors whose value would be determined in a competitive labor market. It was not until a decade after the Civil War that those funds were finally found. While Yale and Harvard temporized by supporting research and research training as ancillary activities, the new, bold Johns Hopkins of 1876 not only had the mind, the will, and the program but also began with a financial base equal to what Harvard, the richest college, had taken two and a half centuries to amass. *That* was the kind of money that helped the American university to be born. Only a few years later, new institutions in Chicago and Palo Alto were to start out with endowments many times larger than the initial Johns Hopkins bequest.[12] Notably in cross-national comparison, nowhere in this funding and interaction of universities was a significant role played by the national government, or by a royal commission, or even by academic oligarchs assembled in committee to plan a design.

In the post-1875 experimentation that worked out the two-tier form of university, efforts were made at first, particularly at Johns Hopkins University and Clark University, to create a university that did not include undergraduates. But this approach would not wash: the undergraduate realm could not be dismissed from the emerging university framework. Undergraduates were needed for institutional viability; they produced income, they served as local recruits for the graduate level, and they were the centerpiece of public expectations of what education beyond high school was all about.[13] Hundreds of existing small colleges choose to remain stand-alone colleges centered on undergraduate teaching. But in the case of those old leading colleges that sought to seriously invest in research and to offer some education based on research, the new institutions, led by Johns Hopkins, forced their hand by providing a general model of two-tier organization. Even as the four-year segment was maintained, it became essential in the American context, in notable contrast to Britain, to develop a formal graduate level with the power to grant master's and doctoral degrees.

Interactive experimentation also ensured that what was already in place in the secondary schools and the colleges would heavily condition the university form. In Europe, as we have seen, general preparation was considered the property of such secondary schools as the German Gymnasium amd the French lycée; the few students who completed such schooling and went on to the university then entered directly into professional programs and specialized disciplinary work. But in the United States, the secondary schools were less academically concentrated. Specialized schools, both academic and vocational, gave way to public comprehensive schools—Horace Mann's common school—that embraced a variety of students and offered a medley of programs. Students then went on to "college," not "university," and at a younger age, seventeen or eighteen, than in Europe, and the four-year uniform college program was defined as the right place for the broad preparation of the educated person. Even as the colleges gradually loosened their ways in the early and mid-nineteenth century to accommodate emerging scientific fields, their curriculum was still considerably oriented to the education of the generalist rather than the specialist. Hence, in this context, the college in itself could not be a promising home for science. Richard Storr put it well: "However open the minds of some academics might be, the mode of instruction in the college was not designed to promote inquiry.... The advancement of knowledge and the promotion of the disciplines appropriate to it, as distinct from mental discipline, were not the goods of the college."[14] At the same time, the college form could not be waived aside in the construction of universities. The general undergraduate program was the immovable object.

The research imperative was the irresistible force: the thousands of American academics who had been to Europe and returned home as enthusiastic converts were but part of an interest in science and specialization that was steadily growing at home inside and outside the academy. Competition among institutions then turned that interest into a particularly strong force requiring an institutional accommodation. The new Johns Hopkins showed the way: define one's institution as a research-centered university and set out to attract faculty from other places that care deeply about research and the Ph.D. Other new private universities of the 1880s and 1890s—Clark, Cornell, Chicago, Stanford—took the same posture. The advanced traditional colleges that had already begun to award an occasional Ph.D.—Yale in 1861, Pennsylvania in 1871, Harvard in 1872—met the competition by establishing their own attractive arrangements for the new breed of scholars. Within a spreading university sector, relative ranking rapidly became dependent on apparent excellence in the production of new knowledge and an output of highly trained talent. With greatly enlarged resources, the universities were soon seen as higher and mightier than the smaller, freestanding colleges.

As other options were tried and foreclosed, the institutions that wanted to have it both ways settled into a clear-cut two-tier arrangement that was more assertive than anything existing in Europe. The universities then either had to build two faculties, one for the undergraduate level and one for the advanced tier, each to span a wide range of fields, or allow one faculty, subdivided by department, to teach at both levels. The first option had, and still has, much educational logic. It offers better protection for the undergraduate level in faculty assignments by providing a faculty of its own; it serves interdisciplinary efforts better, particularly in the undergraduate program; and it frees research-minded professors from the constraints of undergraduate work. It has been considered often and has been tried a few times, notably at the University of Chicago and Columbia University, but it tended not to last.[15] The two-faculty solution has suffered heavily from the fact that the college faculty sooner or later becomes defined as a lower faculty, even a second-class one. Critically, it does not serve disciplinary interests as well as the one-faculty solution. Through decades of development, American faculty and administrators have found much utility in the basic operating units, the departments, covering both levels. The departments can then flexibly and differently, from one university to the next and one discipline to the next, allocate resources, especially faculty time, to the two levels. As is stressed later, the vertical department can use allocations based largely on the number of undergraduate students to subsidize graduate programs. It can better free up time for faculty members to do research by assigning its graduate students to teach its undergraduates. And the involvement of professors in research and graduate research training, particularly in the long term, may invigorate their undergraduate teaching, an unproven doctrine that university professors much prefer to believe than the unsubstantiated charge of their critics that research works to the general detriment of undergraduate education. The vertical university became a framework within which disciplines cum departments could maximize their strength, drawing on large student enrollments at the base and competitively projecting attractive advanced programs based on the research interests of specialists.

If competitive local initiative provided the dynamic that brought the graduate school and the Ph.D. into existence on the American shore, sheer competition could not in itself produce the graduate school that became increasingly standardized in the twentieth century. In the context of competitive struggle, some common interests emerged which were served by voluntary forms of cooperation. One such interest was the international reputation of the American Ph.D. What did it mean? Did it have a standard? Such questions led fourteen institutions, eleven private and three public, to establish the Association of American Universities (AAU) in 1900. Under its auspices, presidents and deans came together to discuss such matters as entrance requirements for graduate programs and the publishing of doctoral dissertations. For the use of universities in Europe, the AAU began in 1913 to serve somewhat as an accrediting agency, compiling a list of American colleges and universities whose graduates could be assumed to be ready for graduate study (a practice discontinued much later, in 1948).[16] Graduate students also sought by means of voluntary association to determine common ground and standard meanings. They formed campus graduate clubs, then in 1896 linked them in the Federation of Graduate Clubs whose annual meetings debated, among other things, the requirements for the Ph.D. degree.[17] Much later, in 1961, the Council of Graduate Schools (CGS) was established as a forum for graduate school deans, with annual meetings and committee reports that over the years led to some agreed-upon norms and understandings of what constituted permissible practice and effective procedure; for example, common dates for accepting applications and notifying applicants of acceptance or rejection; the use of broad written and oral examinations before students were moved on to full candidacy for the Ph.D.; the insistence on original research in the doctoral dissertation.

Other largely informal and indirect means of convergence and standardization that are often found in competitive markets also became operative: the migration and therefore interchange of personnel among institutions; the sheer emulation of successful practices and winning ways. Mobile faculty members, moving, for example, from Clark and Cornell to Chicago and Stanford, brought with them particular conceptions of graduate studies, even their old catalog of graduate courses. Most of all, each aspiring institution had compelling reasons to watch closely the efforts of others to find out what succeeded and what did not. Among the universities, old and new, public and private, voluntary convergence was in place by the first decade of the twentieth century as arguably the central mechanism of coordination and standardization. Ph.D. degree programs were kept "in sight of each other."[18] In more than a nominal sense, a graduate education system was emerging. Competing institutions found they shared the same worries.

PRIVATE PATRONS AND GOVERNMENT FUNDING

The academic revolution that took place in the last quarter of the nineteenth century, as already suggested, had two lasting results in the structure of American universities: it established the graduate school and its programs as a second stratum, combining it with the traditional college; and it brought the department to the fore as the basic operating unit that organized subjects vertically, linking the first and second tiers. Observing the persistence of these basic forms, not much has changed in the nature of the American hybrid university in the course of a century of development. While institutions grew much larger and much more complex, what was in place by 1900 would seem to largely tell the story of the broad research foundations of American advanced education. But much change was yet to come, including several large shifts in the whole nature of the research foundations that would make the practices of the graduate school of the 1980s essentially unrecognizable from those of a century earlier. The graduate school, the department, and the Ph.D. program have been durable forms because they have been able both to adapt to a shifting base of resources and to accommodate enormous expansion in faculty and students.

THE ACQUISITION OF PRIVATE PATRONS

In the beginning the resource base of the American graduate programs was internal, located almost entirely in the institution itself. It then acquired external sponsors, first mainly private ones in the 1900–1940 period and then governmental patrons increasingly from World War II onward. And what the successive revolutions in the research underpinnings contributed to the great advantage of the universities was a diversified resource-and-funding base—partly institutional, partly private patrons, partly national and state governments—that gave institutions a backbone of autonomy even as they depended increasingly on the public purse. In cross-national perspective, the university research funding system that developed in twentieth-century America became increasingly notable not just for its size but also for its diversity of funding channels.

After 1900, those in and out of government who wanted to develop American science had various options open to them and experimented accordingly. One possibility was to turn to the governmental scientific bureau, then much in evidence in European countries, and form research units that in the United States would be approved by Congress largely on the basis of practical need, for example, the U.S. Geological Survey, the Bureau of the Census, and the Bureau of Mines.[19] Such research agencies were problem oriented and largely interdisciplinary; therein lay their long-term limitation and their great weakness in the eyes of scientists. While they could attack specific problems, they were not oriented to act broadly along the frontiers of the natural and social sciences. They commonly could not do basic research, and they could not attend to the needs and interests of the various emerging disciplines. A decade or so of experimentation and experience soon showed that collectively they would not be the American home for science.

A second option, one that early engaged the imagination of the leading American philanthropists, John D. Rockefeller and Andrew Carnegie, was the privately supported research institute. This attractive choice could concentrate pure research in well-funded centers that would be both independent of specific governmental mandates and situated away from the complications of university settings, especially the requirement that professorial researchers teach as well as do research and work with nonspecialized undergraduates as well as specialized graduate students. This option was pursued in a major way early in the century in the form of the Rockefeller Institute for Medical Research and the broader Carnegie Institution of Washington. But the model was not to dominate. For only a while did it appear possible that the private research institute could be likened to "a university in which there are no students"—a phrase used by the second president of the Carnegie Institution. Instead it became more like a governmental scientific bureau unencumbered by government. Operating with limited funds and mindful of serious practical problems of the day, institute directors could not resist choosing research topics and thereby focusing their programs. Then an institute's research agenda became "concen-

trated within a few chosen niches: it was hardly an alternative to university-based investigations in the basic disciplines."[20] It turned out between 1900 and 1920 that the independent research institutions could
no more offer leadership for broad-based science than could the government institutes.

Meanwhile, the universities, public and private, were steadily growing, thereby enlarging the pool of academics eager to do research. Between 1900 and 1915, in a period of relatively stable prices, the leading state universities quadrupled their facilities; the private universities,
more fully developed in 1900, doubled or tripled the value of their
buildings and grounds.[21] By 1920, in the dozen or so leading universities, the growing faculties were trained at a level that met international
standards. A quantum leap in scale was accompanied by a rising level
of scientific competence. But this competence was relatively underfunded. The general institutional budgets made little provision in the
form of funds set aside for the purpose of internally allocated research
grants. Special funds were needed, and it was the leaders in the private
foundations who could make those funds available. Searching among
the major institutional alternatives available to them, the foundation
officials gradually came to see that *the* resource of greatest value to
American science was the talent of the numerous faculty that had steadily accumulated in an enlarged university system. As they turned to the
proven specialists within the established university disciplines, they in
effect anointed the universities as the winners in competition among
the major institutional alternatives.

Outside funds earmarked for the support of university research actually came first in the form of ad hoc individual philanthropy. Individual gift giving, a habit well established before the turn of the century,
took off in the first two decades of the twentieth century, for buildings,
special endowments, institutes, and general funding of research.[22] This
enabled the financially stronger private universities to begin to develop
a significant level of *embedded* resources for research in such forms as
up-to-date laboratories, large libraries, and research equipment. Such
individual philanthropy also gave the universities the beginnings of *incremental* resources for research, funds added year by year which went
beyond the limits of regular institutional support. This was the beginning of what Roger Geiger has called the university research economy,
a pool of resources located outside the universities that is made available for their research endeavors.[23] As that economy developed, the pri-

vate universities were able in effect to endow research, beyond the sub-sidy of faculty, as well as to raise research funds from year to year.

The big players in this economy were soon the major private founda-tions. No longer limiting themselves to in-house studies and the support to freestanding institutes, the foundations assumed responsibility in the 1920s for the long-term development of the research capability of the universities. Following a best-science policy calculated "to make the peaks higher," the foundations, preeminently Rockefeller and Carnegie, concentrated at the outset on supporting research at a hand-ful of leading private universities, especially in the sciences.[24] By the early 1930s, that support had also been extended to such state univer-sities as Michigan, Wisconsin, and California. In the process, at least five different lines of support were fashioned: grants for "research capital"—buildings and equipment—that could be expected to have large multiplier effects through matching requirements and competitive emulation; direct allocations to establish new research institutes and even to initiate new professional schools such as the enticement to the University of Chicago by the Carnegie Corporation to establish the first "graduate school of library science";[25] grants to support re-search projects; long-running schemes for graduate and postdoctoral research fellowships, of which the Guggenheim postdoctoral award, begun in 1925, was to be *the* outstanding success story; and, signif-icant in building a network of support, major sustaining grants to a set of national "intermediate" organizations—the National Research Council, established earlier (1916) during World War I, the Social Science Research Council (1923), and the American Council of Learned Societies (1919)—that were capable of making informed judg-ments, essentially through peer review, on relatively small grants to numerous scholars in such broad areas as the sciences, the social sci-ences, and the humanities.[26] In a university–foundation relationship that evolved through trial and error, such channels became the opera-tional components of the university research economy. Under essen-tially private support, the universities became "the engines of American science."[27]

The takeoff in the support of research that occurred between 1900 and World War II, particularly in the 1920s and 1930s, may thus be seen as a second revolution in the life of American universities, one that greatly enlarged their scope in the direction of research activity and thereby helped establish research underpinnings for graduate education. Beyond the regular payroll and the ordinary expenditures for library and laboratory, grants and contracts from external sponsors were now a fact of university life.[28] Where in other countries governments had long assumed the support, or were increasingly taking over the financial support, of all university functions, patronage for research and advanced study in the American case was significantly nongovernmental. Foundation support at its peak apparently never exceeded 10 percent of the income of all U.S. colleges and universities taken together. But at a small number of universities, mainly private, the foundation contribution is estimated to have been in excess of one-fifth and, critical for our interest, heavily concentrated at the graduate level.[29] Beyond endowment and tuition and general state institutional support in the public universities, institutions could now reach out for special funds that would greatly augment their development as research-centered universities. Thus, long before the national government took over as the primary sponsor in the research economy, the universities, bidding for support from private external sources, had learned how to extend their portfolio of initiatives. The habit of financial diversification was early put in place.

THE EXPLOSION OF GOVERNMENTAL FUNDING

This second academic revolution saw great expansion in U.S. graduate education, along with the undergraduate realm, out of all proportion to growth in the relevant age group. Between 1900 and 1940, the age group did not even double, but "institutions offering the doctorate more than tripled, college faculties became five times as large, college enrollments six times, baccalaureate degrees seven times, and graduate enrollments and degrees from thirteen to seventeen times."[30] College-going increased from about 4 percent of the age group in 1900 to over 15 percent in 1940, putting the United States first in the transition from elite to mass higher education.[31] The percentage of baccalaureate holders who took graduate degrees increased from about 6 percent to 15 percent. Earned doctorates multiplied, increasing by about 250 percent between 1900 and 1920 and by over 500 percent between 1920 and 1940.[32] During the two interwar decades, the number of institutions giving the doctorate doubled, from about fifty to nearly one hundred.[33] By World War II, the research university sector was a towering presence in the system of higher education at large. And by international standards, it was already huge. Where else would one find anything like one hundred institutions offering the doctorate, with the top ten, even the top twenty, individually offering a quantitative production of Ph.D.'s hardly approached by more than a few institutions in all the rest of the world?

But changes that began during World War II soon dwarfed this major prewar stage of development. Wartime involvement in "national defense" set in motion a shift in research-fund patronage from private to public sources. The universities became systematically related to a set of federal mission agencies, in particular, the Department of Defense (DOD) and the new Atomic Energy Commission (AEC), two agencies that were to become principal funders of university applied research. Riding the crest of war-generated goodwill in government circles and in the general population, scientists sought in the years immediately after the war to convince the national government that it should generously support basic university research much more generously. They were successful. The early 1950s saw the establishment of the National Science Foundation (NSF) as a nonmission agency charged with providing broad support of research. NSF's divisional structure soon reflected the natural and social science array of academic disciplines, and from the beginning its funds, guided by peer review, went largely to the universities. At about the same time, the National Institutes of Health (NIH), which had originated in 1930, moved decisively from intramural research alone to extramural grant making, with favorable funding from Congress that was to provide budgets for the support of biological and medical research far in excess of NSF expenditures. Located within the health segment of the Department of Health, Education, and Welfare (later the Department of Health and Human Services), the NIH complex is often classified as a mission agency. But it has played an increasingly important role in the support of basic science in the universities as well as in its own laboratories and should, at the least, be seen as a supporter of "categorical basic research," that is, involved in a search for new knowledge needed for the solution of practical problems, which often generates research that can hardly, if at all, be distinguished from "noncategorical basic research" defined as the search for new knowledge without reference to solution of practical problems. Between them, NSF and NIH became the main channels of government support of academic basic research.

The inclination of the federal government to turn to the universities for both basic and applied research—more broadly, for research and development—was well in place by the mid-1950s. In a space of five years, between 1954 and 1958, governmental expenditures for university research rose 60 percent.[34] Then came the Sputnik scare of 1958, which greatly increased the willingness of elected and appointed officials to turn to science in the name of national defense and economic strength. The reaction to Sputnik forged new and substantial commitments to science, space, and education, all redounding to the benefit of the research universities. A new space agency, the National Aeronautical and Space Administration (NASA), soon became a major funder, supplying by 1966 almost 10 percent of the federal funds for academic R&D, with some thirty-six universities each receiving more than one million dollars.[35] The 1958 National Defense Education Act ushered in federal support for graduate students that was to flourish in the 1960s. Research grants and contracts poured out of the national government and into the hands of the universities. The decade of 1958–1968, a period of relatively stable prices, saw a *sevenfold* increase in federal funds for basic university research (from $178 million to $1,251 million).[36] The 1950s and especially the 1960s were a golden age for American academic science.

The leap in magnitude of the university research economy included support for the infrastructure of university research, building up to the point where the federal government supplied one-third of the universities' capital funds (later decline led in the 1980s to a share of only about one-eighth).[37] Through both direct research grants and the funding of research capital, the federal government encouraged the multiplication of research universities. More academic institutions emerged which stood out from the crowd of hundreds of four-year and two-year colleges on the basis of a major research capacity and substantial Ph.D. program. New funding was spread more widely: by 1968, over forty universities were receiving more than $10 million annually in federal research funds; the share of the total pocketed by the first ten was down to 28 percent.[38]

The drift of institutions toward the values of the graduate school was thereby accelerated in a round-robin of interactions. As research became a financial asset for institutions, in addition to serving as the main basis for university status, more universities aggressively sought the academic researcher. As they built doctoral programs, more institutions turned out research-oriented Ph.D.'s who entered the academic labor market looking for university posts centered on research. Hence the new federal funds extended and intensified institutional competition for research resources and research-minded personnel. This competitive mode of distributing funds was the opposite of standardized state allocation characteristic of most European systems and, as we will see later, of Japan. The intensely competitive world of university science observed in American higher education in the 1980s was set in small part in the late nineteenth century and then in larger share in the private funding takeoff of the 1920s, but it only achieved its full force in the vast government-assisted expansion of the 1960s. In the operation of American universities, the research genie was then fully out of the bottle.

However, the course of federal support for university research and graduate education was not a smooth one. The great expansion in all lines of federal support that took place between the mid-1950s and the end of the 1960s was followed by a "stagnant decade." As conservative administrations, beginning with the presidency of Richard Nixon, turned away from basic research, the funds for research grants and contracts leveled off. Funds for research capital—"R&D plant"—were cut drastically, falling from a high point of $126 million in 1965 to about $35 million annually during the 1970s. Fellowship support for graduate students stumbled badly, falling from a high of $447 million in 1967 to only $185 million a decade later.[39] But just as it looked as if this period of stagnation and decline would predict the future,[40] there was a gradual turnaround, leading to a reasonably prosperous decade after 1978. At a time of little growth in students or faculty, the university research economy grew by over 50 percent in real terms.[41] Academic R&D spending increased over a decade at an average annual rate of 12 percent (5% per year in constant dollars), totaling over $12 billion by 1987 for separately budgeted R&D activities in the sciences and engineering. An additional $1.8 billion (from all sources) was disbursed that year for capital investment in facilities and equipment, a 17 percent increase over the previous year.[42] For the research universities overall, instructional budgets grew by 30 percent in real terms between the mid-1970s and the mid-1980s.[43]

INSTITUTIONAL EMBODIMENT OF RESEARCH

If the research enterprise in American universities was far more vigorous in 1990 than it was a dozen years earlier, the federal government, it turns out, deserved only part of the credit. The federal increases in support during this return to prosperity were smaller than the increases from nonfederal sources: for the 1977–1987 period, 4 percent a year compared to 7 percent, respectively. The nonfederal sources, for *separately budgeted* R&D university expenditures, increased from less than one-third of the total in 1977 to almost two-fifths in 1987: the federal government share declined from 67 percent to 61 percent.[44] Whereas the federal government at the end of this period provided $7.3 billion, the other sources put up a not inconsiderable $4.8 billion. Topping the list of other providers were the institutions themselves, able to provide over $2 billion (in 1987 dollars). Second were state and local governments, offering over a billion dollars. Industry had become a third sponsor, at three-quarters of a billion dollars. And all others, including private foundations, contributed over $800 million. Critically, for the separate item of capital investment or research infrastructure, the $1.8 billion mentioned above for 1987, over 90 percent came from the nonfederal sources.[45]

Such data reveal the hidden story of how American research universities have learned to buffer their research interests and advanced programs from environmental turbulence, specifically the ups and downs of federal commitment. They developed under their own control certain long-term means of supporting research and graduate education; they drew on multiple levels of government as well as industry and foundations. By increasing tuition, enlarging endowment and annual private support, and turning to industry, the private universities enlarged their financial base for all kinds of activities, not the least for the construction of research facilities, the purchase of research equipment, the salaries of professors, and the support of graduate students. Similarly, the state universities increased their own more modest tuition, greatly increased their year-to-year capacity to elicit voluntary contributions from alumni and other potential supporters, continued to depend on state allocations based on student numbers for their core support, and turned to their own state government as well as to industry for special funds for research, pure and applied.

In cross-national comparison, the state component is particularly noteworthy. In a federal system of government in which the many states compete with one another, the 1980s saw many states define their future as lying in scientific innovation, high technology, and an intensely professionalized service economy. The interest of states in the subsidy of university research grew accordingly, even in a grossly exaggerated fashion in many cases as state leaders imagined the growth of a Silicon Valley as a spinoff from a state flagship campus. The governmental interest in science and technology thus spread from Washington, D.C., to the state capitols, encouraging governors and legislators to go beyond student-based institutional allocations to special allotments, large and small, for research. The organized research units (ORUs) that continue to proliferate on state university campuses generally have their sustaining funds built into state allocations, much like the ongoing support of research institutes by national governments in most other advanced systems.

In general, the four decades since the end of World War II have witnessed a growing prominence of the state research universities. Not that private universities did not prosper. A small group of them continued to serve as national pacesetters, providing quality undergraduate settings virtually impossible for larger and cheaper state universities to match, while offering graduate programs and conditions for faculty research that place them at the top of research university rankings. Harvard, Stanford, Chicago, Yale, Cornell, Princeton, and Columbia, all private, appear in many reputational rankings of the top ten U.S. universities. In addition, the Massachusetts Institute of Technology (MIT) and the California Institute of Technology (Cal Tech) have prospered as preeminent centers of science and technology difficult for anyone to match, domestically or internationally. But the state universities, as a general group, have prospered even more. Considerably larger in size on the average, they have developed huge embedded resources in the form of regular state allocations based on student numbers that may be many times larger than private counterparts; for example, in 1990, 35,000 students at UCLA compared to 10,000 at Yale, and 36,000 students at the University of Michigan compared to 6,000 at Princeton. Their capacity to elicit federal grants and contracts and to otherwise raise R&D monies placed twelve of the state universities among the top twenty institutions in 1987 in R&D expenditures in the sciences and engineering, with such fast climbers as Texas A&M and the University of California campuses in Los Angeles and San Diego rising in two decades to appear high on that critical list (see table 2). Wisconsin, Michigan, Minnesota, Texas A&M, Illinois, Washington, and four campuses of the huge University of California system all stood higher in total R&D expenditures than did the pride of the Ivy League: Harvard stood 15th, Yale ranked 20th, and Princeton did not appear in the top twenty. Public universities in the South and Southwest, for example, the University of Texas at Austin, the University of Georgia, and the University of Arizona, became significant research universities on the national scene. Thus it should come as no surprise that more of the U.S.

TABLE TWO   TOP TWENTY AMERICAN
UNIVERSITIES IN SCIENCE AND ENGINEERING R&D
EXPENDITURES, 1987

	Total from All Sources	Federal Contribution	Federal Percentage
	(dollars in millions)		
1. Johns Hopkins University[a]	511	476	.93
2. Massachusetts Institute of Technology	264	207	.78
3. University of Wisconsin, Madison	254	150	.59
4. Cornell University	245	145	.59
5. Stanford University	241	204	.85
6. University of Michigan	225	138	.61
7. University of Minnesota	222	109	.49
8. Texas A&M University	220	75	.34
9. University of California, Los Angeles	189	131	.69
10. University of Illinois, Urbana	189	104	.55
11. University of Washington	187	145	.78
12. University of California, San Diego	183	143	.78
13. University of California, Berkeley	175	109	.62
14. University of California, San Francisco	169	117	.69
15. Harvard University	169	120	.71
16. University of Texas, Austin	169	88	.52
17. Pennsylvania State University	166	94	.57
18. University of Pennsylvania	158	111	.70
19. Columbia University, Main Division	150	133	.89
20. Yale University	146	117	.80
Total, leading 20 institutions	4,233	2,917	.69
Total, all other institutions	7,849	4,409	.56
Total, all institutions	12,082	7,326	.61

SOURCE: National Science Foundation, Science Resource Studies Highlights, August 25, 1989, 5.

Note: Data do not include R&D performed by university-administered federally funded research and development centers.

[a] Includes Applied Physics Laboratory with $342 million in total and $338 million in federally financed R&D expenditures.

research literature came from the state universities in the 1980s than in the past. These universities, as a general enlarging group, have shown a relatively greater expansion of research.

Finally, looming large on the American scene is the huge state and institutional subsidy of faculty salary and time that is only poorly factored at best and often entirely overlooked in American figures on university research and national R&D. This form of subsidy is outside all the figures presented above, operating as a wild card that renders highly problematic the global sums reported for the United States in basic research and, more broadly, R&D. In the state universities, faculty salaries are covered primarily by state allocations; in the private universities, they are covered considerably, if not primarily, by tuition, income from endowment, and annual fund-raising from private sources. In this central feature of institutional core support, the federal government is therefore only a supplementary player. Then, within the bounds of the state and institutional subsidy of faculty time, in any university seriously invested in research, the time spent on teaching is held to such a level that a third or a half or more of professorial time is available for research. This distribution contrasts sharply with that found in nonresearch universities and the many nonuniversity sectors that contain most U.S. students, where teaching loads of twelve and fifteen hours or more in the classroom signify the priority given to teaching, often to the virtual preclusion of research. (We return to the American development of teaching-only institutions and their differentiation from research universities under the concept of teaching drift in chapter 6.) In the top one hundred universities and sometimes beyond, classroom contact hours are in the range of six hours a week, more often tailing down than up, amounting to a seminar a week, for example, when professors are able to "buy off" more time from monies available in their research grants, use generous sabbatical leave plans, and have teaching assistants assist them or even substitute for them in the undergraduate classroom.[46]

The subsidy of faculty time for inquiry is the most basic of all research subsidies. In every country it is difficult to estimate, and it may even go unreported in calculations of financial support for academic research. It is a particularly hidden feature of the American system, buried in the individual funding of private universities and in the diverse allocations of fifty states to their university and nonuniversity sectors. But a broad pattern may be discerned: a funding division of support exists in which the private universities themselves, and the state governments, in

the case of the public universities, provide mainline institutional support across the disciplines—the embedded resources of faculty as well
as of facilities—while the federal government largely provides the additional allocations—the incremental resources—that make possible
modern scientific research. But even in this latter provision, as we have
seen, nonfederal patrons, including the institutions themselves, offer a
significant share, in considerable contrast to the funding patterns observed in Germany, Britain, France, and Japan. The U.S. funding pattern helps to set a system framework within which national initiatives
supplement state initiatives and, more important, institutional initiatives. Individual universities exercise an uncommon degree of self-direc-
tion, based on a multiplicity of patrons and a diversity of funding channels. They thereby develop stability and resilience, especially a capacity
to buffer governmental turbulence. The federal government has been an
unsteady "partner"; for example, federal support of graduate students
in science and engineering has ridden a roller-coaster of change, from
10 percent of all such students in 1954 to a peak of 42 percent of all
such students in 1967 and then back down the slope again to 20 percent in 1985.[47] The institutions themselves have picked up the slack,
along with students relying more on their own funds and loans.

Diversified patronage has helped to give the higher education sector
relatively strong footing within the four major sectors that compose the
huge American R&D establishment. American R&D expenditures in
1990 amounted to over $150 billion across all sectors of society, com-
pared to about $67 billion for Japan, $32 billion for Germany, $24 bil-
lion for France, and $20 billion for Britain.[48] This huge difference in
absolute size is reduced considerably when adjusted for size of population, since then the Japanese sum should be doubled and the European
figures quadrupled, for populations that are about one-half and one-
fourth the American. But while the relative comparison is an appropriate "per capita" indicator of national effort, the absolute figures remain
a primary phenomenon. By all worldly standards, the American R&D
enterprise is immense.

Within this huge realm, the higher education sector has clearly been
defined as the home of science in the sense of basic research. In the 1990
figures, academic R&D totaled about $22 billion (including university-
administered federal laboratories, a $5 billion item), virtually all dedi-
cated to basic and applied research. R&D funds in industry, a second
major sector, have been much larger, totaling over $108 billion, but
they are overwhelmingly devoted to development rather than research.

In per capita magnitude of investment, American industrial R&D is somewhat less than that found in German and Japanese industry, while distinctly ahead of the British and French industrial sectors. American R&D mounted within government establishments, the third sector, has been more moderate in comparison to higher education and industry (approximately $16 billion), especially since many of some five hundred governmental laboratories are located on university campuses and are supervised by individual universities or consortia of universities. The fourth sector, independent, nonprofit research establishments, totaled about $5 billion.[49] This sector has not had the organized strength of nonuniversity sectors in France and Germany, where CNRS and Max Planck structures have developed as significant homes for basic as well as applied research and development. In short, in comparison to other countries, basic research has developed and has remained most fully in the universities.

One highly significant outcome of a huge research base located in universities, where publication of results is a primary item in faculty rewards and institutional reputation, has been an outpouring of research literature across a wide range of basic disciplines and professional subjects. As measured in the databases of publication and citation analysis, the U.S. share of world scientific literature in the early 1980s was between one-third and two-fifths (36.8%), a share greater than that of Germany (5.9%), Britain (9%), France (4.7%), and Japan (7%) combined (see table 3). The elaborate but crude machinery of publication and citation analysis, covering over 2,600 scientific journals at the time, was and is clearly biased toward English-language publications; it underestimates publication by Japanese researchers in Japanese, French researchers in French, and, to a lesser degree, German researchers in German. And it captures applied research less well than basic research. But the orders of magnitude still hold,[50] and, even for French researchers, English continues to spread as the language of scientific publication.

As citation analysis has grown in sophistication over several decades, analysts have been able to report research literature output by individual scholar, research group, department, university, region of country, whole nation, and, notably, discipline, both in quantity of papers and in quality as indicated by frequency of referenced use in the work of others. Thus the world share of a country can be studied field by field and aggregated by such major groupings as life sciences and physical sciences. For example, as table 3 shows, the U.S. share in life sciences was about 40 percent in sheer volume of research articles and over 50

TABLE THREE   WORLD SHARE OF SCIENTIFIC
LITERATURE, BY COUNTRY, 1981–1985 (PERCENT)

Indicator	Country				
	U.S.A.	U.K.	Japan	West Germany	France
All Scientific Fields					
Publication[a]	36.8	9.0	7.0	5.9	4.7
Citations[b]	50.8	9.6	5.8	5.8	4.2
Life Sciences[c]					
Publications	40.8	10.6	5.9	5.5	4.4
Citations	53.2	10.8	4.8	4.8	3.6
Physical Sciences[c]					
Publications	34.9	6.8	7.1	6.3	5.3
Citations	50.5	6.7	5.7	7.4	5.9

SOURCE: A. Schubert, W. Glänzel, and T. Braun, "Scientometrics Data Files: A Comprehensive Set of Indicators on 2,649 Journals and 96 Countries in All Major Science Fields and Sub-Fields, 1981–1985," *Scientometrics* 16, nos. 1–6 (1989): 3–478.

[a] Authors of articles *counted* in 2,649 journals in all major scientific fields.

[b] Authors of articles *cited* in other articles in the journals.

[c] 108 subfields were aggregated into five major fields: life sciences, physical sciences, chemistry, engineering, and mathematics. Only the first two fields are reported here.

percent in frequency of citations; in physical sciences, about 35 and 50 percent, respectively. Trends can also be identified which show, for example, the Japanese share overall and in a number of critical fields markedly increasing, the German and French shares rising slightly, and the English portion showing distinct signs of decline. As the shares of a few other countries rise, the U.S. contribution is marginally less dominating. In sheer volume of output of scientific papers, however, the U.S. gain during the 1980s was the largest of all.[51] The American base, heavily university grounded, is huge, deeply institutionalized, and relatively stable.

A second highly significant macro-outcome of the American framework of academic research has been the positioning of a large number of universities (and departments) to become world leaders. As places of inquiry, it is difficult for universities in other countries, even Oxford and Cambridge in Britain and the Universities of Tokyo and Kyoto in Japan, to measure up in breadth and depth to the top ten American institutions and even to the top twenty and beyond. For example, citation analysis in four subfields of chemistry found in the several cases that 18 to 20 of the top twenty-five universities internationally and 8 to 9 of the top ten were American; in the field of electrical engineering, as a second example, 20 of the top twenty-five, with 4 in Britain and 1 in Japan (the same type of analysis for industrial firms showed less dominance: 13 were U.S. companies, 8 were Japanese, 3 were British, and 1 was Dutch).[52] A special inquiry mounted by a British economist for his own discipline, using a varied set of indicators of research productivity, showed that among the top twenty-five economics departments in the world, 21 were American, 2 were British, and 2 were Israeli.[53] A knowledgeable American observer, Henry Rosovsky, former Dean of Arts and Sciences at Harvard University, had considerable justification when he stated in the late 1980s that "between two-thirds and three-fourths" of the leading universities in the world were in the American system.[54] For the purposes of research and research training, an institutional base in the form of strong universities is very substantial.

INSTITUTIONAL DIFFERENTIATION OF GRADUATE EDUCATION

When the master's degree is included, institutions that offer "advanced degrees" in the American system number more like 800 to 1,200 (according to different classifications) than 200.[55] Beyond the 200 universities that are "doctoral granting," in the definitions of the Carnegie classification, another 600, composing a large, loose, and growing category known as "comprehensive universities and colleges," award the master's as their highest degree.[56] In the late 1980s, while the doctoral-granting universities, large in average size, possessed about 28 percent of all higher education students, the master's-granting group contained another 27 percent. The other half of student enrollment is found in some 600 small private institutions that define themselves as "liberal arts colleges" (5%); or in the huge community college sector, consisting of over 1,400 two-year institutions (37%); or in a miscellany of detached specialized institutions in such fields as theology, business, technology, teaching, medicine, and the arts (4%).

The basic Carnegie classification divided the approximately 200 doctoral-granting institutions into four categories. Those in the first two
categories, entitled Research Universities I and II, "are committed to
graduate education through the doctorate degree *and* give high priority
to research."[57] Seventy institutions were placed in the top category on
the basis of receiving at least $33.5 million in federal research support
in the years of the mid-1980s, in addition to awarding at least fifty
Ph.D. degrees per year. Another thirty-four universities were assigned
to the second category on the basis of receiving between $12.5 and
$33.5 million (and also awarding at least fifty Ph.D.'s). The 100-plus
institutions thus defined as research universities constitute the heart-
land of academic science. At the end of the 1980s, they were receiving
about 80 percent of the federal research dollars. The remaining universities were allocated to two additional categories simply defined as
"Doctoral-granting Universities I" and "II." They are also committed
to graduate education through the doctoral degree but had in the mid-
1980s something less that $12.5 million in federal dollars for research
and offered, respectively, at least forty Ph.D. degrees in five or more
academic disciplines, twenty or more in at least one discipline, or ten
or more in three or more disciplines.

    While serviceable in making elementary distinctions in the vast array
of over 3,500 formally accredited institutions, these arbitrary categories, noticeably indistinct, reflect the great difficulty of composing an
accurate and meaningful classification in an extremely heterogeneous,
nonformal national system. In all the assorted categories, there is
much range. For example, the top category, Research Universities I,
contained institutions that received over $200 million annually at the
end of the 1980s from the federal government for research and ones
that just crawled over the $33.5 million cutoff point, hence a six to
one or seven to one difference in capacity to obtain federal research dollars. Institutional resources and funds from nonfederal sources exhibit a
similar magnitude of difference.

    To complicate matters further, institutions are individually mobile
and readily move from one category to another. Among 213 institutions counted as doctoral-granting institutions in 1987, 58 had moved
from one category to another among the four types of university during
the decade since 1976. While no Research I universities had fallen out
of that category, 16 institutions classified earlier as Research II had become Research I. Ten that earlier had placed in the third category of
Doctorate I had moved up to Research II, and 2 had jumped two cate-

gories to Research I, while another 10 institutions had moved down-ward to Doctorate II. Most prone to institutional shifting were the master's-level "comprehensive universities and colleges" and the tradi-tionally four-year "liberal arts colleges." In a decade, 23 master's insti-tutions moved into doctoral-granting ranks; 73 Comprehensive II be-came Comprehensive I; and 63 liberal arts colleges, broadening their undergraduate programs toward occupational fields and reaching for the master's, became reclassified as comprehensive colleges.[58] The insti-tutional drift is clear: toward comprehensiveness, university status, and greater involvement in research.

In the construction of institutional foundations for advanced teach-ing and study, the competitive dynamics of the American system have produced both intense concentration, allowing some of the rich to be-come considerably richer, and extensive diffusion, involving more insti-tutions that are strung out along a lengthened core-to-periphery contin-uum. Conditions in the core of the institutional complex are the best in the academic world, while at the periphery they are quite weak, amounting at the low end to not much more than a hope of building more satisfactory arrangements after another decade or two of struggle and perhaps a little bit of luck along the way. Always complicating the picture are the growing differences among disciplines in all the institu-tions, particularly between the sciences and humanities.

Four universities illustrate well this simultaneous concentration and diffusion.[59] Studied in the late 1980s, they were selected for analysis from a list that ranked two hundred universities and colleges according to the amount of separately earmarked or "sponsored" research monies they obtained from outside sources, with the federal component ranging between two-thirds and three-fourths. The first university, in the top ten, brought in over $300 million; the second, ranked about twenty-fifth, $125 million; the third, ranked about one hundredth, $50 mil-lion; and the fourth, standing about two hundredth, brought in about $3 million from federal sources in an overall research budget of $5 mil-lion.

University A, a private university, has been able to link graduate edu-cation to research across all departments. As major research universities go, it is not inordinately large, with a total enrollment of about 13,000, but over half of that enrollment was lodged at the graduate level, mainly in graduate professional schools but with over 2,000 students in the "nonprofessional" graduate school of the arts and sciences. Post-doctoral researchers numbered 600. Nearly all incoming graduate students, highly selected from across the country and from around the world, were guaranteed at least four years of financial support to cover tuition and room and board, a very sizable sum. Although students in the sciences obtained greater support, students in the humanities and social sciences were also covered at a relatively high level compared to other universities, by means of financial packages that departments and the graduate school fashioned from institutional budgets for teaching and research support, research assistantships built into research grants, and fellowships and traineeships obtained from foundations as well as national agencies. Like other well-funded universities, University A can, in effect, roll funds toward the disciplines that would otherwise become poorer. Although faculty staffing of departments is not large by American standards, mostly in the range of twenty to forty faculty, the university is able to offer about seventy doctoral degree programs and a similar number of largely subsidiary master's, with a substantial output of over five hundred Ph.D.'s a year. Doctoral training is foremost: the aim is to train researchers and scholars (not "teachers"); there is an abundance of "time to do research, research facilities [and] student-faculty interaction";[60] and across the many basic disciplines, graduate education and research are seen as inseparable activities.

University B exhibits institutional conditions that reflect recent hard-driving institutional mobility. Self-defined to be on the move, ever climbing, the institution has been extremely entrepreneurial in the research economy: in the ten years ending 1987, external research funds grew from $40 million to $125 million (in constant dollars), moving the university close to the top twenty. In a total enrollment of about 35,000, graduate enrollment was about 7,500, heavily concentrated in science and engineering programs that have been the cutting edge of institutional ambition. The organizational magnitude of this type of American public research university is highlighted in density of the biological sciences: in 1989, this general subject area was spread across thirteen discipline-based departments and seventeen interdisciplinary programs.[61]

But development is uneven: compared to University A, the humanities are not well funded; there are many part-time students (one-half of all graduate students) who take a long time to complete the program. The university actually has a greater range of doctoral and master's programs—about 100 doctoral and 150 master's—than University A, but fewer degrees are conferred, approximately 300 Ph.D.'s a year.

But in University B as in University A, the numbers are very large when seen in cross-national perspective; for example, in the late 1980s, about 125 Ph.D.'s a year at the University of Sussex in Britain and about 60 a year at the University of Nagoya in Japan. This second university exhibits in its own nature the comparative view that the American university sector is "the 800-pound gorilla" of national academic research.

University C, falling outside the top one hundred in research support, is even more uneven in the development of graduate programs. Sponsored research brings in about $50 million. Out of a total enrollment of about 26,000, graduate enrollment is over 6,500, with two-thirds of the students in professional schools. Most financial aid for graduate students comes in the form of state-supported teaching assistantships. Located in a state known historically for weak support of even its flagship campus, this university struggles to maintain its current weak position as a research university. It has managed to obtain a research reputation in a few departments, mainly in pure and applied sciences. But even here, far down the line, the competitive effort to build research foundations goes on. "Graduate education and research are inseparable.... If it's good for research it's good for graduate education." Linking graduate education and research is seen by central administration as "symbolically important." It may be "too big for us to do well" at the moment, but "change comes slowly and from the bottom up.... We're still feeling our way."[62] Even as a weak player, this third-level university operates about fifty doctoral programs and, in 1987, issued over 300 doctorates and 900 master's degrees. Faculty research prevails across departments. Generally part-time (only one-fourth full-time) and lacking research assistant appointments, graduate students are less integrated into faculty research or able to concentrate fully on their own projects. The difference in graduate school climate between this university and a top ten institution is large.

University D sinks virtually out of the picture as a place for well-supported academic research and intense research training, despite having about twenty-five Ph.D. programs and, at the end of the 1980s, certifying about 100 Ph.D.'s and 1,000 master's degrees each year. Though its graduate student enrollment of about 3,500 students (out of a total of 20,000) approximates the total student enrollment of, for example, Keele in Britain, it represents the tail end of the American institutional progression in relating research to advanced teaching and learning, ranking as it does about 200 nationally in university research monies. Having evolved out of a normal school–teacher's college background, it is far from being a flagship campus even in its own state. But not content with just offering the bachelor's degree, or even with a range of practical master's programs, this fourth-level institution has managed to establish some "small groupings of doctoral activity, referred to as 'research strengths ... in selected areas.'"[63] With research dollars amounting to about $5 million in the late 1980s, the sum for the entire campus was less than that possessed by many individual departments in the first and second universities. But, encouraged by the administration, the faculty seek outside funds for themselves and to support graduate students as research assistants. The problem is stated this way: "We don't compete very well. When we line up against Stanford, Washington, Minnesota, Wisconsin, and eastern schools, we can't compete." And if you cannot compete, you have to teach—teach more, and teach more undergraduates. Teaching assignments of three courses per semester are then exacted, "loads" that are more like those in all-teaching institutions than those found in the leading universities. And only about one-eighth of the 3,500 graduate students are full-time. In short, the university is a service university for its state and region, but at the same time it goes on trying to establish more research activity and doctoral training.

Crisscrossing these large institutional differences are disciplinary differences that in the first instance parallel the differences found in the German, British, French, and, as we will soon see, Japanese system. For advanced students, the sciences offer increasingly a laboratory-intensive or team-research setting. Students are trained while contributing to professors' research projects or large multiperson efforts headed by an institute or laboratory director. The training may rest on a virtually ideal mentoring relationship or on one that includes much linkage and a sense of colleagueship among research staff, postdoctoral students, and graduate students of several levels of experience. In contrast, the training may consist of only training in narrow skills with the students essentially used as cheap labor: in pejorative British terms, "dogmeat"; in American, "stoop labor." The increasing deployment of graduate students in large research teams in the sciences and engineering has caused concern that narrow-skill training may be increasingly common and not in the best interest of the students. But the realities of different campuses and research clusters are complex on this point and frequently seem to combine narrow routine work and broad learning experiences: "Some days you are a peon. Other days you know how ... and you're king for a day."[64] Or: "I feel like an employee, but I like it ... —an employee on a long leash."[65] The better science students also go on to postdoctoral positions, since in most fields in both the biological and physical sciences, the "post-doc" has replaced the Ph.D. as the terminal point in student training. More personal autonomy and greater responsibility are found at this level, including supervision of graduate students.

As found in the other countries, graduate students in the humanities (and extensively in the social sciences) work in the dissertation or research phase of their studies considerably on their own, independently from the faculty members' own research. They may go months at a time with little or no faculty contact. The dissertation research may be carried out in a faraway library or residence, with perhaps chapters occasionally mailed back to a professor or a whole draft submitted at one time after a long period of work. This individualistic mode is a far cry from laboratory-intensive interaction. It contains little risk of student exploitation, but it is an uncertain and chancy path. Time to completion increases in this less structured mode of graduate student research; dropping out and noncompletion are more likely.

Disciplinary differences produced in the first instance by the nature of disciplinary knowledge are extended by a widening gap in funding. The sciences grow richer and hence can more likely support their students in continuous study. The humanities grow poorer, absolutely and relatively, and their students must scramble for means of support that lead to part-time study and financial self-sacrifice. But, as we have seen, the impact of such funding differentials varies greatly according to the extent of institutional wealth. In the fourth-level university described above, even students in the sciences are likely to have little or no financial support from research funds; they can be virtually as poor as their counterparts in the humanities. Teaching assistantships, based on undergraduate student numbers, are the common ground of financial aid. But in University A, even students in the humanities possess four years of financial assistance for full-time study, with the likelihood, if needed, of fifth-year assistance. First-line U.S. universities, especially private ones operating on a diverse financial base, compose such support by utilizing contributions from different sources, including the institutional self-support they generate out of tuition, endowment income, annual private contributions, and research grant overhead income rebated to departments. Institutional riches permit some subsidy of disciplines "that do not pay their way," or, as in departments of history and English, that pay their way by heavier-than-average teaching of undergraduates.

DEPARTMENTAL MICROSTRUCTURE

Across all the many institutional and disciplinary differences found in American graduate education there looms the common ground, distinctive among the five countries of this study, of an elaborate microstructure in the form of course work and other requirements specified and monitored by departments in cooperation with the office of the graduate school. Under broad rules enacted by the administration and senate-type faculty bodies, new students are selected by subject departments, in sharp contrast to undergraduate admission performed on an all-college basis by a central admissions office. On entry, students move into a department-arranged institutional setting in the form of two years or more of mandatory and optional courses. New graduate students may possibly also enter research groups, but they do not thereby escape the ubiquitous departmental requirements; dominating the first two years, course work typically comes first. In history, for example, a set of prescribed courses may aim "to map out what has been done" by requiring students to cover such major subareas as American history, European history, and Latin American history. Intensive reading in chosen subfields is then needed as preparatory for a comprehensive examination prepared by faculty on behalf of the department or major subunits within it.

Serving as the culmination of the course-work component of advanced study, the comprehensive examination is *the* breakpoint between course-dominated and research-dominated activity. Generally a written examination, sometimes both written and oral, it reflects multiple substantive interests of the faculty and tests mastery of knowledge covered in courses, basic principles of the discipline, and an acquaintance with major subfields. But course work and the examination are not the only means of enforcing breadth in preparation. In the sciences, the department may even rotate students through faculty laboratories, from a few weeks to three months at a time, providing exposure to three to four subfields. Faculty members may then latch onto promising students and offer part-time research assistantships. But distinctively different from what we have observed in Germany, Britain, and France, extensive course work is always present in patterns decided by the department faculty as a whole or by major subsections as large disciplines become more specialized. For example, in biology, a department may mount a required year-long course in which "different faculty members come in each week to describe their research specialties, which range across plant biology, marine biology, molecular biology, neurobiology, population biology, and ecology."[66] On behalf of the department, faculty members, individually or as committees, also advise students in these early years, before dissertation advisers are lined up or assigned. Then, too, a part-time teaching assistantship is likely to be assumed somewhere along the way for a year or so, serving as another form of instructional involvement.

Thus at the graduate level the department is an organized teaching setting as well as a research setting. Primarily by means of course requirements, it can insist on disciplinary breadth that is not attainable in specific dissertation research. At the same time, the department can plunge students into research activity quite early by rotation through laboratories and research-oriented seminars or even sometimes by beginning multiyear commitments to specific research groups. Then, after the comprehensive examination, the department establishes a three- to five-person committee to oversee the choice of dissertation topic and the adequacy of the proposed research. In this framework, mentors can have apprentices, and apprentices mentors, generating intense personal relationships; but both mentors and apprentices are part of a more embracing operational unit that exacts teaching-based requirements set in a broader framework of disciplinary knowledge and even interdisciplinary coverage. Viewed in a cross-national frame, this type of basic unit is a counterpoise to training in narrow skills and the tunnel vision of exclusive specialization.

University organization matters; departmental organization in the American case matters a great deal. We return in chapter 7 to the conditions thereby established for the relating of teaching and advanced study to research. To anticipate: strong local organization in an advanced tier of study is a highly favorable condition, even an essential one, in late twentieth-century universities for the forging and maintenance of a research-teaching-study nexus.

MAGNIFICATION OF THE GRADUATE LEVEL

Extensive course work at the graduate level in America serves as a basis for faculty employment. Around it, student clientele can be assembled and faculty time deployed. Much more than in the undergraduate realm, graduate courses are staffed in a way that reflects proliferating

specific interests of individual faculty, subfields, and research clusters.
The array of courses needs to approximate some considerable share of
the inordinate specialization entailed in a modern discipline. Here is
where the student as generalist and beginning specialist must be transformed into an accomplished specialist. Good reasons abound for a
strong departmental impulse to multiply courses.

The result is an assortment of general and specific graduate courses
that often equals or surpasses in sheer number the courses offered at the
undergraduate level, even when undergraduates are many times more
numerous. While useful comprehensive data are scarce, a Carnegie
Commission "catalog study" carried out in the mid-1970s offered striking data on the average number of separately titled courses offered at
undergraduate and graduate levels in different types of universities and
colleges distinguished by the categories of the Carnegie classification
(see table 4). In the top fifty universities (Research Universities I), al-

TABLE FOUR   UNDERGRADUATE AND GRADUATE
COURSES IN AMERICAN INSTITUTIONS, BY TYPE OF
UNIVERSITY AND COLLEGE, 1977

| | Average Number of Courses per Institution | | | |
Type of University	Total	Undergraduate	Graduate	Percent Graduate
Research Universities I	4,517	2,385	2,132	47.2
Research Universities II	4,039	2,285	1,754	43.4
Doctoral Degrees-granting Universities I	2,878	1,835	1,043	36.2
Doctoral Degree-granting Universities II	2,683	1,767	916	34.1
Comprehensive Universities & Colleges I	1,524	1,226	298	19.6
Comprehensive Universities & Colleges II	982	874	108	11.0
Liberal Arts Colleges I	591	579	12	2.0
Liberal Arts Colleges II	504	501	3	0.6
Two-year Colleges	463	463	0	0

SOURCE: Carnegie Catalog Study, 1977.
Note: Research Universities I were the fifty leading universities in federal support of
academic science between 1968 and 1971.

most as many courses were offered at the graduate as at the undergraduate level: 47 to 53 percent of the total. In the next fifty universities (Research Universities II), the graduate share fell off but was still as high as 43 percent. The proportion lessened in the remaining categories, but even in the fourth category of universities (Doctoral Degree-granting Universities II), graduate courses amounted to over a third of the total.

Specific information can be obtained on particular university departments by examining course listings. For example, the chemistry department at UCLA, a public university, is in itself a huge operation.[67] In the late 1980s, on top of an undergraduate realm of about 700 students majoring in chemistry and about 4,000 students enrolled in different chemistry courses at any one time, the graduate level of the department had about 250 students, virtually all full-time and well supported. While undergraduate instruction was organized in about fifty courses, the graduate level had more than that number. Some fifty faculty, of whom thirty-five or so were full professors (the contrast to foreign systems in top-rank staff is startling) taught at both levels, batching students in large undergraduate classes, especially in some twelve introductory courses in the first two years ("lower division"), while grouping students in small lecture courses and seminars at the graduate level, with much one-on-one informal instruction both prior to and especially during the dissertation stage.

Such an extensive commitment to the graduate level, evidenced in over fifty courses for 250 graduate students, is made possible by a number of national, state, and institutional conditions. Departmental core support comes from annual allocations of the state of California and whatever special funds the university has accumulated for its own disposal and made available to this particular department. In addition, at the end of the 1980s, this one department controlled about 150 research grants or awards from external funders, governmental and non-governmental, indicating a high degree of entrepreneurship by the department as a whole and on the part of many faculty members. The university operates as a strong mediator, obtaining and reallocating the state funds, developing its own resources, and strongly encouraging departmental and faculty entrepreneurial behavior. As developed in chapter 7, such macroconditions can be seen as enabling a bringing together of advanced teaching and study with research activity and research training. But, in the end, the conditions of enactment are located in the departmental framework. There, the buildup of course work looms large.

    Magnification of the graduate level is clearly exhibited in student en-
rollment as well as in the buildup of courses. Even a university of the
second rank, outside the top twenty, as we saw earlier, may have a
graduate enrollment of 7,000 or more, equal to or surpassing in sheer
size the total enrollment of many British universities. Critically, among
the top twenty, many American universities are surprisingly top-heavy
in enrollment (see table 5). The University of Chicago is only about one-
third undergraduate, despite the inordinate amount of attention paid
nationally to the ideas of Robert Hutchins and his plans for the undergraduate years. In sheer enrollment, Columbia University has twice as
many graduate students as undergraduates; Harvard is about 60 percent graduate; and Stanford, 50 percent. Among the public universities, where undergraduate enrollments are much larger, the graduate
share is less: approximately one-third at Michigan and UCLA, one-
sixth at Pennsylvania State University. But the graduate numbers are
still large, for example, over 3,000 at Michigan and 6,000 at Berkeley
in letters and science departments alone, thereby providing enrollment
for the abundant provision of courses that calls for a great deal of faculty time. Thus, despite all the attention the general public and academic critics give to the undergraduate segment in public universities
and the sentiment that alumni invest in "the college years" in private
institutions, American research universities are structurally grounded
in graduate-level dominance. At the extreme of research orientation in
leading private universities, some departments function much like subsidized think tanks deeply involved in research and scholarship that include a few advanced students—and also happen to teach some classes
for undergraduates.
    Financial cross-subsidization also plays a part in this vast American
construction of an advanced level that combines much instruction with
much research activity. As elsewhere, the most advanced level is expensive. In the United States, as computed by an economist, costs per student compared to the undergraduate level may run three to one, or six
to one when the costs of research are included.[68] The president of Harvard University claimed as far back as the 1960s that the "costs of educating graduate students are from three to ten times as great as those of
educating undergraduates."[69] Since departments largely control the deployment of faculty to undergraduate and graduate work, faculty time
can be rolled to the graduate level even though funds based on student
numbers are largely undergraduate based. The result is a process in
which the undergraduate realm often subsidizes graduate work. This

TABLE FIVE   UNDERGRADUATE AND GRADUATE ENROLLMENT IN LEADING AMERICAN UNIVERSITIES, 1991

	Enrollment	Undergraduate Enrollment		Graduate Enrollment		Letters and Science Graduate Enrollment		"Professional" Graduate Enrollment	
		No.	%	No.	%	No.	%	No.	%
Private Universities									
Columbia[a]	17,191	5,802	33.8	11,389	66.2	3,449	20.0	7,940	46.1
Chicago	9,364	3,478	37.1	5,886	62.9	2,992	32.0	2,894	30.9
Harvard	18,437	7,038	38.2	11,399	61.8	3,391	18.4	8,008	43.4
Stanford	13,549	6,527	48.2	7,022	51.8	2,045	15.1	4,977	36.7
Public Universities									
Michigan	36,228	23,126	63.8	13,102	36.2	3,409	9.4	9,693	26.8
UCLA	34,787	24,368	70.0	10,419	30.0	3,135	9.0	7,284	20.9
UC, Berkeley	30,372	21,660	71.3	8,712	28.7	6,423	21.1	2,289	7.5
Penn. State	38,911	32,397	83.3	6,514	16.7	2,422	6.2	4,092	10.5

SOURCE: Data supplied by individual universities on request; compiled and analyzed by Françoise Quéval.
[a] Columbia also listed 2,432 students as "special students" who were neither undergraduate nor graduate students, mainly nondegree students in general studies. They are excluded here.

cross-subsidization is basic to the solidity of American graduate education. As a general phenomenon, local financial reallocation is an increasingly important issue in the changing patterns of finance evidenced in Germany, Britain, and France—and indeed in all countries considering the alternatives of blended funding and funding that separately earmarks support for teaching and support for research. At first glance, the U.S. form of cross-subsidization is suspect as a hidden and unfair maneuver that takes resources from first-tier instruction. But further analysis (see chapter 7) indicates that such subsidy is an institutional way, even perhaps an essential device, for supporting a close relation between research, teaching, and study that otherwise will not obtain under modern conditions. When the alternatives are considered, this local way of reallocating funds has sustaining advantages.

The American form of a modern university complex, with its graduate-level emphasis wrapped in institutional competition, presents a wide array of problems, some unique and others shared with other national systems. In the system as a whole, as we have noted, national government funding for graduate education and academic research has been unstable. The vaunted "partnership" between research universities and federal government has dissolved under the pounding of separate interests and the strain between governmental mandates and university autonomy. Robert M. Rosenzweig, president of the American Association of Universities during the 1980s, has argued effectively that the concept of partnership is an inaccurate and dysfunctional myth, that "the federal government is not, in any meaningful sense of the word, a 'partner' with universities, and to believe that it is is to court bad policy and deep disillusion." Rather, "the term 'purchase order' is a better description of the transactions between the government and the research universities." The government is "a long-term, perhaps even permanent patron, who is sometimes generous, sometimes inattentive, at times quite coldly indifferent, rather flighty and changeable, given to taking action unilaterally, never to be wholly relied upon, and always to be watched carefully." Proof of undependability is found in the simple fact that during the twenty years leading up to 1988, there was "virtually no federal investment in the physical infrastructure of research, and investments designed to replenish the human resource base have been episodic and uneven."[70]

In turn, the national practice of funding research by means of short-term grants exacerbates the problem of a huge labor force of researchers exercising an insatiable appetite for support under the whip of competitive selectivity. Fewer winners and more losers make for disturbing problems of research continuity and researcher morale. "Proposal writing" becomes a research disease, taking time from research and teaching and heightening cynicism. With intense demand from the field for research support and with research costs everywhere rising sharply, tension between concentration and dispersion of resources across institutions also sharpens, placing on the agendas of central scientific councils and funding agencies the possibility that more hard choices will need to be more deliberately made rather than left to the outcomes of unbridled competition. And there are always nagging problems of weaknesses in the pipelines of research talent that are given a particular American twist by the deficiencies of elementary and secondary education and the constraints that have held back the advancement of minority-group members. A much-noted shortage of domestic students in science and engineering has been compensated for only by a major influx to these fields of foreign students who find American training pastures much greener than the ones in their home countries.

At the institutional level, *the* generic problem of the American vertical university is the inbuilt tension between undergraduate and graduate levels. Balance between the two tiers is difficult to maintain: with a strong tendency to tilt upward, preadvanced work becomes an Achilles' heel that elicits student and popular discontent. Much effort in reform during the 1980s and continuing in the 1990s has been devoted to ways of strengthening undergraduate education. Racial and ethnic group conflict on American campuses also feeds into this tension, fixating attention principally on student life in the undergraduate years. Faculty who "escape" to their research (and by implication to their graduate students) are often viewed as chief culprits in whatever is wrong with undergraduate education. The place of research in the training offered in professional schools, in such areas as medicine, business, and education, is also contentiously ambiguous—arguably appropriate to some degree but easy to carry too far as professional school faculties tilt toward the scholarly values of the letters and science "core" and away from the nitty-gritty of professional practice. As elsewhere, American universities have not escaped the growing gap among major clusters of disciplines in the nature of their knowledge, modes of thinking, and available resources. Troubles in American universities break out more often than not in the poorer fields: in the 1980s and early 1990s, the humanities were in considerable institutional as well as intellectual disarray. Finally, even in the richest institutions, the constraints of rising costs and lagging funding dictate that universities increasingly cannot cover all fields of advanced knowledge, no matter how comprehensive they seek to be, sharpening the problem of what to include and what to leave out.

At the level of basic units, departments are internally rent by increasing fragmentation. The growth of campus research institutes and interdisciplinary programs intensifies the problem of how to provide them with constructive, funded autonomy and at the same time integrate them with departmental control of faculty appointments, student selection, and program requirements. Too little autonomy hobbles the effectiveness of these nondepartment units; too much strength on their part means a drift of the campus's intellectual center of gravity from departments to, for example, research institutes. And as new specialties emerge and old ones wither in all the disciplines, whole sets of departments, as clearly seen in the biological sciences, stand in need periodically of recombination and restructuring.

As elsewhere, the American university scene exhibits increased tension between the Ph.D. defined primarily as research training and the doctoral dissertation that in itself provides a contribution to knowledge. Within the research training component lies the increasingly thorny problem, again as elsewhere, of whether students employed in research projects are used more as laborers for the good of the project or are treated as apprentices who acquire serious, long-lasting training. Growing attention has been given in the 1980s also to lengthened study time between the bachelor's degree and the Ph.D. and to noncompletion, with disciplinary variation exhibiting relatively favorable outcomes in the sciences—short time, high completion—and worse conditions in the humanities—long time, low completion.[71] Firm financial support and (relatively) firm knowledge go a long way in easing student progress through American graduate schools.

Many of the American problems are problems of affluence and success. As such, other systems may prefer these problems to their own. But taken in the aggregate, they give rise to a drumbeat of concern in the United States about "the higher education crisis." Simplified views of the complex university also add greatly to the problem of operational realities outrunning old expectations, especially old definitions that view one part or function of the university as its "essence" or "essential mission." Seen as a problem of all modern systems of higher education, the gap between simple expectations and complex realities is explored further in the concluding chapter.

THE GRADUATE DEPARTMENT UNIVERSITY: A SUMMATION

On the worldwide stage, the American twentieth-century graduate school has been a great anomaly. Out of a competitive, chaotic laissez-faire system of small colleges, a formal graduate level emerged in the late nineteenth century as the clearly recognized second tier of a new vertical or hybrid form of university that was not only original at home but new among the nations of the world. While the old college program continued, within the setting of a new university framework, as a first tier committed largely to general education, the higher level was increasingly given over to specialized education, including that provided by professional schools. The vertical division of labor placed competing functions somewhat out of each other's way, at least to the point of viable accommodation. The first four years could still be college, even in some institutions to the virtual exclusion of professional or vocational studies. But after the first degree, specialization fully took over. Notably, the graduate school became a home for science and, as such, a place where doctoral students joined their professors in the laboratory and the seminar.

In the vertical university, the academic department became the integrating unit that held together lower and upper levels, stretching in the basic disciplines from the introductory courses of the freshman year to the final approval of the Ph.D. dissertation. Serving as the backbone of this type of university, the department has determined its capabilities and weaknesses. More flexible and expandable than the European chair, the department replaced hegemony of the single professor with collegial controls of the disciplinary group. While general educationists have seen its disciplinary concentration as the bane of their existence, towering over more interdisciplinary arrangements, disciplinarians and central administrators alike have used it as a form that can be stretched to serve many purposes. For disciplinarians, it has been the mother of all virtues, not least in its bias toward advanced work. University departments clearly take recognition from their parental disciplines, not on the grounds of introductory instruction and service to nonmajors, but on the quality and quantity of faculty research, advanced student training, and doctoral output. In the top one hundred universities, and often stretching beyond them, most constituent departments find their primary interest in the graduate school function; the undergraduate operation then provides a sustaining base and secondary rewards.

Startling in cross-national perspective has been the minimal role played in the development of the graduate school and the academic department by national planning and coordination. The university complex overall is characterized by a heavy preponderance of local and state initiatives. Private sector styles of responsibility and interaction that developed first, historically, long ago spread into the public sector, itself radically decentralized and much prone to engage in competition. In both sectors, institution building has favored the wishes of research-minded professors and institutional forms they found supportive of their efforts. The minimal standardization that has taken place has been largely field led, more emergent than planned, with competitive emulation the main source of convergence. Professional controls, pluralistically exercised through a maze of voluntary associations, have provided more guidance than bureaucratic controls exercised through government departments. Few, if any, monopoly controls have been in the hands of one or more departments in a discipline, one or more institutions in the institutional pecking order, one or more disciplinary or administrative associations, or one or more government agencies that fund institutions and students. Steerage has stemmed primarily from market-type interactions that are only secondarily bounded by professional regulation and guided by state mandate. One may speak of an institutional complex that is a spontaneous order.

The balance of power in favor of local and state initiative as against national direction has had deep import for the research underpinnings of graduate education. Centralized control favors mandated science, while decentralized control more readily supports disciplinary science.[72] Centralized control favors isomorphism among institutions, while decentralized control encourages institutional divergence.[73] Highly decentralized, the two hundred and more American universities range widely as settings for academic research and graduate education. The differences among settings are greatly extended when an additional six hundred institutions or more are included which provide at least master's-level training and seek to fashion at least some minimal research underpinnings. So variously located, the academic research infrastructure is at once strong and weak, resilient and fragile, deeply institutionalized and sustained by a diversified funding base in some institutions and marginalized and poorly funded in others. In its totality that infrastructure evolves largely as a result of niche building and competitive emulation on the part of many institutions.

In contemporary American research universities, the Humboldtian ideal of the unity of research, teaching, and study is played out in late twentieth-century form in the context of the world's leading case of nigh-universal higher education. In this context, diversified by both widening disciplinary differences and increasingly large differences among types of institutions, graduate education is a massive, heterogeneous operation. In pure nineteenth-century form, the Humboldtian ideal is hardly to be found. But as an evolved and adaptive overarching set of beliefs, the ideal has wide play. Each passing decade sees additional institutions investing deeply in academic research and building doctoral programs that incorporate research training. The institutional struggle for eminence brings an assertion of the unity principle and some partial implementation of its mandates.

What is finally most distinguishable about the evolved arrangements for linking research, teaching, and study in late twentieth-century America is the operational conjoining of advanced instruction and research activity. In Germany, France, and Britain, as we have seen, those who continue beyond the first major degree with research-oriented training and degrees in mind largely become "research students" or junior academic staff cut free from organized instruction. In contrast, the American department bristles with course work: teaching carries on. All sorts of department-guarded requirements for entry, measured progress, and certified advanced preparation for embarking on a research dissertation are in place. In short, an instructional frame looms large. At the same time, together with related on-campus organized research units, the department is ever more a nest of research groups that become the places where prospective mentors and apprentices forge working relationships based on research. In these local settings, faculty research activity becomes a mode of teaching and student research activity a mode of learning.

If for the purpose of grasping the conditions of the research-teaching-study nexus in the operation of modern universities we have distinguished the German university as "the institute university," the British as "the collegiate university," and the French as "the academy university," we can appropriately characterize the American university as "the graduate department university." Here, a powerful operational formula for integrating research, teaching, and advanced study is written large.

In the late twentieth-century context of mass universities and sophisticated disciplines, advanced students, no matter how accomplished their mentors, can hardly receive adequate training on the grounds of a preadvanced degree, a single research project, and a related dissertation, even if the project issues from a fortunate appointment in a major research institute. The preadvanced level increasingly cannot carry the student far enough in the discipline: it is overloaded with mass instruction, even as disciplinary knowledge becomes more extended. Systematic instruction at the advanced level is then required: The nexus highlighted in this study requires an advanced teaching program as a framework for a research program. At its best, and somewhat distinctively among the operational units found in other university systems, the American university provides this linkage in great abundance. Its features provide the footing for many of the generic formulations set forth in Part Two.

CHAPTER FIVE

Japan
Displacement to Industry

Compared to higher education structures in Europe and especially America, Japan's most advanced level of education is radically under-developed. Graduate schools exist, but their main strength is the train-ing of engineers as far as the master's degree. Long devoted principally to preparing practitioners in professional fields, chiefly medicine and engineering, doctoral programs are otherwise surprisingly weak in a country that has stressed education and possesses a highly trained workforce; the humanities and social sciences are particularly impover-ished. Interlocking barriers, inside and outside the universities, stand in the way of improvement, leaving Japanese reformers with ample reason to wonder whether they can develop a more robust system of advanced teaching and study founded on academic research. With an "industry option" displaying considerable strength and more promise than the university sector, the research-teaching-study nexus in Japan is hightly problematic.

THE CONSTRAINT OF GRADUATE EDUCATION

A constrained state of affairs for graduate education in Japan is not sim-ply the result of recent developments and current governmental actions. A diminished capacity has evolved over a long period from seeds of weakness planted at the outset and from early traditions and practices that became deeply embedded. Graduate education in Japan is virtually as old as in the United States, formally introduced long before the

appearance of the modern doctorate in Britain. It was officially initiated
in 1886, just a decade after the founding of Johns Hopkins, when a new
national law stipulated that the first Imperial University, the University
of Tokyo (then about a decade old), should be composed of an undergraduate component that would emphasize teaching *and* a graduate
level that would be based on research.[1] The time frame in Japan and
the United States is not all that different.

But institutional conditions differed like night and day. The American development was bottom-up and institutionally organic: as we
have seen, it emerged from the desires of academics and the interests
of individual institutions in the extremely decentralized context of a
multitude of small colleges, more private than public, fixed on a general education bachelor's degree. Professors who sought to specialize
and institutions that wanted to invest in academic research had to devise a local organizational response if they were to develop disciplinary
departments and research laboratories capable of doing science and
training researchers to the pacesetting level then evident in Europe, especially in Germany. As chapter 4 highlighted, extensive experimentation led to a two-tier structure that included structured doctoral programs. Sharp competition among a dozen or more universities then
spurred the spread and consolidation of the graduate school innovation, with a high premium placed on research productivity and quality
Ph.D. output. In this American emergence, the national government
was distinctly not involved. Without any top-down guiding hand, adaptive imitation and voluntary agreement became the main sources of
linkage and commonality among the graduate school components of
different universities.

Categorically different, the graduate school in Japan was willed into
existence by governmental decree and applied in the beginning to the
one university that had been founded in the late 1870s by the national
Ministry of Education as the cutting edge and model for all that was to
take place in the modernization of Japanese higher education. The flagship university, Tokyo, was formed around specialized professional
schools, beginning with a law school that had been run by the Ministry
of Justice and a school for technology that had been under the aegis of
the Ministry of Industry. The university soon took the form of a set of
professional field faculties in law, medicine, technology, and agriculture, with broader faculties also assembled for the natural sciences and
the humanities.[2] In this essentially European mode of university organization, the faculties committed their energies to a first tier of specialized

training, offering degrees that signified competence in many fields and led to professional certification. Thus while in the American case the undergraduate level remained committed to liberal or general education, with specialization postponed to graduate programs, in the Japanese case the undergraduate level in its early stage of development was preempted by professional or specialized work. Relatively few students would then require additional graduate study; those who did go on would mainly pursue advanced professional degrees, not a research-centered Ph.D. As other national universities were formed, beginning with Kyoto in 1897 and then followed during the next two decades by Tohoku at Sendai (1906), Kyushu at Fukuoka (1910), and Hokkaido at Sapporo (1918), they essentially followed the Tokyo model. Kyoto, for example, was founded around the three faculties of engineering, medicine, and science. "Because of the intense demand for more engineers and physicians, having faculties in those areas was a foregone conclusion."[3]

Hence in Japan there was nothing like the competitive and heady pursuit of doctoral programs on the part of universities, faculties, and students alike that characterized the American setting by 1900. The scale of the emerging official university system also remained comparatively small, consisting of just Tokyo and Kyoto as would-be major universities at the turn of the century, compared to over twenty notable institutions in Germany at the time and to an even larger but quite uneven set of private and public universities in the United States from among which fourteen, as noted earlier, crowned themselves fully qualified when they organized the American Association of Universities in 1900. However, private colleges also existed in Japan, some shaped by British and American missionaries, and the government granted the privilege of university status to some of them, notably Keio and Wasada, in 1919. Thus by 1920, the country counted sixteen universities, a number that was to triple during the next two decades, to forty-seven before World War II.

For the Japanese, even more than for Americans, foreign study (ryū-gaku) was a compelling means for assembling a competent university professoriate, one equipped with modern scientific knowledge and infected with research values. A large leap had to be made from the feudal past of the prior Tokugawa period (1603–1868), and much catching up with Western nations had to be accomplished. Scientists from other countries were employed, even generously subsidized, and translation of scholarly materials into Japanese greatly improved. But most

important was the "foreign-study student" (*ryūgakusei*) sent abroad
for two years or more, particularly to Germany. "Overall two-thirds
of the man-years of study [abroad] were spent in Germany during the
period 1869–1914."[4] Across many fields, the pattern was the same:
two-thirds of the chemists and 70 percent of the physicists went there,
90 percent of those pursuing advanced work in medicine.[5] Under the
direction of a determined government, personified by autocratic ministers of education, and despite meager stipends, the "*ryūgakusei* were
supposed to go abroad when sent, study particular subjects, work with
particular professors, come home when directed, and assume the positions the government gave them."[6] The official directive was clear: subsidized trainees were to go where the best scientific work was done,
absorb knowledge and technique as fast as possible, and come home
to an assigned position.

There was hardly any doubt that Tokyo, Kyoto, and other imperial
universities that followed in their footsteps, as officially defined national
instruments of modernization, would have a decidedly pragmatic orientation. For a sponsoring governmental elite committed to rapid change,
"national need" in the late nineteenth and early twentieth century
hardly required essays on Shakespeare or theses on Melville. It certainly did not first require a devotion to the classics of other countries
as well as Japan, however admirable that might be. Port and sherry in a
faculty common room would have to wait. There was serious business
to attend to, and that meant industry, technical administration, science,
and especially its applied partner, engineering. In a striking Japan–
Britain comparison that stressed the lasting effects of university origins, Ronald P. Dore and Mari Sako noted that "Japan has no Oxfords
and no Cambridges. Its elite universities have never been places where
reverend clerks prepared young gentlemen for a life of, hopefully cul-
tured, indolence or nobility-obliged public service. They started off ...
as meritocratic as the *grandes écoles*, and they were built for a country
which took industrialization, and especially manufacturing, seriously.
... Engineering as well as science was an integral part of the first university foundation."[7] Indeed, integral to the university at the outset, engineering went on to become the king of the academic hill, a field to
which favors were to flow.

This Japanese version of first-degree specialization with emphasis on
professional field preparation became deeply institutionalized in the
twentieth century, supported by emerging interests that downplayed
the importance of graduate work. Early on, the awarding of the doc-

toral degree in Japan became a classic case of how to detach degrees from educational programs. As Morikazu Ushiogi has detailed, the great bulk of doctorates in the late nineteenth and early twentieth century were obtained not by completion of a specific research project and a related dissertation, or by course work and examinations, but by "recommendation," first at the pleasure of the minister of education and then later, after a 1898 Degree Ordinance, by a national association of degree holders (*Hakase-kai*) or by the minister after the endorsement of a university president.[8] The highest degree became an honor awarded for distinguished scholarship and long service. As such, it was used in the early decades of modernization to reward those who stayed at home to labor in the academic vineyards as well as those colleagues who went off to Europe or America for two or three years, long enough to acquire some advanced training but not long enough to earn a foreign doctorate. This practice of degree by recommendation soon lent itself to abuse—"bamboo-shoot doctors" were turning up everywhere—and was abolished in reforms enacted shortly before 1920. However, in its place, as the much preferred route to the doctorate, a practice of "dissertation only" took over which also allowed for gaining a doctoral degree without any graduate training at all. While the master's degree might require two years of course work and also a thesis that grew to be substantial in many fields, particularly in the humanities and social sciences, the doctorate could be taken without further participation at the university. This practice became thoroughly institutionalized during the interwar period: four out of five doctorates conferred during the 1920s and 1930s were obtained just by submission of the dissertation. The door was now opened, through which industry was to march, to a displacement of the location of research training and early research accomplishment from the physical setting of the degree-awarding university. A half-century later, in the 1980s, this route still dominated: course work and even physical appearance at the university were still not necessary for the majority of those awarded the most advanced degree of the system.

Also critical in the development of this pattern, in sharp contrast to American practices, was the simple fact that the doctorate did not become a requirement for entry into and promotion within the academic career. From the time that the first universities were founded until today, the doctorate has not been required. In place of graduate school course work and early completion of a dissertation, those who wanted to become academics took paid positions as university assistants, thereby assuming an apprenticeship with a mentoring professor. The assistantship, not the doctorate and not systematic course work, became *the* route to academic positions. Once in place, it had a self-fulfilling logic: if even the chair-holding professors had not attained a doctorate and yet had progressed through the ranks to positions of dignity and respect, with an associated self-concept of high competence, why would younger people need it? Even as late as the 1980s, in the humanities and social sciences, they did not. "Earning a doctorate is not a critical step, nor is it a routine part of the early stages of an academic career."[9]

Even more constraining in the long evolution of graduate education in Japan has been a low demand from the outside labor market for the holders of master's and especially doctoral degrees. At no time in the twentieth century has Japanese industry and government shown a substantial appetite for doctoral graduates. Japanese firms have long made clear that they want the best and the brightest as soon as they can get their hands on them. Hence, especially in the decades since World War II, they have vigorously recruited among bachelor's degree recipients, able young people, overwhelmingly men, who have shown that they are high achievers in Japan's selective and competitive system of secondary education and who also have been vigorously selected by means of highly competitive examinations for entry into the leading universities.

In the special case of engineering, for good reason, the firms have also prized those who hold the master's degree. Post–World War II reforms under the American Occupation formally reserved, for all students, the first two years of university study for general education.[10] Hence a follow-on four years of concentrated study in engineering could not be completed in less than six years. Once recruited, whether as bachelor's or master's degree holders, university graduates could then be molded into loyal and devoted members of firms in the classic Japanese pattern of lifelong employment, without intense disciplinary identification getting in the way. If further training were needed, it could be carried out within the firm, closely tailored to the firm's needs and indeed even to its identity. In this context of early seizure of talent, those who pursued the doctorate came to be seen as having little "value added"; instead, they were viewed as overspecialized.

This pattern of first-degree talent absorption supplemented by advanced training within employing institutions has in recent decades become a remarkable phenomenon, growing apace the dynamic expansion of Japanese firms to positions of world dominance. A correlated step was then almost inevitable: research work done in the firm could be written up and submitted as a dissertation to the university for the awarding of a doctoral degree. This preferred route, the *ronbun* doctorate, in place today, offers clear advantages for the student cum scientist or technologist. The young person who pursues doctoral work at the university needs to study for three or more years beyond the master's, pay tuition, receive little income subsidy, lose three or more years of seniority time in the firm, forgo corporate salary for that period, and possibly end up tarnished as "overqualified" or "overspecialized," hence a less desirable recruit. Additionally, research equipment at universities has been deficient in comparison to that found in firms. Thus students have been well advised to take an early offer from industry, acquire a steady income, settle in as loyal members of the corporate work group, and start research with favorable funding and equipment, aware that the doctorate can still be earned along the way by submitting a dissertation based on firm-supported research. The material rewards are better, the firms provide further training, and industry-based research can provide the dissertation that earns the Ph.D. A virtuous circle for industry thereby became a vicious one for the universities, inducing, among other effects, a brain drain from university study to industrial work.

Such major long-standing and even intensifying constraints on the development of graduate education have induced exceedingly small enrollments beyond the bachelor's degree in virtually all fields outside of engineering and medicine. Graduate students per one thousand inhabitants in the 1980s numbered about half a person in Japan, compared to about one in Britain and five in the United States, or ten times as many. The proportion of graduate students to undergraduates was approximately 4 percent compared to about 14 percent in the United States. Doctoral degrees conferred each year per ten thousand inhabitants numbered about 0.5 in Japan in contrast to American and German outputs that were three (1.5) and four (2.2) times higher.[11] The humanities and the social sciences have been especially weak; in these fields, the demand from industry and government has been nil, entry to academic work has been by means of the assistantship rather than the Ph.D., and the academic labor market overall has been sluggish. Here the low output approaches the unbelievable; in the mid-1980s, all Japanese universities together annually produced only about 150 doctorates in the social sciences and about 100 in the humanities.[12] Year after year openings for new students in these fields have gone largely unfilled: in 1986,

only about one-third of the government-allocated openings in the
national public universities in the social sciences were filled, only about
three-fourths in the humanities. In science and engineering, enough students apply to fill the master's openings, but still in the 1980s many
openings at the doctoral level went begging. Thus, even in the fields
most critical for scientific and economic purposes, the doctoral level
has gone undersubscribed.[13]

The point is clear; the pursuit of education in Japan has stopped well
short of the doctoral degree, even short of the master's in the humanities and social sciences. Higher education is overwhelmingly undergraduate centered, with emphasis on the point of entry. Japan has not
yet had a takeoff in the growth of advanced education, compared, for
example, to Korea, let alone to Germany, France, or Britain, and especially the United States.[14]

The undergraduate fixation is even more extensive in Japan's many
private institutions than in the national public universities. Private sectors of higher education come in many forms: they may serve elite functions and clienteles, or operate in ways that parallel the public institutions, or may absorb mass demand.[15] Possessing up to three-fourths of
all postsecondary students, the Japanese private sector is largely a case
of the mass-demand type. From the beginning of modernization, the
national public universities have possessed the elite programs, the sharpest selection of students, and the strongest claims to excellence. Their
resource base has been comparatively high. In contrast, the private sector overall has been more open in admission, serving generally as an
arena of second and third choices. Lacking substantial endowment,
the private institutions have been heavily dependent on student tuition,
hence are more demand led. Their limited resource base has not favored
investment in expensive disciplines, pulling them away from equipment-
laden engineering, the field that is the backbone of Japanese graduate
training, and, in general, away from the physical and life sciences.
Hence the private institutions have found their center of gravity in
undergraduate work in the social sciences and the humanities; in 1987,
about two-thirds of their undergraduate enrollment, 46 and 17 percent,
respectively, was in these two broad areas. And graduate education has
clearly not been their wont. Among some 340 private institutions in all
of Japan, master's enrollment totaled only 18,000, compared to twice
that in the national universities. Enrollment in doctoral courses was a
minuscule 8,000,[16] a number less than the doctoral students at just
two or three leading American universities combined.

Where Japanese higher education has taken off is in the sheer number of universities that have deliberately set up graduate schools within their midsts. In a burst of activity that virtually amounted to a graduate school mania, the number of universities ready to declare themselves and be recognized formally as in the business of offering advanced degrees grew from 47 in 1955 to 294 in 1988. In the latter year, about 200 institutions could claim they offered doctoral as well as master's work. This great formal proliferation of advanced programs in the face of small student enrollments and even smaller outputs of degree recipients has created the phenomenon of the "empty show window."[17] While a handful of leading institutions, beginning with Tokyo and Kyoto, have substantive numbers of graduate students, most institutions claiming the attributes of a modern research university do not.

The existence of so many lightly used graduate schools in a system where much top-down planning and control has been in the hands of a national ministry seems odd, even formally irrational. But graduate schools are a prestige item, and the normal scramble for institutional prestige in complex systems of any considerable diversity is here coupled in a compelling fashion with funding patterns applied by the Ministry of Education across the national public universities. Bureaucratic rules have helped establish and maintain a host of empty show windows.

THE BUREAUCRATIC FUNDING BASE

A Japanese national university is generally composed of several schools. Each school has several departments, and each department is composed of several chairs. Responsible for both research and teaching, the chair (*koza*) is the base unit. Looming large as the operational anchoring point of the system, the notorious koza is sometimes playfully likened to a sofa, since it consists not only of a full professor but also of seats for an associate professor and one to three research assistants. Hence the chair is essentially a team of three to six people, with a full professor in charge. The budget for chairs has been the most important source of research funds. Highly stable, it has been allocated routinely each year by the Ministry of Education on the basis of a standard national formula and without any review by the administration of each university, thereby weakening campus initiative and coordination. Notably, salaries have been separately covered in the national support system and are not subject to even marginal reallocation by campus bodies.

Chairs can also apply for research grants administered separately by the Ministry of Education, grants from several mission agencies, such as the Ministry of International Trade and Industry (MITI), and grants from private foundations. Chairs can also obtain funds from private companies, primarily in engineering and medicine. But the "institutional" or mainline budget for chairs has been the most significant source and, in the humanities and the social sciences, often the only source.

Most important, the chairs have been systematically funded according to the levels of education they embrace together with the nature of the discipline or professional area of study in which they are involved. Three levels are defined as undergraduate only, undergraduate plus master's, and undergraduate plus doctoral as well as master's study; fields are defined as "clinical," as in the medical school, "experimental," as in the natural sciences, engineering, and some social sciences, and "nonexperimental," as in the humanities and most social sciences. An official cross-hatching of these two criteria produced (as of 1987) seven categories that offer great differences in funding, from 958,000 yen for a nonexperimental chair for undergraduate courses to 8,078,000 yen in the case of a clinical chair responsible for doctoral work, a ratio of 1:8. All along the line experimental pays much more, generally over three times more, than nonexperimental. Hence it pays, and pays well, to have one's discipline listed in the experimental category. And it also pays, and pays very well, to have one's university recognized officially to be in the graduate school business, in as many disciplines as possible, and especially to be giving doctoral courses. Between undergraduate-centered chairs and ones approved for doctoral programs, income roughly doubles, for example, in experimental fields, from 3,400,000 to 7,443,000 yen and in nonexperimental fields, from 958,000 to 1,903,000 yen.[18]

Since these funding categories are applied across all national universities, the primary providers of graduate education, they offer a uniform foundation of institutional funding. They reflect a bureaucratic impulse as well as the democratic inclination toward "fair shares," an important concept in Japanese public administration.[19] But at the same time they create and maintain great differences in funding between graduate and undergraduate levels as well as between the sciences, engineering, and medicine, on the one side, and humanities and social sciences, on the other. Thus it has been centrally and bureaucratically determined that there will be richly and poorly supported fields, that earmarked funds flow from ministry to chair, and that chair holders individually and collectively are central players, despite the formal structure of command. Operational feudalism has been the result.

This ministry-to-chair mode of funding was increasingly viewed in the 1970s and 1980s as overly rigid and adverse to the promotion of centers of excellence. Critics have claimed that it rewards seniority too much, since it allocates budgets to senior professors who hold the chairs while paying them on the basis of years of service. Referring to such funding as "a feudal system,"[20] they charge that the worst researchers and the worst universities get as much support as the best. The adaptive response of the ministry has been similar to ones we observed earlier in European systems, namely, to attempt to shift funds from the mainline of institutional support to the research grant portfolio, one the ministry also controls, where funds are awarded competitively to individual applicants after some limited and rather closed peer review. The grant funds increased in the 1980s but remained a minor secondary source to the basic chair budgeting.

Meanwhile, the chair budgets have been allowed to decline in value. One analysis of the trend in chair-based university funding between 1965 and 1983 showed that while the number of academic researchers (largely the personnel of the chairs) had almost tripled in those two decades, the yen allotted, in absolute figures, had stayed relatively constant: with inflation added in, "the amount given to each *koza* has decreased by about half since 1964."[21] Thus, in their general institutional support, the operating units of Japanese national universities were considerably worse off in the 1980s than they had been in the 1960s. The resulting worsening of conditions in even the best universities has not escaped the attention of the international scientific community. From as far away as London, *Nature*, the world's leading journal in the natural sciences, asserted editorially in 1989 that "the best of Japan's national universities are parochial and static institutions," that "even at the University of Tokyo, there are buildings so shabby, ill-equipped and dust-ridden that they seem hardly to have been touched since they were built, mostly in the rebuilding programs following the great earthquake and fire of 1923."[22]

While evenly applied across universities, the chair budgeting categories, as we have seen, differentiate to an extreme degree by type of field and degree level. The overall financing of academic science and scholarship in Japan thereby becomes a strong case of the Matthew principle: to them that have, more shall be given.[23] The national public universities are, for the most part, considerably better funded than their private counterparts; among the national universities, those that have doctoral programs are better funded than those that reach only to the master's level and the latter, in turn, more than undergraduate-only institutions; and, finally, within the universities, clinical and experimental fields receive more support than nonexperimental fields. Since all along the line it pays to be among the blessed, how, then, if ever, do the non-blessed become blessed? The ministry controls the categories. Therefore the ministry needs to be lobbied for a higher-funded definition of one's field. For example, sociology successfully lobbied its way in the halls of the ministry to be reclassified from nonexperimental to experimental, a feat that, as of 1989, economics and political science had not managed to pull off. The lobbying effect thus somewhat offsets the principle that only the rich can get richer: the political route to the camp of the privileged intrudes on the cycle in which the poor stay poor. Then, too, the bureaucratic norm of fair shares also enters the equation as annual equal increases or decreases that raise or lower everybody. The 1970s and 1980s witnessed largely a leveling down, causing much anguish among scientists and officials who wish to concentrate resources so as to support a limited number of centers of excellence.

In sheer bureaucratic determination of the operation of higher education, the Japanese *national* university sector ranks with the French university sector among the five countries in our comparison. The initial ministerial sponsorship of the late nineteenth century—modeled on French centralism and highly charged with an impulse for rapid development—has during a century of development become transformed into an elaborately rule-bound macrostructure that straitjackets the adaptive capacity of the universities. Such constraint hits harder at research than at the great bulk of teaching: if compelled, most teaching in the mass university can be creditably carried out within the bounds of standardized curricula based on traditional knowledge, while research, requiring openness in the pursuit of new formulations, is inherently more resistant to uniformity. Bureaucratic constraint also hits harder at graduate than at undergraduate education: preadvanced programs, particularly when the first two years are given over to general education, are organized considerably around introductory and intermediate materials codified in previous decades, while graduate education, particularly when oriented toward research activity and training, is less specifically defined. It branches into a thousand and one disciplinary specialties that follow specialization close to the frontiers of knowledge. By the 1980s, as much as the French, the Japanese system had tested the limits of a unified structure that attempted to command finance, personnel, and curricula. The limits were found severely wanting, especially in providing conditions that bring research, teaching, and advanced study into a mutually supporting relationship.

DISCIPLINARY DIFFERENCES

The constraints on the development of graduate education in Japan that are lodged in national and institutional settings, as we have seen in a preliminary fashion, operate in different ways in such major areas as the humanities, the social sciences, and the sciences and engineering. In pursuit of further clarification of these differences, research carried out by Tatsuo Kawashima and Fumihuro Maruyama (and colleagues) in departments of history, economics, physics, and engineering illuminated a range that extended from grave weakness at one end of a spectrum to embedded strength and overwhelming centrality at the other.[24]

In history, graduate students are so few (only about 1,700 in the entire country during the 1980s) that they are like disciples apprenticed here and there to individual masters. In 1985, for example, just 129 history students finished their doctoral programs, and out of that cohort, just 16 finished with the Ph.D. degree in hand. In comparison, in the field of history in the United States at the time, about 500 students received the Ph.D. annually. Moreover, the most common path to the Japanese doctorate in history remained the *Ronbun-hakase*; that is, the dissertation was prepared and submitted while the candidate was employed, often outside the university, and without doing course work. The few students enrolled in doctoral programs are also heavily concentrated in a few institutions, about ten among ninety-five national universities, which means that for the great number of institutions that formally permit graduate work, the history showcase is indeed empty. History has remained a traditional field in which the doctorate is not a qualification needed for entry into an academic career; it is still not ordinarily obtained by those entering the academic ranks. Instead it has remained largely an honorable award for the great scholar and hence a certification to be received by a few in middle age or later.

Taken as a representative field for the social sciences, economics exhibited a profile surprisingly similar to history. Two hundred thousand students majored in economics at the undergraduate level in the 1980s with an eye on the business world, but less than 2,000 show up as graduate students, a yield of one in a hundred. Among the 2,000, only about

700 registered in doctoral programs, and about 50 persons in the entire country were annually awarded a doctorate, in sharp contrast to the United States, where economics produced during the 1980s over 800 Ph.D.'s a year. Among some 4,300 university economics teachers, only about one in seven held a doctorate. Notably, the teachers outnumbered the 2,000 master's and doctoral students by a margin of more than two to one. Thus, as in history, the graduate student who stayed the course and obtained a doctorate by means of matriculated status and supervised dissertation was a rare bird who deserved to be treated as a valuable disciple; for a handful of students, such discipleship meant closely sponsored mobility. A small number of settings, consisting all together of a few advanced students clustered around a few patrons, survived, in effect, as exceedingly constrained elite niches in a system of mass higher education.

Private sector employers, including financial institutions, do not hunger for the economics Ph.D., as they do in the United States, or for the master's graduate. As in manufacturing firms, companies in the service and finance sectors see the holders of advanced degrees as overeducated or otherwise unsuited for their own purposes. They make their enticing job offers to younger persons finishing the bachelor's degree. With these graduates facing a favorable job market in white-collar employment, economics has become an attractive, relatively low-cost operation at the undergraduate level. Hence it has become a field attractive to private universities that have built large economics faculties to handle large undergraduate enrollments. From this base they expanded into master's and doctoral programs: three-fourths of the recognized doctoral programs in eonomics (36 out of 49) in the late 1980s were in private universities. But public or private, the graduate schools cannot get the best students in economics, since they have gone off to employment, and as elsewhere in the social sciences and humanities, the graduate economics programs cannot even assemble a critical mass of students. They have been able to fill only about one-third to one-half of the admissions quota that even a restrictive government is willing to fund. And even though few doctorates are produced each year, mainly in a handful of public universities, the job market is so bad that "overdoctors" exist. Finally, the academic job market is also stagnant, since when only one in seven of the existing professoriate has the doctorate, the vast majority of faculty are predisposed to think of the highest degree in the land as something less than a necessary or even useful requirement.

The steady undersubscribing of graduate student openings in such fields as history and economics, with resulting small numbers, give the Japanese universities a problem of scale of operations that we noted in Britain. In many fields, in many universities, the discipline does not have enough enrollment to justify and sustain courses. Chair atomization further weakens the possibilities of grouping students into curricular clusters. According to Kawashima and Maruyama, "Even in the largest departments, the institutional staff for each research unit, assembled around one or a few chairs, is at most five. The entering graduate students also number about five, with perhaps only one student in a particular specialty. Highly structured sequential curricula are then clearly not feasible."[25] Graduate study must then necessarily become something of an individuated or do-it-on-your-own enterprise, reinforcing the legacy of obtaining the doctorate by just submitting a dissertation, perhaps considerably later in life. Old expectations constrain the modern pattern; modern conditions reinforce the traditional ways.

The constraints on advanced study lessen somewhat in physics, taken as a representative field for the sciences, compared to the dire situation in the humanities and social sciences. But given the international standing of physics in the late twentieth century as a primary academic discipline and Japan's well-known technological prowess, weaknesses here are equally remarkable. Physics is a high-status field in Japan, and the government has seemingly stood ready to finance its expansion. Concentrated in the early years of modernization at the Universities of Tokyo and Kyoto, it spread in some strength to about ten major universities. Minor universities have also been motivated to add and develop graduate courses in physics as a noteworthy part of their attempt to rise to the high-status and income-producing category of "graduate school university." Finally, given the magnitude of theory and method in this highly advanced science, four years of undergraduate work, especially with the first two years given over largely to general education, surely cannot produce physicists at a high level of competence. Graduate work seems a virtual necessity.

Under such conditions favoring graduate-level development of this particular field, competitive entry to master's programs has occurred at the ten major locations: quotas were filled and, in 1987, about 1,700 students were enrolled. Further, the physics students are much more likely than students in history or economics to complete the doctoral dissertation on the projected normal schedule of five years. But seen in cross-national perspective, the numbers are still small; in 1987, throughout the nation, only 184 physics students finished their doctoral programs, and just 132 of them finished completely with the degree in hand; while in the late 1980s, U.S. physics departments annually graduated over 1,200 Ph.D.'s. Again, much constraint stems from attitudes and hiring practices in job markets: the doctoral graduates in physics have faced poor job prospects in industry and recently in academia. Here, too, the Ph.D. recipient has been confronted in industry by the view that those trained to this level are too specialized. The academic job market, in turn, has been for some time more filled up than vibrating with demands for newly minted physicists. Secondary school teaching has been the one dependable job market. In stark contrast to its striking weakness in the American high school, physics is well established in Japanese secondary schools. For this outlet the master's level of preparation is sufficient. Hence graduate students in physics typically stop their graduate work after doing master's course work and a master's dissertation and apply for the competitive examination that will take the more successful ones into teaching posts at the secondary level, thereby stocking it with talent.

An additional formidable constraint on the development of graduate work in physics comes from the great strength of the bordering field of engineering. A long-established and enormously powerful field, Japanese engineering has in effect swallowed up applied physics, and applied science generally, leaving the physics departments with pure physics. While the physics departments place their graduates in high schools, the engineering schools place their graduates, including the applied physicists, in the huge pipeline that flows to industry. Engineering has become the monster discipline in Japanese national universities, with large enrollments in large departments in large schools of engineering. A single *department* organized around an engineering specialty in an engineering school may have as much enrollment as an entire *school* embracing a set of disciplines in the social sciences or humanities. But since employment opportunities at the master's level are outstanding, only a few pursue a doctorate: in 1987, over 88 percent of the master's graduates went to major industrial companies, while 8 percent entered doctoral programs.[26]

The preeminent place of engineering in Japanese universities has roots in the origins of the first universities. As noted earlier, the universities were largely formed around professional areas of study, with engineering and medicine particularly strong carryovers from the Tokugawa (pre-Meiji) period. The early dominance of these two fields in advanced work is shown in sharp relief in the number of doctorates in technical or scientific fields awarded between 1888 and 1920: in descending order, medicine, 656 (48%); engineering, 366 (27%); agriculture or forestry, 138 (10%); and in all other fields (physics, chemistry, veterinary medicine, mathematics, and geology), 200 (15%). In most of the latter fields, there was less than one doctorate per year.[27] The "doctorate" was actually a set of specialized professional degrees, not the Ph.D. awarded across a wide range of disciplines. In the 1980s, virtually a century later, the dominance of medicine and engineering is strikingly similar, with medicine (health sciences) awarding over 60 percent of all doctoral degrees (including those offered in the humanities, the social sciences, and such "nontechnical" professions as law), while engineering, a strong second, awarded 17 percent. No other field came close. Moreover, engineering completely dominates the master's degree, with about 45 percent of all such awards.

Engineering graduates not only have been avidly recruited by Japanese industry but also have long enjoyed excellent prospects of promotion. In explaining the great success of the Japanese economy in the decades since World War II, the British economist G. C. Allen has emphasized the relentless concentration by industry and government on the "single objective of industrial growth."[28] Embedded in that concentration has been the recruitment and promotion of engineers. "Most of those who have administered the leading companies for decades past were systematically trained in higher educational institutions in subjects appropriate to their careers."[29] Those subjects were not finance and accounting, let alone the liberal arts. "In the early post-war years, when Japan was about to launch herself on her career in the high-technology industries, firms set about recruiting the staff they needed by offering relatively high salaries to graduates in engineering. With this pecuniary stimulus, the number of such graduates rose markedly in subsequent years."[30] Further, with Britain in mind as the main point of contrast, Allen noted that

> the Japanese business world has little use for the "inspired amateur" with a general education but no systematic training in the disciplines relevant to the work that has to be done. The majority of those in high authority in industry have received an education in science or technology. A recent inquiry [late 1970s] showed that 67 percent of all seats on the board of directors of the leading companies were occupied by professional engineers (the term "engineer" in Japan covers men educated in some branch of applied science).[31]

A study carried out in the early 1980s by the American National Science Foundation noted that in all of Japanese industry, combining finance and service enterprises with manufacturing firms, "about 50 percent of all directors have engineering qualifications."[32]

Success in climbing the corporate ladder in an increasingly wide range of firms has added to the high esteem in which engineers are held, giving great weight to the idea that university training in engineering is the best preparation for leadership in private industry. As a passport to management circles, the engineering master's degree in Japan is more than the equivalent of the master's in business administration in the United States, with the striking difference that engineers know about production technique while business school graduates do not.

Japanese engineering graduates have even bulked large in public sector employment. Allen observed that "a high proportion of the administrative civil servants in the departments that have to do with industry have had a scientific education," whereas "only 7 percent of those recently recruited [late 1970s] to the administrative grade of the British civil service took papers in science at their examination."[33] In a detailed study of Japan's governmental administrative elite, the higher civil servants, B. C. Koh has shown that for the quarter century 1960–1986, between 30 and 50 percent of the new recruits came from engineering and natural sciences, surpassing until 1972 all those drawn from law and the social sciences and still in 1986 amounting to 36 percent compared to 41 percent for law and social science, with "agriculture and related fields" contributing the remaining 23 percent.[34]

All available evidence thus indicates an exceedingly attractive job market for those who enroll in engineering. At the bachelor's level, Japan has about as many engineering degree recipients as the United States, a country twice as large in general population and some four to five times larger in higher education student population, and about eight to nine times as many first-degree engineers as the United Kingdom—in one comparison drawn in the late 1970s, 80,000 to 9,000.[35] A comparatively high flow of engineering students continues through the master's level. Growing tremendously during the 1960s, 1970s, and 1980s, along with the huge expansion of Japanese industry, the engineering master's has been the great success story of Japanese graduate education. Far and above all other sectors of Japanese higher education, the field of engineering has been at the cutting edge of Japan's industrialization and economic progress. While in Britain the tradition of the "inspired amateur" has had quite a run, with reflected strength in the humanities, and in the United States, management has found value in MBAs, accountants, lawyers, and economists, in Japan, the land of the engineer, the preferred route to management in production firms has been to be "well trained in the technique of the occupation."[36]

At the same time, Japanese engineering has not been as narrow and technical as an outsider might first suspect, given the exceedingly practical orientation of business and government. The engineering students, like others at the university, have had a general academic preparation in quality secondary schools; like others, they have then spent their first two years at the university largely in the hands of a general education faculty. As put by Dore and Sako, "The curriculum remains a broad one until the end of high school.... It is still almost as broadly based in the first two, general education, years of the university course. Real specialization begins only in the last two years of university." Then, when they take up the more specialized subjects, they receive an engineering education that "is rather more theoretical than practical," one that "leans more toward basic science than is common in Britain or the United States."[37] This surprising emphasis is part of a pattern in which Japanese firms stress the recruitment of bright, highly motivated people when they look to selective departments in selective universities. They need not look for narrow, specific training; *that* they can do themselves. According to E. H. Kinmouth, "Japanese companies do not expect engineering graduates to possess substantial mechanical skills on graduation.... [F]lexibility is more important than immediately applicable mechanical skills. Studies of Japanese engineers show that within 2-3 years of hiring more than 40 percent will be following a technical specialty substantially different from that which they studied in college."[38]

Engineering also requires, more than most other fields, that students engage in serious study while pursuing undergraduate degrees. Students in many academic fields, particularly in the humanities and social sciences, have been prone to use the four undergraduate years as a "moratorium period" between a workaholic adolescence, up to secondary school graduation and university admission, and a workaholic life at work after leaving the university.[39] With entrance itself conferring an "ability label" used by later potential employers, students in many fields can let down in their studies and turn to part-time jobs and recreation. But this is not the case in engineering, since undergraduate performance there affects entry to master's programs that are both selective and offer a valuable degree. Connected substantive learning also weighs most heavily in "hard" subjects such as engineering and science, where the nature of knowledge dictates an orderly sequence of course work. In short, engineering students have strong incentive, from top to bottom of the university pecking order, not to treat their undergraduate years as a time for diversion from the grind of study and work.

Finally, as one more twist in the connection of universities to industry, beyond the recruitment linkage the ties have not been close. Instead university attitudes have generally stressed the autonomy of scholarship, even to the point of hostility toward any direct involvement in the world of commerce. Dore and Sako have noted that "the university-industry relationship is a good deal more distant than in Britain. The feeling that the citadels of disinterested scholarship should not be corrupted by those who live in the world of the profit motive is a strong one, and one which in the public universities is embodied in regulations which greatly restrict professional consultancies or the receipt of research contracts." Industry more than returns the favor. If it seeks university ties, it seeks them elsewhere, outside of Japan. "As MITI is frequently wont to deplore, Japanese corporations commission more research from universities in the U.S. and Europe than from universities in Japan." A study of Japanese students studying in U.S. science and engineering graduate schools in the early 1980s indicated that there may well be more Japanese *company-sponsored* graduate students overseas than in Japanese universities.[40]

Our review of the enormous differences found among fields of study at the most advanced levels of Japanese universities indicates an extremely high degree of disciplinary hierarchy. That steep rank order magnifies the impact of the sharp institutional hierarchy that has long been viewed as a central feature of Japanese higher education. The peak of the institutional hierarchy consists of the University of Tokyo alone. "The national bureaucracy, including nearly all ministries, is positively dominated by Tokyo University. *This has been true for eighty years*. Middle management in the bureaucracy also comes from Todai, and 50–75 percent of all executive-oriented starting positions in most ministries go to its graduates."[41] In the Ministry of Education in the mid-1970s, at a time when the ministry had been "explicitly assigned the task of disassembling the elite university influence over exams and jobs," sixteen out of eighteen of the top positions were filled by University of Tokyo graduates.[42] The influence of this one university in the business world, while not as staggeringly high as in the realm of government, still measurably outgunned any other university, claiming about one-third of all large company presidents. In comparison, among top American executives, no single university—Yale or Harvard—topped 3 percent.[43] Moreover, the faculty of the University of Tokyo itself has been extremely inbred, made up almost entirely of its own graduates.[44] Descending from the Tokyo peak, the next level in the institutional hierarchy, also relatively fixed, has been occupied by a handful of national universities such as Kyoto, Osaka, and Kyushu and two leading private universities, Keio and Waseda.

To these imposing differences in prestige and placement embedded in a sharply peaked hierarchy of institutions, the disciplinary differences add an accentuation effect. They stretch from a host of fields, here fully represented by history, that have a low degree of elite placement to the special case of engineering as *the* springboard to high office in business and, secondarily, in government. Engineering at the University of Tokyo offers a double advantage, a doubly elevated status of highest discipline in the highest institution—in a country where such preparatory locations are intimately linked to elite jobs. The impact of disciplinary differences then increases at the graduate level: there, as we have seen, the fields divide in an even more radical fashion between relatively weak humanities and social sciences and relatively strong sciences, with engineering towering over all others.

THE APPLIED UNIVERSITY: A SUMMATION

Japan's expenditures on research and development, in gross international comparisons, appear relatively modest: as a proportion of national income, they have been less than in Britain, France, West Germany, and the United States. But the other countries spend a higher proportion of R&D funds on defense, particularly Britain, France, and the United States, while Japan spends less than 5 percent, thereby elevating its investment in nondefense R&D to a high level. Most important, the R&D monies have been put up by industry, with 80 percent coming from private firms rather than from government, and are spent by the firms themselves largely for development work that exploits imported as well as home-generated applied research and technology. Until recently, little has been spent on basic research.[45]

Japanese industry has thereby built up a tremendous applied research base of laboratories and equipment that has made Japan a technological powerhouse, one that has increasingly also become technologically inventive. For example, to take patents as an indicator of inventiveness, between 1975 and 1985 the share of U.S. patents issued to Japanese inventors doubled, from about 9 percent to 18 percent; the 1985 share was greater than that of West Germany, France, and Britain combined.[46] In 1987, Japanese firms obtained over 17,000 American patents, a 25 percent increase over the previous year.[47] By that year, the top three U.S. patent recipients were Hitachi, Canon, and Toshiba; the top American firm, General Electric, had dropped in two years from first to fourth place.[48] In short, Japanese technologists now invent as well as borrow, having moved beyond the copycat pattern of imitation for which they were well known throughout much of the twentieth century. As summarized by Francis Narin and J. Davidson Frame, "Data on patent counts demonstrate a burgeoning Japanese inventive vitality, and the patent citation data suggest that the impact of the inventions is high. The U.S. patent statistics do not support the view that the Japanese are unoriginal copycats."[49]

But technology is not as closely connected to science in Japan as it is in the United States and Western Europe. Japanese science remains relatively weak. In 1985, as shown in patent citations to the nonpatent literature, the science linkage of U.S.-invented patents was twice as great as for Japanese-invented patents. Further, American scientists published about five scientific papers for each paper published by a Japanese scientist; scientists in West Germany, France, and Britain publish about two and a half times as much. The Japanese papers also have been relatively undercited, a phenomenon to which language is a contributor. The most heavily cited Japanese papers have been in engineering and technology. Overall, "the publication and citation data show Japanese scientific performance to be much less impressive than Japanese technological performance."[50]

The comparative performance of Japanese technology and Japanese science has clear and direct manpower underpinnings in the production of Japanese universities at the three levels of bachelor's, master's, and doctoral degrees. As we have seen, all along the line in higher education, in comparison to other fields of study in Japan as well as to subject emphases in other countries, Japan has achieved a staggeringly high and self-amplifying output of engineers. We have noted that Japan graduates as many engineers at the bachelor's degree level as does the United States, that the engineering master's program is the crown jewel of the Japanese graduate school, bulking large among graduates and accounting for over 40 percent of all master's degrees, and finally, that

even at the doctoral level, engineering is second only to medicine, granting in recent years approximately 17 percent.[51] With an ever bleaker
picture at ascending levels, the output in the sciences does not begin to
compare: about 800 doctoral recipients annually in all the fields of the
physical and biological sciences taken together in the late 1980s is a
minuscule output compared to an American output of 7,800, ten times
higher. Financially, the basic sciences are poorly supported, receiving
less than one-fourth of the total research expenditures in Japan's
national universities, while approximately three-fourths goes to the
engineering fields.[52]

The Japanese system of research and development thus has a clear
formula of relationship of technology to science that translates into a
relationship between industry and higher education. Japanese technology is abundantly equipped, and it has overwhelmingly found its
home in industry. It has not needed a foundation in basic research, or
even in university-generated applied research: the industrial home has
been more than enough for its flowering as the world's best. But, as a
result, basic science has been downplayed, even robbed of manpower.
And the Japanese graduate school has been essentially robbed of its
scientific research foundations. In a pragmatic fashion, government
and industry have asked the universities to select talent, hence to make
entry the critical matter, and then at the more advanced levels to train
in such applied fields as engineering and medicine. Over a long period
of time and in a parallel fashion, a pattern has become entrenched in
which technology dominates science while, as a location for research
and advanced training, industry dominates the university.

This technology-and-industry constraint on the development of Japanese graduate schools has extended, as we have noted, beyond the
sciences. The scientific fields altogether at least turn out 10 percent or
so of all doctorates: in 1986, 820 out of 8,533 awarded degrees. But
the social sciences have shrunk to insignificance, with 136 new degree
holders in 1986, amounting to about 1.5 percent; and the humanities
have virtually disappeared, with 91 awards totaling about 1 percent.[53]
Indeed, beyond the dominance of medicine and engineering in the
awarding of doctorates, a third applied area, agriculture, turns out
two to three times as many doctorates as the humanities and social
sciences combined. At the master's level, the same relationship of
applied to basic science holds, with engineering instead of medicine
as the prime producer to the point of *five* engineering degrees to every
one in the sciences combined or in all the social sciences or in all the

humanities: in 1986, 10,390 compared to 2,261, 1,701, and 2,156, respectively. With over 2,300 master's degrees, agriculture alone at this level also outproduced all three clusters of science, social science, and the humanities.[54]

The weakness of Japanese graduate education as a home for science and a place for research-based doctoral education thus runs deep, rooted primarily in a displacement of commitment, interest, and resources to technology and industry that puts levers of change considerably outside the purview of university staff and ministerial officials. Various reform measures have been taken in the 1970s and 1980s to place more money in competitive research grant funding, to start up major research institutes within and among universities, and to initiate whole new enterprises designed to be special homes for science and advanced degrees. But such affirmative action for a lagging, deprived institutional sector encounters the major constraints within and outside the system of higher education that this analysis has highlighted. Foremost remains the dynamism of Japanese firms that know how to attract talent, do their own training, and perform the research they need. As put by Edward R. Beauchamp and Richard Rubinger, "The major Japanese firms which are fueled by research results generally prefer to provide the equivalent of graduate training within the confines of the firm."[55] These highly entrepreneurial firms do not wait for Japanese graduate schools to become world-acclaimed centers of excellence; instead they move ahead on a worldwide stage. By the early 1980s, in their search for productive and prestigious ties to universities, they were giving twice as much money to universities in other countries, preeminently the United States, than they were to universities in their own country. Such funds from large Japanese firms go beyond research grants: one American university alone, MIT, had, by the end of the 1980s, nineteen Japanese-endowed chairs.[56]

This considerable displacement of research activity and even research training to industry in Japan suggests a model for other countries of an industry-based mode of connecting research to instruction and learning. Why not have young recruits learn research by doing research in the context of industrial (and even governmental) research programs? Those programs are largely applied in nature, but they also increasingly include basic research: much two-way interaction takes place and distinctions between basic and applied have, in the event, grown less clear. In this industrial mode, the university mainly provides some ratification, a laying on of the hands, by means of token advanced course work and especially the awarding of advanced degrees that have international meaning. We observe an extreme case of research drift, the movement of research from the university to other sites (see chap. 6), largely propelled in Japan by dominating industry interests. Such drift has also been abetted by governmental constraints on the research and research training capacities of the universities that we have highlighted *and* by institutionalized limitations of the universities, some self-imposed, to compete with industrial firms as research sites. Since this pattern has worked well for Japan as an intrinsic part of strong industrial capability and striking economic development, it poses the question of whether research-based graduate programs are perhaps not necessary, indeed *not* the wave of the future, despite their great success in the United States and the movement of European systems toward more structured advanced programs.

However, the industry mode is clearly a limited pattern that does not extend effectively outside of applied science and engineering. It does not apply well to the full and ever-widening range of disciplines and professional fields that the comprehensive university and the university complex at large embraces. In observing the distribution of research effort among the four sectors of university, government, industry, and nonprofit organization in Germany, Britain, France, and the United States, we have seen that the nonuniversity sectors are all considerably more focused in their research efforts than are the universities and are thereby more limited. American philanthropic foundations, we saw in chapter 4, engaged in a major exploration in the early part of the twentieth century of locales in which to fund "best science." The university became the clear choice when it became apparent that neither the government laboratory nor the independent research institute could fulfill the twin tasks of productive research and first-class research training. And so it has remained: the government-supported research sector in France has arguably come closest to the comprehensive coverage possible in universities but still falls far short.

Thus late twentieth-century Japan is a great experiment in the possibility of industry dominating the university in both research and research training: a displacement to industry is a pragmatic way of achieving technological development propelled by industrial R&D. But it is arguably not a long-term solution for basic research and research training, since industry cannot be a university system. Industry is not positioned to commit fully to a wide and expanding frontier of research; it is particularly poorly positioned to commit fully to research training in a host of subjects that have no short-term payoff or even a discernible prospect of long-term profitable returns. In short, the Japanese firm is no substitute for what in the American case we have called the graduate school university. Compared to a well-developed sector of research universities, a set of industrial research establishments is a weak base for a broad band of research and scholarship in which disciplinary judgment, idle curiosity, and knowledge for its own sake all have a place.

This view has increasing currency in Japan. We have noted that Japanese corporations with a sharp eye for best science and quality research training but disappointed in their own universities have turned to American universities, endowing chairs and laboratories, fashioning university-firm research linkages, and sending personnel for university study. Leading scientists and government officials highly critical of current conditions and bent on reform were by the end of the 1980s mounting major experiments in research-based university advanced education, from the well-known Tsukuba Science City established as an elite science-oriented complex outside of Tokyo consisting of two universities and over fifty research centers to a consortium of university research institutes (the Graduate University for Advanced Studies) chartered to enroll only doctoral students, opened in 1989, to individual new graduate schools with an interdisciplinary orientation such as the Graduate School for International Development formed in 1990 out of old faculties and schools at Nagoya University. Such efforts reflect a view that, whatever their current weakness in Japan, universities are indispensable for discipline-led basic research. That indispensability includes the need to bring forth research-centered academics to staff the universities. As part of a larger search for the conditions of strong basic research, graduate school initiatives are under way.

But the "empty show window" of Japanese graduate schools is their iron cage: the conditions behind that phenomenon remain as interlocked constraints that resist reform. The entrenched combination of bureaucratic funding at the system level and chair organization at the local level is noticeably dysfunctional in producing a universal small scale of the operating units. The impoverished size of base units raises severe problems of scale and scope similar to what we observed in Britain. Commonly there are too few students in an operational cohort to justify systematic disciplinary instruction or to mount large research projects. Bureaucratic and chair atomization is clearly a root defect that has to be overcome: organizational fragmentation robs the universities of adaptive capacity at the graduate level in an age when substantial expansion in students and staff is required to cope with irresistible expansion in knowledge. At the beginning of the 1990s, aware of the depth of constraint in the historic structure, Japanese reform had at last fixed on a general decentralization of control from state to university as *the* underlying requirement. When Japanese public universities have more self-control over budget, personnel, and curriculum, as promised at the beginning of the 1990s by the government, some among them may be able to move seriously to solve the graduate school problem.

In the event, we have arrived at a global characterization of the modern Japanese university as viewed against the patterns of other advanced systems in relating research to advanced teaching and learning. If for the purpose of cross-national comparison of this major university function we have characterized the German pattern as "the institute university," the British instance as "the collegiate university," the French configuration as "the academy university," and the American provision as "the graduate department university," the Japanese configuration can be aptly designated "the applied university." It is here that industry has most fully taken over as the home for research—and research training. It is here that applied science dominates the universities. The seeds of this pattern were planted a century ago when the Japanese began their search for a pragmatic form of the research university. A century later the pattern has been deeply institutionalized, intertwined with the great strength of industrial firms, the detailed steerage of the government, and the historically evolved allocation of resources and personnel to professional fields and disciplines within the university complex. All along the line, historically and structurally, the "engineering interest" has been magnified.

As a fifth distinguishing pattern, this highly unusual Japanese configuration further extends the analytical warrant in comparative analysis for first establishing the central peculiarities and uniquenesses of the systems in point. As we sum national profiles, even in a first approximation, we learn volumes about the grave weakness of all the plentiful discussions of "the idea of the university" that are voiced without regard to national contexts. Just on the research dimension alone, the idea of the university takes many forms: five countries, five ideas. And operating within the scope of the national idea, the realm of national practice is even more special. The striking distinctiveness of the Japanese system is most powerfully voiced not in the vague rhetorics of officials and academics but in specific practices that have long endured. As elsewhere, it is by means of their patterns of action that we know what the participants are about and how the system works.

PART TWO

The Research-Teaching-Study Nexus

CHAPTER SIX

Forces of Fragmentation

The integrating theme of this study is higher education viewed primarily as a place of inquiry. In harmony with this leitmotiv, Part One depicted research organization and advanced education in five major national configurations as a way of identifying educational settings that incorporate research activities and link them to teaching and study. Each country account entertained complexities and uniquenesses that flow from national context, thereby giving weight to historical determination and the interlocking of components in a national mosaic. Chapter 1 emphasized the vicissitudes of the Humboldtian ideal of education through science under late twentieth-century conditions in the Federal Republic of Germany of rapid expansion in higher education and research. Enduring structures that continue to have great symbolic importance experience much difficulty in handling the expanded tasks now forced on both the educational and the research domains. The historic ideal is still capable of steering behavior where conditions favor its cause, but for an increasing share of that system it is a misleading definition. Confusion reigns as the system as a whole attempts to simultaneously accommodate mass higher education and maintain "the institute university."

In turn, amid the complexities of the British scene, chapter 2 stressed the depth of the undergraduate fixation of the donnish tradition and the related small organization of departments and universities, features that led to craftlike relations among professors and students in postgraduate studies but on a highly limited scale. A thoroughgoing nationalization of higher education during the 1970s and 1980s in effect nationalized these features, limiting resources in ways that sharply constrain doctoral programs. In "the collegiate university," adverse conditions for a wholesale deployment of research resources have helped cause dismay among academics to the point of serious exodus from the system. The British system faces great difficulty in enhancing research-based advanced education to the point where it can continue to be internationally competitive.

Chapter 3 depicted the highly unusual French configuration, born of long evolution, in which the universities, now places of greatly expanded mass enrollment, neither contain the principal routes of elite preparation nor receive the bulk of government-allocated funds for basic research. Poorly financed and organizationally weak, the universities maneuver from a subordinate position in the research world, striking bargains as best they can with externally constituted research units that possess greater power and prestige. In a byzantine set of nationally specified levels, programs, degrees, and university–research center linkages, advanced students scramble to reach the main sites of research. Overall, in "the academy university," the research foundations of advanced education are markedly uneven among universities and across disciplines.

Chapter 4 highlighted the magnitude and dynamics of American research organization and higher education in a large national setting characterized by competition and institutional initiative. Semimarket conditions have favored graduate school development that incorporates a strong investment in academic research. Comparatively, the American graduate school is a great success. But as postbachelor education becomes a virtual necessity for professionals in American society, to the tune of 400,000 advanced degrees a year by the end of the 1980s, the graduate level itself experiences the problems attendant on mass higher education. With the populist theme of "any person, any study" carried to the advanced level, graduate programs are ever more diversified and the vast majority of graduate students do not pass into elite sectors of research. The problem of providing a general education for university undergraduates in an environment of specialized research and focused professional training also does not go away; instead, in "the graduate department university," it steadily intensifies.

Chapter 5 stressed the high degree to which Japanese industry has come to dominate higher education as the site for research *and* increasingly as the site for research-based advanced training. When young people are well advised to avoid the graduate school and the doctorate can be taken by submitting a dissertation from an industrial laboratory, graduate education hardly has sturdy research underpinnings. "The applied university" is characterized by much displacement to industry. We also observed in Japan the operational results of a vast bureaucratization of the university complex in the form of atomized chairs and rigid budgets. Arguably more than anywhere else, disciplinary differences have also been magnified by enormous investment in engineering and applied science coupled with benign neglect of the humanities and social sciences.

Within each of these five major national systems, the relationship of research to teaching and study has been under increasing strain from many sides and in many quarters. However sacred the unity principle in faculty sanctuaries, it seems less and less applicable. At the same time, the research-teaching-study nexus clearly has not disappeared in any of these countries. Near the end of the twentieth century, it may well flourish in quantity and intensity as never before. The modern linkage is not the one Wilhelm von Humboldt had in mind: even in the practices of the German university, his idealism was long ago subordinated and given a practical twist by academic specialists. But the intimate blending of teaching and study with an orientation to research and even deep immersion in research activity can still be found in many quarters. The commitment to such activity seems so prevalent among leading American universities that it appears to many observers as a dominating feature that marginalizes everything else, especially the general education of undergraduates.

The chapters of Part Two shift attention from country configurations to analytical categories that identify and explain the systemic bases of research-based advanced education. A two-sided organizational approach is developed which portrays the maintenance and support of the research-teaching-study nexus as a struggle between "forces"—conditions, structures, ideologies, interests—that act to tear the nexus apart and opposing ones that uphold it. Among innumerable features that stretch from government control to department organization, parsimonious explanation is found in a limited set of conditions that stand out sharply in one or more of the five national portraits and also appear to be in train in all five systems.

This chapter concentrates on drifts in the very nature of modern research and higher education that promote a breakup of the relationship in question. Certain generic impulses of research activity tend to drive research away from teaching and learning. In turn, operating on a massive scale, certain thrusts of the teaching mandate remove teaching from research. These dissolving drifts find encouragement in identifiable interests of government and industry. National variations in the operation of these forces can be established to bring in the role played by idiosyncratic features of national settings. Taken by themselves in analytical isolation, the fragmenting forces appear so overwhelming as to lead to the conclusion that the nexus, the unity principle, is now sunk without a trace.

But in pursuit of the other side of the coin, chapter 7 teaches otherwise, identifying primary features of modern organization of higher education and science that counter fragmentation and uphold integration. There is ample reason to assert that *some* meaningful integration of research with teaching and learning will always exist in an advanced university complex. But how much, in what quarters, under what conditions? Here, at the heart of the analysis, with the American case as the prime example but the experiences of other countries also weighed in the balance, primary supporting conditions are nested within one another. They extend from the broad setting of the national system as a whole to the university as the main organizational actor to the university basic units in which professors, researchers, and students are located. While certain conditions at the higher levels contribute significantly, specifiable conditions in the "units of production" are finally crucial. In the workings of departmental groups we find how integration is operationalized on a wide scale.

Chapter 8 returns to the conceptual and practical advantages of adopting a perspective that views universities as knowledge institutions oriented by inquiry, thereby to understand the importance of the research-teaching-study nexus both for the most advanced level of instruction and learning that has been little studied and for the beginning and intermediate levels, "undergraduate education," where extensive analysis and criticism has been little informed by the necessities of the advanced programs in the arts and sciences and in the professional schools. When the university is understood first of all as a place of inquiry, the activities of research and teaching are seen as more than interfused. They possess an essential compatibility.

First, the fragmenting forces. As a first approximation, the preceding volume published from this study identified four common trends in higher education internationally that tend to disconnect research and advanced education: the movement into mass higher education; increased labor market demand for professional experts; the increasing gap between frontier knowledge and teachable codified knowledge; and increased governmental patronage and supervision.[1] Building on country analyses presented in the first part of this volume, these categories are here recast in simplified, generic terms as two forms of drift—research drift and teaching drift—that inhere in these trends. General tendencies for research to drift away from educational settings and for teaching activities in turn to pull away from research locales are also encouraged by governmental interests that are impatient with traditional academic blends of activity and by industrial interests that see research primarily as the handmaiden of technological development. Some countries currently exemplify the patterns of drift more than do others. But in differing intensity at a given time, systemic separation of these mainline academic activities can be everywhere noted.

RESEARCH DRIFT

As widely observed in the five country chapters, modern higher education experiences self-amplifying substantive growth. Research and scholarship steadily fashion more cognitive domains in the form of disciplines, specialisms, and interdisciplinary subjects. As a result, each major discipline, each major cluster of academic fields, and especially the research enterprise at large simultaneously intensifies and diversifies. Specialization knows no bounds: by 1990, those who track the volume and cited usage of research papers internationally could identify in the sciences alone some eight thousands topics that exhibited related networks.[2] Highly focused and exceedingly diverse, the specialties are widely and unevenly scattered. A growing host of these high-knowledge specialisms require a concentration of funds, equipment, and personnel that are difficult to contain in traditional locales of teaching and study. And the specialized networks need not be bounded by universities: all evidence is to the contrary.

   Thus the research imperative itself can be seen as containing a strong divisive tendency. The needs of specialized knowledge and research seemingly are often best served by groups that do not have teaching programs and student needs on their minds. Specialists committed to moving ahead in the research world as fast as possible frequently find the main educational sites clogged and diffuse. Where research comes first, fully and completely, its agents are notably willing to have science education and even research training take a back seat. Instructional concerns may readily be defined as falling in someone else's domain. Hence it is generic and not incidental that core needs of much modern research will promote a flow of research activity from normal university teaching locales to research centers, laboratories, and institutes. If located at universities, these units may not have teaching responsibilities: frequently and increasingly they are operated by research staff serving as nonteaching academic personnel.

Critically, research proliferates beyond the boundaries of universities as a common activity in civilian government agencies, the military establishment, and the nonprofit sector as well as in industry, all structurally divorced from the university. Then, too, from medicine to fashion design, each profession or would-be profession develops a research wing. As hordes of knowledge workers in the general labor force have come to claim a research role, they too generate specialized literatures. Such self-amplifying production of basic and applied research turns substantive growth into a societal phenomenon rather than one just characteristic of research-based higher education. It also carries across nations. As the means of communication among nations have dramatically improved, highly specialized researchers have been driven more than ever by both intrinsic motivation and extrinsic reward to reach out not to others unlike themselves who happen to be nearby but to others of "their kind" who are variously scattered around the world. The research impulse and its related specialization are steadily internationalized.

For purposes of both training and employment, eager researchers are attracted to universities known to be strong in particular disciplines and specialties. Such willing mobility expands the international trade of talent—brain influx and brain drain—in which some countries win and others lose. Such trade is an essential part of an international competition for best science and cutting-edge inquiry thought essential for scientific and technological progress. A host of personal, departmental, institutional, and system interests interact to encourage the development of internationally recognized centers of excellence that will serve as intellectual magnets for attracting talent from the worldwide pool of researchers, professors, and students. The competitive construction of such institutional magnets becomes yet another major force in the intensification of research, and the related concern to concentrate research, that tends to pull research activity out of departments and other university basic units that are responsible for teaching and student training.

The process of divorce affects first the introductory and intermediate levels of instruction and then finally the advanced programs.

In short, restless research moves out in many directions from traditional university settings to establish new outposts whose members prospect full-time for whatever gold lies at the frontiers of knowledge. Teaching and study lag behind, fixed in older settlements where the fruits of exploration are finally consolidated in forms appropriate for systematic transmission and wholesale consumption.

NATIONAL VARIATION

Research drift that undermines the research foundations of advanced teaching and study has long been prominent in France. For half a century, the CNRS-university schism has significantly divided a public research sector from a teaching sector. A host of major mission agencies in a powerful executive branch in a centralized government have served their own interests by increasingly promoting research within their own borders and in units they directly support, without any necessary connection to education. Such drift has also been strongly evident in Germany. Max Planck institutes have systematically provided a place, a nonindustrial home, for research outside of universities. With other concentrated research sectors recently created, scientists and government officials in Germany can directly aid scientific and technological advance by supporting such locales more than they do universities that are less focused, if not totally confused. Such direct concentration on research tasks seems particularly attractive when a valued structure and a respected tradition of institutes are firmly in place. The institutes constitute a set of interest groups whose high prestige translates into power and influence in the allocation of research funds.

Research drift in Britain has been weaker than in France or Germany. No separate research realm of the magnitude of the Max Planck establishment, let alone of the French CNRS, has existed. British universities traditionally have been relatively free to blend research, teaching, and study within their operational units at their own discretion. However, at the same time, mission agencies in the British government have long supported their own research institutes. Moreover, the research councils that control the main money stream for research have allocated substantial funds to nonuniversity institutes and laboratories, sometimes more than what they assigned to the universities. Most important—a point to which we return—an increasingly dirigiste government has become impatient with the old "soft" ways of the universities and much inclined to concentrate and isolate research.

Research drift occurs in the American system, but less than in the European systems that have a substantial public research sector independent of universities. The historic and entrenched strength of American research universities as places of inquiry has slowed the drift of research to outside public sector or third sector locales. But research has tended to drift out of campus departments as campus scientists have sought to create organized research units as tools for supporting and concentrating research. The campus ORU is the university answer to keeping focused research groups within the university when they cannot be suitably housed within teaching departments. Additionally, such major mission agencies as the Departments of Defense and Energy have created hundreds of national laboratories, some of them huge, many of which have been placed under university administration. Overall, even in a system quite dominated by a research university mentality, a larger share of research increasingly appears outside the university framework.

Finally, research drift has a distinctive shape in the Japanese system. With institutional funds that include time for research distributed by bureaucratic formula equally across a large number of universities to chairs in departments, research has been anchored in settings of teaching and study. But its moorings have also thereby been highly atomized. The departments and the graduate schools for the most part lack advanced students. Campus ORUs are also in short supply, hobbling the capability of the universities to handle large-scale research. No government-sponsored structures approaching the strength of a CNRS enterprise or a Max Planck establishment have arisen to serve as independent public research sectors. But the drift of research away from universities has been considerable, as chapter 5 highlighted, in the form of exceedingly heavy industrial involvement. We return below to the vast flow of research into that sector under the twin conditions of strong industry and weak university.

In sum, whatever the system, the research imperative contains the seeds of separation of research activity from teaching and learning, Ever more specialized research frequently requires separate quarters. It needs its own modes and lines of support that are unfettered by the complexities of the channels that support the educational dimension of universities. Or so it will seem to many specialists deeply dedicated to research. A commitment to full-time pursuit of research can be tantamount to a decision to leave to someone else the tasks of teaching and the provision of places for training. Critically, in an inquiring society, one major societal sector after another—business, the health-care complex, the prison system, the church—will craft its own apparatus of self-exploration and improvement. Any university monopoly of research is sooner or later rendered obsolete. As seen in five leading nations, the diffusion of research activity by 1990 has been sufficiently advanced to cause concern in each national setting about the fate of research training as well as the access of even university-educated people to the knowledge possessed by clusters of specialists separated from the halls of learning.

TEACHING DRIFT

While components of substantive growth tend to set research aside from teaching and learning, a second form of growth acts directly on teaching and study components to encourage a divorce from research. "Reactive growth," as specified in chapter 4, is growth in institutions and staff that follows as a reaction to expanded student demand and enlarged labor force requirements.[3] Advanced nations move over time into mass secondary education and then into mass access to postsecondary education, well away from the old elite pattern of 5 percent or less age-group participation. Between the push of such expanded access and the pull of enlarged employment of qualified professionals, national systems move to include 30 percent or more of relevant age groups, a marker surpassed by a half-dozen countries at the end of the 1980s.[4] Without doubt, more nations will join the club of mass-to-nigh-universal higher education by the year 2000.

Such growth exerts irresistible pressure for differentiation based largely on varied distribution of teaching and research: concentrating on teaching, certain settings are removed from research. Such differentiation, bearing decisively on the unity of research, teaching, and study, appears in at least three major forms: among types of institutions; across program levels within universities and colleges; and, finally, within the most advanced level of university study itself.

The interinstitutional mode can be widely observed in the form of pure teaching institutions deliberately set apart from ones that are research centered. The pretense that all students, preadvanced and advanced, will be trained either for research or in research is surrendered, even if academics do so reluctantly and official rhetoric lags behind a changed reality. Across a large set of institutions, explicitly or implicitly, different research-teaching-training linkages are delineated. The historic principle of close unity is then expected to apply in one type of institution, the university, but not in other types, the nonuniversity colleges and especially the short-cycle colleges. The system as a whole becomes more "postsecondary," less "higher." Even among the universities substantial differentiation occurs: various ones are officially designated, or evolve in an unplanned fashion, to be full research universities, while others are only partially invested in research, and still others operate without a research base and give themselves over largely to teaching. By permitting certain universities to concentrate heavily on research, this ongoing separation of institutions also serves oppositely to intensify the research-teaching-study nexus, a critical feature stressed in the following chapter.

The second form of differentiation, occurring within universities, accentuates levels of instruction and degree attainment. In mass higher education, much attention must necessarily gravitate to introductory teaching. No longer do virtually all students come from selective academic secondary schools and highly educated families. More preparatory work is needed beyond that provided in secondary education to bring students even up to the first stages of specialized study. The students may seek to enter a specialty, the pattern that remains dominant around the world, or stand in need first to immerse themselves in a general education that was not completed at the secondary level, as in the American system. But in either case, a first tier of instruction of a relatively introductory kind becomes necessary: entering students are not sufficiently advanced in a domain of knowledge whereby immersion in research, or direct training for research, is deemed appropriate. Instead an introductory cycle is established as prerequisite to a second level, which then leads to something like a true postgraduate level: in French terms, first, second, and third cycles; in American terms, lower division undergraduate, upper division undergraduate, and graduate school. Most teaching within the modern university takes place at the first two levels, with research-based teaching largely reserved for the highest tier.

This key form of internal differentiation has been further operationalized in many countries in the establishment and growth of the "university lecturer," a position defined as full-time teaching with little or no research involvement.[5] The university creates two classes of faculty:

the "professors," as traditionally understood, are expected to do research and are granted appropriate time and resources; and members of the newer class who are formally designated "teachers," or are known to be just that. Since the second type of position has marked similarities to the teaching role in upper secondary schools, it is sometimes viewed by staff and students as one that converges on the practices and ethos of secondary education. At the least, it is a striking structural adjustment to the huge instructional needs of mass higher education, an organizational recognition that the teaching of beginning students is a different operation from teaching of their advanced counterparts.

Third, the inclination to have teaching programs that at best have only a small base in research also extends into the most advanced tier. Steadily growing in importance, graduate programs that have little or no research footing take two forms: terminal degree programs in the arts and sciences that are explicitly designed for nonresearch students; and professional degree programs in an expanding array of practice-oriented fields. Both types reflect the growing amount of specialized knowledge in a large number of occupations that the labor market defines as the initial threshold of recognizable competence. The two types together have led to what we can call the triumph of the master's degree. As observed by Stuart Blume and Olga Amsterdamska in a 1987 report for the Organisation for Economic Co-operation and Development (OECD) on postgraduate education in the 1980s, expansion in postgraduate enrollment has occurred more at the master's than at the doctoral level, largely in professional training programs directly relevant to the labor market, with business management and administration a main case in point.[6] For the OECD catchment of over twenty industrially advanced nations, they noted a growing need in a range of occupations for "people with advanced training and *some* knowledge of research methods."[7]

Seen from the perspective of research foundations, the three levels of bachelor's, master's, and doctoral degrees represent a vertical differentiation in which the research base of teaching and learning varies greatly. Knowledge of research methods shifts from minor importance to some relevance to central place. Notably, advanced higher education itself has its own forms of massification. Increasingly popular, it has many tracks and speaks in many tongues. Driven by expansion in enrollment, knowledge, and professional preparation, advanced higher education becomes something more than a place for the research student and the awarding of the research-based doctorate. It is increasingly also a home for nondoctoral programs, nonresearch students, and the attainment of nonresearch degrees.

NATIONAL VARIATION

Teaching drift has figured prominently in the American system, where relatively early expansion into mass higher education, as highlighted in chapter 4, took place in a market system characterized by radically decentralized control and intense institutional competition. Across more than three thousand institutions, the vast majority of professors and students have been and are not now located in research environments—not in the majority of public and private four-year colleges and especially not in the innumerable community colleges that account for a third of all college enrollment. In addition, as earlier stressed, among two hundred doctoral-granting universities (and several hundred ambitious "comprehensive universities" that want the "higher" status) huge differences in research funding and infrastructure exist which translate into extreme ratios of ten to one, twenty to one, and more, in amount of research funds. Many universities must be sensitive primarily to the market demand for undergraduate education, secondarily to the provision of master's programs for professional training, and only finally, as much as they might wish otherwise, to the demand for research productivity and research training.

As the most advanced case of mass higher education, the U.S. system also exhibits most acutely the phenomenon of teaching drift at the graduate level. Well known as an enormous producer of doctorates, with an output by 1990 that had risen to over 35,000 a year, the American graduate level, as we have seen, is many times over an even larger source of master's degrees (300,000) and "first professional" degrees (75,000) that are awarded at a stage beyond the bachelor's degree. Some master's students proceed to the doctorate and hence may be viewed as on a research track. But four out of five are not and, along with the professional-degree students, are not positioned to receive substantial training for research, let alone be involved in research. They are located in what the British call a "taught master's," a program that for the most part seeks to transmit codified knowledge.

That extensive separation and concentration of teaching is characteristic of advanced systems of mass higher education is indicated also by long-run developments in Japan, where enormous demand for undergraduate education has been met by the development of over seven hundred private institutions that have captured three-fourths of all enroll-ment. Heavily dependent on tuition income, these mass institutions have invested only lightly in research, especially in scientific fields, and only a mere handful are serious players at the graduate level. In turn, among the national public universities, the vast majority exhibit the empty show window phenomenon in their graduate schools, leaving as of 1990 only some ten to twelve institutions as major centers of inquiry. Then, too, as chapter 5 highlighted, output at the graduate level is con-siderably concentrated in two professional areas, the master's degree in engineering and the doctoral degree in medicine.

Teaching drift has also become increasingly evident in France and Germany. In France, beyond the devotion of the grandes écoles to teaching and learning without benefit of a research orientation, the 1970s and 1980s saw the addition of the nonuniversity sector of IUTs as a major form of differentiation in which research, particularly basic research, is not a prominent feature. As earlier stressed, French univer-sities have also long been comparatively poor, underfunded by the stan-dards of other northern European systems, leaving less slack for the support of research in the face of the demand for first- and second-cycle teaching occasioned by greatly expanded enrollments. Similarly in Germany; there, the allocation of much instruction to teaching-based institutions is found particularly in the creation and growth of the Fach-hochschulen sector. Student overload in the universities has also notice-ably drawn faculty time toward the immediate demands of teaching, leaving less time for faculty research and placing more students at inter-mediate as well as introductory stages outside of research settings.

Finally, beginning in the 1960s, Britain attempted to develop a major nonuniversity sector, centered on polytechnics, that would concentrate on teaching and practical training without heavy university-type invest-ment in research. But the institutions in this sector had sufficient auton-omy to influence their own emerging character and they chose to be-come more like the universities, thereby becoming *the* classic case of convergent "academic drift."[8] The binary arrangement was thereby eroded and, in the early 1990s, was officially declared null and void. Within a now-unified national system, all institutions could claim to be universities, greatly broadening the meaning of the term. As else-where, however, the symbolism of institutional equity is one thing, the reality of dissimilarity quite another, with difference centered on the balance of teaching and research. Extended differentiation within the extended family of institutions is officially intended and is occurring.

British academics struggle to hold research, teaching, and study together throughout the system, but they will manage this feat only in
some institutions. Additionally, at the postgraduate level, British institutions are steadily investing in taught master's programs for nonresearch
students that grant an end-point degree and lead straightaway to the
job market.

In sum: national systems of higher education undergoing reactive
growth steadily invest in (a) "teaching-dominated" institutions, (b)
teaching-centered introductory levels of university work, and (c) nonresearch tracks for students at advanced levels. Much more teaching is
needed which does not have to be intimately blended with research activity or serve significantly as training for research. In wholesale lots,
teaching drifts away from the traditional nexus.

GOVERNMENTAL AND INDUSTRIAL INTERESTS

The above conceptual isolation of research drift and teaching drift as
forces of fragmentation found reason in the very nature of modern research and modern mass higher education. The imperatives, in effect,
were found within the house, inside the research enterprise and within
the higher education system. In addition, two external institutions,
modern government and industry, play such an important stimulating
role that they must be brought into the picture.[9] Turning to certain of
their interests, we can again proceed to identify generic tendencies in
conceptually pure terms and then briefly describe national variation in
degree and type of expression.

GOVERNMENTAL INTERESTS

Several observable impulses of modern governments in their efforts
to support and steer science and higher education undermine the
research-teaching-study nexus. Foremost is the concern to limit costs.
Particularly in scientific fields, research-based educational programs
are increasingly expensive and possess an insatiable appetite for enhanced budgetary support. When totaled up, they present huge bills
that governments are unwilling to pay. Cost containment then encourages governmental officials to fund universities differentially, distinguishing subsets by extent of research commitment. Governments are
thereby much inclined to separate research funding from the funding

of teaching, primarily by taking the support for research, including subsidized research time, wholly or partly out of blanket institutional allocations and placing it in a separate line devoted to research support
where funds are awarded competitively and hence selectively. Equity
funding based largely on sheer number of faculty and students is replaced by funding that allows certain fields, projects, and academic
researchers to be favored over others. Costs are also contained by the
deliberate creation of a stratum of university lecturers—or, we should
note, by allowing such posts to emerge incrementally and unofficially
when university staff who are not funded in research competition find
their duties shift toward teaching. From the standpoint of governmental cost containment, economy and efficiency are promoted by limiting
the distribution of research across institutions and insisting on more
teaching in research-poor locales. When and where mass higher education means more education "on the cheap," as it inevitably does in
certain sectors of higher education, the old nexus is downplayed.

Certain other concerns of government strengthen the tendency to
separate research in domains of its own that in the first instance is
brought about by the sheer intensification of research that we have
already noted. In part because of their sheer expensiveness, some scientific specialties are formally and spatially designated by governmental
patrons to be set apart on university campuses from teaching units,
with only some students invited to these more distant concentrations.
Modern governments also develop an interest in deliberately placing
research concentrations outside the university framework altogether.
Ostensibly, focused laboratories can be better managed and oriented
to produce quick results. As outside centers, they escape the encrusted
bureaucratic and professional practices of the universities. They may
also offer clearer research accountability, since assessment of research
outcomes is less clouded when research performance is separated from
teaching and training activities. Without intruding into the collegiate
halls of university decision making, investment in preferred fields in
science and technology can be heightened while support for contentious and apparently nonproductive disciplines in the humanities and
certain social sciences, in comparison, gently fades. And a not-to-be-
missed benefit for harassed ministers and senior civil servants in a
number of countries is the simple fact that direct support of outside
institutes offers the opportunity to move desired research more fully
out of "the university mess," that is, away from university politics,

especially left-wing protest, and away from the frustrating resistance of academics to top-down control that is individually and collectively pre-figured. Ministerial revenge is sometimes not far from the surface.

Finally, governmental steerage that undermines the research-teach-ing-study nexus is promoted by time horizons that are considerably shorter than those normally found in universities. Governments face economic, technological, and social problems that cry out for immedi-ate solution. In democratic societies, political elections are never far away and incumbents need to garner support by showing results from current programs. A naturally created need to get things done in a definable time span then strongly supports the inclination to steer re-search by concentrating it in settings that seem to promise immediate results. A short time horizon also produces a bias in favor of special-ized institutions, particularly research units that can be funded and evaluated on a one- or three- or five-year cycle. For government offi-cials in a hurry, the slow ways of basic research and academic depart-ments may seem a luxury and a gamble on long-run returns on which they cannot wait. In the urgencies of political agendas and executive action, governments find potent reasons to seek to steer research and support it in concentrated centers.

National Variation   As the classic case among major Western coun-tries of centralized control and related ministerial funding of higher education and research, the French system offers the strongest profile of deliberate governmental separation of research and teaching. State-led differentiation on a grand scale has produced a massive formal de-marcation of a research system and a training system. At the same time, the truly elite part of the training system, consisting of the leading grandes écoles, breaks off from whatever research values are upheld at the universities, giving pride of place to non-research-based professional training. Differential funding of disciplines is also great, as seen in chap-ter 3, and universities based on the humanities and the softer social sciences seem fated for a future of more teaching, less research. Since there is little CNRS assistance to build third-cycle and doctoral pro-grams in the nonscientific fields, faculty attention must all the more flow to the huge demand for first-cycle and second-cycle teaching.

Fascinating for our analysis, if painful for British academics, is the long and recently accelerated evolution in Britain of universities from a high degree of independence to crypto-dirigisme to full-scale dirigisme in which in the latter stage the government is much inclined to fund research separately from teaching, discriminate among types of universities, and distinguish academic researchers from academic teachers. Together with heavy-handed steerage, the national government has insisted that the universities increasingly raise their own funds "in the market," where, we now know in Britain and elsewhere, those institutions that are deficient in ability to compete for research funding from government funding councils, industrial firms, and private foundations will be obliged to fund themselves on the basis of student demand for undergraduate education and practical postgraduate training.

British dirigisme of the 1980s became in many ways more precisely intrusive in the lives of universities than the long-standing French mode of ministerial control. French academics have had decades of experience with the ways of ministers and ministries during which they have developed coping mechanisms in depth, from the autonomy of major faculties (law, medicine, the sciences) to unionization by rank. Post-1968 reform opened up so much leeway for local maneuvering that academics were even able to decompose whole universities according to local taste, with, as chapter 3 made clear, the scientists able to separate themselves from social scientists and humanists in science-concentrated universities, while social scientists and humanities professors fashioned specialized universities of their own—a perverse, undesired effect of the governmental "Big Bang" effort to engage in wholesale reform. Meanwhile, in Britain, the drift to state control has been nasty and brutish, fought out against long-standing faculty traditions of autonomy by a government deeply suspicious of academics and committed to rapid movement toward a system that will be leaner in research, lower in cost per student, and more responsive to industrial and governmental interests.

In the case of Japan, the government has saved a great deal of money over the decades of the post-1945 period by allowing private universities to become the mass-demand sector, a massive set of institutions concentrated on tuition-subsidized teaching of undergraduates and of those interested in practical advanced training. Exercising a high degree of bureaucratic centralism, the government in turn has funded the national public universities differentially by field of study and level of instruction as well as by number of students and faculty. Officially reaching directly to the basic units, the chairs, governmental budgeting has supported the distribution of research across the chairs but in an atomistic and impoverished fashion. Detailed governmental steerage has meant much diffusion of limited research support; procedural rationality has rested heavily on this system, often to the detriment of substantive rationality. Reform efforts in the late 1980s and early 1990s have sought to move some support for research from institutional allocations to research council-type competitive awards. In general, governmental influence has been significant in differentiating teaching-dominated institutions and programs from ones rooted in research.

German universities have been under the double support and supervision of Länder governments and nationally centralized offices and bodies. Both levels have been inclined in recent decades toward steerage that, on the one side, increases research drift by giving more support to research institutes outside of universities and, on the other, increases teaching drift by expanding student numbers much faster than faculty and facilities and hence increasing the burdens of teaching. Compared to the levels of support common in the days of elite higher education, and the level that professors presuppose for across-the-board application of the Humboldtian ideal, Germany has found, like other countries, that the combination of expensive science and mass higher education means that much of higher education will not have deep research foundations.

Last, the United States has exhibited since World War II a drift toward more governmental control at both state and national levels. State plans have flowed toward a tripartite differentiation of public university, public four- and five-year college, and community college that effects a radical separation of much research and teaching. Much committed rhetorically to equal access and higher education for all, state governments at the same time have not been in the habit of making equal allocations to all institutions within their purview. Rather, they fund at different levels according to the mix of research and teaching, the mix of disciplines and professional fields, and the mix of preadvanced and advanced programs. In this far-flung system, much higher education is on the cheap for state funders, while some is inordinately expensive. Additional funding of research by the federal government by means of competitive research grants and mission agency allocations then furthers the differentiation between research-based and teaching-based sectors. Even within the university complex, federal research dollars flow in a discriminating fashion. The competitive pursuit of research funds offered by central agencies leads to vast differences in the research bases of both private and public universities that, while never acknowledged as deliberate governmental policy, are well known by those actively involved in funding circles.

THE INTERESTS OF INDUSTRY

In the last half of the twentieth century, industry has everywhere developed an increasingly strong interest in research that is focused on practical outcomes. In the widely used coupling of R&D, research should lead to application and technological development should in turn have roots in research. The R&D formulation also ties research primarily to the economic sphere and the pursuit of profit and then secondarily to the military establishment and the pursuit of its missions. Thus oriented, "R" is considerably the handmaiden of "D." Sums apportioned to development typically outweigh manyfold those allocated to research; the R&D funds spent by industry and in industry typically also vastly exceed the research expenditures of higher education. In general, as research develops in a major way outside the academic sector, the focus is pulled away from the connection of research to teaching and study.

Thinking counterfactually, we may note that no conceptual couplings such as R&T (research and teaching) or R&S (research and study) have developed as counterweights to the inherent biases of the research-and-development mode of thinking. If in a moment of long-term insight they became widely accepted, they would undoubtedly be poor cousins to the idea of R&D, with its deep roots in economic and governmental interests. Business firms and military agencies may have a hand, even a considerable one in Japan, in the training of scientists, but these sectors, are not positioned to engage across the board in the tasks of preparing future generations of scholars and scientists.

Industrial firms (and mission-oriented government departments) have also increasingly attempted to develop direct connections to universities to gain access to new ideas, encourage "relevant" research, and promote the transfer of knowledge and technology from university centers to their own more development-oriented laboratories. Such connections increasingly involve new institutes and laboratories that stand halfway between higher education and the commercial sector and thereby become located on the margin of the traditional academic core. Such collaborative centers exist primarily to do research, not to teach; they employ nonteaching staff; they may adopt a few graduate students as part-time research assistants, but most graduate students in related departments will be outside their reach. Despite some impressive cases to the contrary, research organized in this fashion moves away from the university settings that sustain the mainstream of teaching and learning.

National Variation   As reviewed earlier in considerable detail, industrial drift characterizes the Japanese research-education complex more than any other. Japan has become the R&D nation par excellence, with industry the center of research as well as of development. Industry is even willing to train its own research cadres, and students opt for employment rather than graduate school after the first degree. The universities have fallen in line, particularly by awarding doctorates to research workers employed in industry who need not have pursued graduate course work.

In lesser degree, the play of industrial R&D interests was also evident in the analyses of other countries in Part One. As revealed in broad figures, industrial investment in R&D has long been a major force in the Federal Republic of Germany and the United States. While traditionally relying primarily on their universities for basic research, both countries have exhibited some flow of basic and applied research into major industrial laboratories. Then, too, within the universities, the old distinction between basic science and applied science has been blurred by elaborate interplay between different forms of scientific and technological investigation and of investigative technique and product development; the practical field of "engineering" has become "the engineering sciences." Across blurred lines of activity and definition, research work and even some research training more readily flow in each of these countries from university settings to industrial locales.

The British and French systems of higher education have traditionally reflected industrial interests the least of the five countries examined here, due to the historic aversion of the donnish tradition in Britain to the practical ways of commerce and, in the case of France, to the historic role of Continental universities, particularly the "Mediterranean" subtype, as places that trained primarily not for private sector employment but for the civil service and the professions. But the pressure on British universities to work with industry, even to be guided and supervised by industry in top funding councils, became enormous during the 1980s in line with a larger joint government-industry effort to recast British industry in a competitive R&D mold. Research, and even training for research, can be expected to grow within industry, even if not at a pace desired by government and industry. Similarly in France: it, too, is committed to building a more dynamic industrial sector in which R&D has a large place. For a long time in France, academics have had to listen closely to ministerial pronouncements. Now they may need to listen more acutely than in the past to industry-led and industry-responsive councils when they offer plans for the reorganization and restructuring of higher education.

NEGATION OF THE NEXUS

The generic forces here simplified as research drift and teaching drift, encouraged by certain governmental concerns and interests of industry, tend everywhere to dissolve the research-teaching-study nexus. They pull research away from the settings of advanced teaching and learning and, in turn, shift teaching and study away from locales characterized as places of inquiry. They even divide universities internally into teaching- and research-centered components. Such forces cannot be avoided in modern systems of higher education: the imperatives of expanded access and knowledge specialization alone irresistibly bring them into play. The forces are also highly interactive; for example, the interests of leading academic scientists in promoting concentrated centers of research located outside university departments often converge with the willingness of governmental officials to subsidize such separate arrangements. However, the national contexts of science and higher education observed in Part One vary the mix and strength of these forces. And national settings always introduce significant idiosyncratic elements that are beyond the reach of common categories.

In modern systems of higher education, it is increasingly clear, not all academic staff will be or should be researchers. It is also everywhere the case that full-time research becomes a career in its own right. As a result, "teachers" and "researchers" in some considerable part become two groups separated by task and location. It is also increasingly unrealistic to expect all university students, even at the most advanced level, to work at the bench with research mentors in the sciences or have a place in advanced seminars and leading research clusters in the social sciences and the humanities. The students are too numerous and too varied in interest and capability. Differentiated implicitly, if not explicitly, they become subgroups that shade from intense to minimal involvement in the practice of research. With students brought forward to intermediate and advanced levels of higher education in much larger numbers than in the past, and notably in part-time as well as full-time status, many more are left largely on their own on peripheries that are far from the core settings in which small clusters or students partake of a tightly woven nexus of research activity, research-based teaching, and research-based learning.

Our analysis supports and extends the Eurocentric 1981 report of the OECD on the future of university research which concluded, "The old view that education and research at the university level are insepar-able has begun to break down.... Research and teaching are tending to grow apart.... [A] declining proportion of graduates are likely to re-ceive their higher education in institutions in which any research goes on [and] a declining proportion of teachers in higher education are likely to engage in research."[10] The "traditional ethos of the European university in which teaching and research are regarded as insepar-able"[11] can at best apply only to selected segments. The Humboldtian idea is no longer, and cannot be, in command across modern systems of higher education and related systems of research. Powerful conditions dictate that much research and teaching, research and learning, will proceed on different pathways.

CHAPTER SEVEN

Conditions of Integration

Complexly organized across levels that extend from central national offices to academic departments and research clusters, a national system of higher education contains an array of nested contexts that shape academic activities. Opposing logics may abound: bureaucratic and political habits of ministries are often dramatically different from the collegial, guildlike ways of departments, chairs, and institutes within which staff and students interact. What may be true at the top may not be the case at the bottom. As we turn to conditions that uphold the research-teaching-study nexus in modern systems, countering and even conquering the fragmenting forces identified in chapter 6, we need to search across at least the three levels of the national system as a whole, the individual university, and the basic unit. From top to bottom, the problem is to identify the structures and related processes that promote a close blending of the primary activities. If "far from being a natural match, research and teaching can be organized within a single framework only under specific conditions," as Ben-David put it,[1] what indeed are those conditions, especially when we add study as a third compelling component that brings in student learning and training? Put slightly differently, what are the settings that have an elective affinity for a three-way integration? Where do we find the thrusts toward unity that conquer centrifugal tendencies? If answers to these questions were simple, they would have been identified and widely applied a long time ago. We confront a problem of integrating academic activities over which governments stumble, administrators puzzle at great length, and academics exhibit more than two minds.

Corresponding to the levels of national system, university, and basic unit, the following analysis characterizes three types of conditions: enabling, formative, and enacting. Broad conditions characteristic of whole national systems are enabling when they help provide the opportunity for, even give sanction to, patterns of action found further down the line. But they do not themselves closely form or enact those patterns: Indeed, they may even be pushed aside by adverse reactions from below. Conditions at the university level, closer to production, may be defined as formative: they are more contextually compelling than broad national conditions in shaping academic activities, while at the same time, they are still external to the operational entities. It is only when we turn to the basic units that we find the conditions that directly determine behavior, contextual features that are literally a part of the patterns of execution and performance. These conditions of enactment are finally the ones closest to being necessary and sufficient in making possible a three-way connection. However created, they get the job done. They are what supportive efforts at higher levels are finally all about. They are the actuating conditions that are undercut when the fragmentary forces isolated in chapter 6 dominate the scene. Distinguishing three levels of organization and related types of conditions provides a clear logic of analysis: we proceed from general systemwide conditions that enable to less general institutional ones that are broadly formative to the local conditions that enact an integration.

ENABLING CONDITIONS IN THE NATIONAL SYSTEM

Within the constraints of modern mass higher education, primary features of whole national systems that most vigorously support the unity principle may be simplified around four concepts: differentiation, competition, ideology, and funding. Favorable conditions at the broadest level consist of a differentiation of institutions that produces and protects a concentrated sector of research-based universities; a competitive mode of interaction among these universities and their constituent units; an adoption of the Humboldtian principle, in modern dress, as the legitimating ideology for this particular university sector; and national funding patterns that deliberately or indirectly support the blending of research with teaching and learning.

DIFFERENTIATION OF RESEARCH UNIVERSITIES

Pride of place goes to the phenomenon of concentrated support within an ever more differentiated and diffused system. By both planned means and unplanned evolution, advanced systems of higher education come to differentiate research universities from other types of postsecondary education. As emphasized in the analysis of fragmenting forces, the other types embody a drift of teaching away from research. But the research university sector itself constitutes a striking commitment to the performance of research within higher education, especially in contrast to the placement of research in government laboratories, nonprofit research enterprises, and industrial settings. At the same time that research is no longer seen as an activity performed in common across universities and colleges, the insistence in the research universities becomes powerfully entrenched. Disciplinary and institutional mandates converge to ensure that research comes first. As much as in late nineteenth-century German universities, research is seen by faculty and administration alike as the essence of the university. Indeed, the research foundations are now cut on a much larger scale, as more disciplinary specialties, with supporting faculty, facilities, and students, are included in the university framework and the research university sector at large.

The massive American sector of over one hundred research universities is the leading case internationally of how differentiation concentrates and intensifies the unity principle. The universities in this set are understood by government and the general public to be *the* centers of basic research within and without the educational system. Defining themselves around research and research training, these institutions are positioned to develop resources and utilize money streams that are qualitatively different as well as quantitatively greater than those possessed by nonresearch universities, public comprehensive colleges, private liberal arts colleges, and community colleges. Overwhelmingly the dominant sector, their strength is based primarily on their research activity. Operating considerably as research conglomerates, the leading members of this powerful tribe, as of 1990, counted their money in the billions of dollars.

Institutional concentration of the research-teaching-study possibility is also exhibited in the Japanese de facto differentiation of universities in which academic research and research training is heavily concentrated in some ten to twelve institutions while all the other universities, at best, have graduate programs that are short on students and are underfunded. The institutional hierarchy is steep, with prestige based in part on research capability and productivity. In Britain, we noted, the binary policy has served as a tool for institutional concentration, protecting the universities as places for basic research while other institutions in a second sector grew as places for practical training and some applied research. Now that at the beginning of the 1990s the polytechnics have joined the universities in a nationally unified system, the incorporation of research activity that begins with Oxford, Cambridge, and London shades off by degrees in a large array of institutions that will not be equally funded and equipped for research. By both state steerage and market interaction, institutional concentration of the unity principle is found to a significant degree in Britain, with research funding as key agent and marker.

In Germany, institutional concentration has lagged, held back by the privileges for all institutions and academics that have been invoked by the Humboldtian legacy and by the inability of universities to select their students. But the trend toward concentration is at work. The Fachhochschulen have grown as a second major sector. Notably, while research may be formally defined as a core task of all German universities, "the allocated regular budget only covers a small part of this task," leaving the individual professor "to compete for grants from the German Research Association and similar institutions or from private sources."[2] Since such competition means selective awards, professors and departments do not end up equal. In France, the extreme case of nonsupportive system structure, institutional concentration has not meant the raising of the unity principle to primacy but rather the opposite: both elite professional training and the center of gravity in research is placed outside the university-funded framework. But even in France, a broad differentiation that supports a research-teaching-study connection is apparent, especially in the separation of universities one from another by disciplinary grouping and the close linking of CNRS units with university units, all serving to give special support to scientific fields.

The long-term flow is clear. *If* a modern system of higher education is going to support and protect an integration of research with teaching and study, it will at the most macro level develop an institutional concentration of the nexus. If spread among all institutions, the nexus will

become too costly, underfunded in unit support, and weakened by diffusion.

COMPETITION IN THE UNIVERSITY SECTOR

Institutional competition strengthens a differentiated research university
sector as an effective place for uniting research with teaching and study.
In a remarkable essay written in the early 1960s, Joseph Ben-David and
Abraham Zloczower argued persuasively that competitive educational
institutions promote research and research training better than do noncompetitive ones.[3] In comparisons of Germany, France, Britain, and the
United States, they gave considerable weight to the element of competition among Land governments and the universities they individually
supported in the international primacy of the German system in the
nineteenth century. They portrayed even more strongly the intense
competitive spirit of American universities as a prime source of twentieth-century dominance in research productivity and training. In both
countries, decentralized control generated the competition: control by
multiple subgovernments in Germany; and control by forty-eight to
fifty state governments *and* the self-vested control of private universities in the United States. As a general system argument, Ben-David
and Zloczower offered an appropriate interpretation that has borne
up well. But what is the invisible hand by which competition works
such effects? Do we find a muted counterpart in less decentralized
and less competitive systems? Is competition perhaps something so
natural in modern science and scholarship that it steadily comes to the
surface in a major university complex and is suppressed only at great
cost?

The steering hand of competition is hardly invisible once we realize
that while business firms show success by turning a profit, universities
(or major subunits within them) become successful by achieving a reputation. As Clark Kerr has put it, "A reputation, once established, is an
institution's single greatest asset."[4] Reputation is basic to the Matthew
effect—to those who have, more shall be given. It is also a prime ingredient in what can be called the Initiative effect—to those who do not
have but strive hard and make the right decisions, more shall be given.
Reputation is an institutional bridge to the environment across which
favorable fiscal resources, faculty, and students naturally flow. Reputation can be largely assigned by a national government, as in Japan, by

initially granting one or two universities a leading place. But such state-specified monopolies or duopolies lead in time to inbreeding and rigidity while greatly limiting the opportunities for other institutions to develop. In contrast, decentralized control creates competitive interaction among a larger set of institutions: various subunits struggle to make themselves attractive to faculty and students. In the competitive struggle, noted scientists and scholars become the crucial item. To attract and retain them, favorable conditions for research and scholarship are required, from well-equipped laboratories to light teaching loads to financial support for advanced students. These conditions then promote research and research training.

In simplified linear form, the formula for favorable outcomes from competition runs as follows: decentralized control leads to institutional competition; the competition centers on relative repute; reputation is dependent on nationally and internationally recognized productive academic staff; the capacity to attract and retain such personnel depends on maintaining work conditions they desire; supportive conditions and able staff lead to productive research and to the institution becoming a research training magnet for talented students.

Notably, the reputation market for institutions is closely intertwined with the labor market for academics: institutional reputation is an aggregate characteristic that follows largely from individual and subgroup achievements in research and training. It is also intertwined with the academic consumer market in which institutions and students find one another. An important characteristic of American higher education, one that has gone largely unnoticed but that stands out in cross-national comparison, is the high degree of mobility of students after their undergraduate degree and on entry to graduate school. A whole new round of selection and self-selection takes place across institutions that is much more affected than undergraduate admissions by reputation of departments. Largely on the basis of reputation, graduate schools and the graduate segments of departments compete, and students, especially the most talented ones, decide where to apply and whose offer to accept. In sharp contrast to the "in-house" barriers to student mobility common in most national systems and particularly observed in France and Japan in this study, the extensive interinstitutional mobility characteristic of an intensively competitive system becomes yet another broad condition that favors local concentrations of best students with best faculty in research-oriented settings.

A competitive dynamic in the research university sector of a national system thus sets in motion an activation effect. Institutions cannot rest on fixed, guaranteed allocations; they especially cannot count on attracting and retaining highly qualified academic staff without close attention to their desires. Faculty avoid or drift away from institutions that cannot offer favorable conditions. Institutions that nod off for a decade or two fall behind: it pays to pay attention. Institutions are activated by the competitive struggle to build the conditions of best science and best scholarship.

Perhaps the clearest empirical macrocomparison in the history of higher education of the importance of competitive setting was the sustained systemic divergence of German and French higher education in the nineteenth century. As argued succinctly by R. R. Palmer, "The much admired and influential German system of the nineteenth century came into being [as] a pluralist and competitive system of twenty universities in all parts of the country, each priding itself on being an independent center of *Wissenschaft*."[5] In marked contrast, as we have seen, a diametrically opposite course was taken in France. Under central control, special écoles were established, scientific academies were revived, and a single Imperial University was laid down in which the faculties of letters and of science mainly served as examination committees for the lycées. These faculties "were nothing like what the rest of the world knew as a university,"[6] since separate universities did not really exist, and the centrally controlled French structure meant that "the creative energies of the French went into the founding of specialized schools of advanced study, the écoles spéciales and the grandes écoles." The result was both "a fragmentation of higher learning and its extreme concentration in Paris. In the nineteenth century Paris was one of the great scientific centers of the world, and the rest of France became nearly a desert."[7] And while the German system insisted on the principle of "serious and creative learning and scholarship at the university level of education," the French system insisted on "the principle of public responsibility, planning, and final control of the educational system *at all levels* in the public interest."[8] It matters greatly which principle is emphasized in system culture and structure. Competition among universities operating under decentralized control supports the first principle, while a centralized and essentially noncompetitive national structure places first the need for coordinated planning and "final control."

Officials and academics in advanced societies and advanced developing societies that are eager to improve the performance of their universities in research and research training have increasingly realized the

activation effect of competition. In their desire to bolster university performance, Germany, Britain, France, and Japan are all "slouching toward the market,"[9] thereby forcing universities to compete more for
their incomes, especially those earmarked for research that in turn help
to build research foundations for teaching and learning. Funding patterns, a topic to which we return, then become critical. Competition in
the American system, already the grand case in cross-national comparison, is destined to intensify even further. Individual states, even regions
within states, increased their pressure in the 1970s and 1980s for their
own research universities to be bigger and better in science and technology for reasons of economic advancement and even of general improvement in quality of life. In the United States, competitiveness is con-
stantly stimulated by the state-federal structure of dual support in
which the states individually back their own state universities in the
pursuit of federal research funds. In turn, the inherent competitiveness
of the private universities only increases as more of them seek to enter
the research lists and the stakes of high-cost research are raised higher.
"A natural and eternal race in the American context," the race to be
better among universities, is "increasing in intensity."[10]

Competition among universities has long had an international component. By the beginning of the twentieth century, French and British
officials and academics were eyeing the Germans, the Germans were
taking the measure of the rising behemoth across the Atlantic, and the
Japanese were embarked on a furious race to catch up with all the other
major powers. With increasing frequency and intensity, disciplinarians
have been disposed to pursue their specialties across national borders.
Hundreds of thousands of faculty and advanced students have long informally ranked universities internationally as they contemplated their
choices of places for training and career development. Specialty by specialty, as bibliographical methods of citation analysis churn out readily
available institutional and national comparisons of research prowess,
such assessments have now even become quantitative and ostensibly
more objective. In either event, by qualitative or quantitative measure,
universities of any serious renown increasingly make themselves known
internationally and compete for reputation and academic talent across
national borders. Research and research training are first-listed items on
their calling cards. And more countries have cause to worry about brain
drains, or to be cheered by brain gains, when such means of international coordination as the Single European Market promise to increase
the flow of academics and scientists across national borders.

THE IDEOLOGY OF UNITY

Among research universities, the long-standing belief in the unity principle helps both to steer behavior and to rationalize it. Beliefs can serve as switchmen, in the famous metaphor of Max Weber, setting tracks along which interests are pursued.[11] In all five countries we have examined, and elsewhere generally in higher education, the belief that research should be the basis for advanced teaching and study glows bright. An OECD overview of university research published in the early 1980s stressed that the dominant ideology in universities is that in all disciplines, teaching and research benefit each other.[12] An intensive study of the beliefs of academics in Australia in the late 1980s revealed a universal commitment among university professors to the inherent necessity of combining research with teaching and hence to research-based advanced study.[13] The minister of education in the government of Finland stated in 1990 that once a separation is made between "higher education" and "postsecondary education"—the latter a more vocational nonuniversity sector—then "all the Finnish institutions of higher education have a duty to undertake research. Their instruction is based on research and all universities ... are empowered to award postgraduate degrees."[14] A Danish researcher observed in the late 1980s that "the 'unity of research and teaching' is an ingrained principle in university policy in Denmark."[15] The unity belief is virtually subsumed in the all-embracing academic faith in which "freedom of research," "freedom of teaching," and sometimes even "freedom of study" stress that the primary academic activities are both self-chosen and freely merged.

A primary point of orientation, in itself a steering mechanism and a source of intrinsic motivation, the unity belief is also a powerful ideology for justifying professorial freedom, power, and privilege. Like a protective blanket it can be thrown over a range of personal and institutional actions that may or may not involve research activity linked to teaching and study. As in present-day Germany, it may still be used to rationalize professors teaching what they please and students studying when, where, and what they please, with little regard for systematic linkage. Protective of the autonomy of basic units and whole universities, it is a powerful ideological counterforce to doctrines of public accountability and national order that rationalize top-down regulation.

The power of late twentieth-century interpretation of Humboldtian ideology to orient academic behavior is enhanced by its apparent rationality. If talented young people are to be trained for research, what better way is there than to put them in the hands of productive researchers who will prepare them for research activity and then put them directly into that activity? To have researchers do research in locales away from students is tantamount to narrowing and distorting the pipeline of recruitment and training. For teachers to work in teaching-only settings, away from research activity, is to dampen their own research capacity and to deny their students any involvement in research. Why do things a second-best or third-best way by divorcing research from teaching and study? In the case of the United States, as put succinctly by Robert Rosenzweig, American universities "have been built on the premise that research and graduate education go together because each enriches the other. Therefore, they are best done in the same place by the same people. This system works."[16] The principle is not only rational on its face but competitively rational as well: students denied access to research mentors in one university or country are free in many instances to vote with their feet and to choose to attend another university at home or abroad. An apparently straightforward rationality is particularly a blessing for an ideology that is much use in educated circles of professors and academic officials who, virtually without exception it sometimes seems, conceive of themselves as logical thinkers.

INTEGRATIVE FUNDING

Different forms of funding in national systems of higher education shape the strength of the research-teaching-study linkage. Amid a bewildering complexity of money streams, we have distinguished three main types that contribute to research foundations. General institutional support, or general university funds (GUF), is the main line of funding for universities from national governments in nationalized systems; and, in federal systems, from state governments alone, as in the United States, or from a combination of provincial and national governments, as in Germany. In most countries this funding line starts in a national ministry—of "education," or "higher education," or "higher education and science," or "employment, education, and training"—and is widely considered the backbone of university support. Funds are commonly based on number of students grouped within major blocs of fields of study and as such are considerably enrollment defined.

The second major money stream, the research line, is the second element in the "dual support" finance structures of European systems. Funds flow through national research-focused bodies, particularly research councils for designated groups of disciplines; they also come in the form of research allocations made to universities by such mission agencies as departments of defense, energy, agriculture, and health. While the research line commonly starts in government, it does not aim to constitute mainline support: neither student nor faculty numbers are at issue. With monies given directly for the support of research and research training, this line commonly operates competitively and selectively. It creates winners and losers among individual professors, research teams, departments, and whole universities. Broadly based bodies favoring basic research, as in the case of a national science foundation, may distribute funds across a host of disciplines and specialties, while mission agencies, favoring focused applied research, generally fund within a narrower band. But in either case the object is not to offer across-the-system institutional support. The focus on research involves competitively sought allocations and institutional selectivity in awards.

The third funding line, which "dual support" perspectives radically underplay if not miss entirely, is nongovernmental support. This multifaceted source includes student tuition and fees, endowment income, private fund-raising (including grants from private foundations), hospital patient revenue and other services sold for a fee, and monies received from industry. In private universities and colleges, this third line may largely replace the first. With little or no governmental institutional support, their mainline support is privatized in a combination of the sources named above *and* overhead or indirect-cost charges on grants and contracts that flow in the second line. Taken together, monies from such sources constitute "untied block grants."[17] For those who want to self-steer, the third pathway is a highly preferred source of income.

The integration of research with teaching and with advanced study is clearly favored by funding patterns that help blend support of these activities. As highlighted in the discussion of fragmenting forces in chapter 6, a favorite way to tear apart the research-teaching-study nexus is to fund research and teaching separately, preeminently by funding a few places at a relatively high level to be research-first universities and funding teaching-first sectors at a less costly level. Governmental interest in cost containment pushes powerfully in this direction. A separate tempting way is to move research out of universities by funding a separate research establishment, either within government or as a nonprofit sector or both. Whether funds are blended or segmented is clearly of great importance.

In support of the nexus, support may be blended at the source. This historic pattern, favoring university autonomy and local decision making and hence much preferred by academics, may be distinguished as governmental core funding.[18] Institutional support is largely lump-sum: the budget is not heavily earmarked for restricted spending within centrally specified categories—"formula funding"—but comes largely as a total sum within which the institution can spend as it pleases. The classic case historically was undoubtedly the funding of British universities in the golden age of the University Grants Committee, 1920–1965, when, as reliable legend has it, lump sums for whole universities were agreed to and then written down on the back of an envelope after lunch discussion in a London club. But such trusting blended support has long been out of favor in nationalized bureaucratic systems, as in France and Japan, and virtually everywhere it has been in decline. Lump sums have given way to earmarked allocations.

A second form of blended support exists at the institutional level when universities develop many money streams, comingle them, and then dispense funds at their own discretion. Diversified institutional support has become the late twentieth-century answer to the decrease in source-blended support, a prime way to enhance university autonomy and to maintain the marriage of research to teaching and learning that university professors fervently desire. We return to this crucial point below. Additionally, with the ascent of government means of control, single-source financing has become an increasingly risky business for universities, somewhat analogous to investment in a single stock in the stock market. In contrast, diversified funding, like investment in a mutual fund or multiasset portfolio, buffers a university against the risk of having all its eggs in one basket.

The primary funding trends set in motion by the great expansion of systems in the last half of the twentieth century became, by the end of the 1980s, reasonably clear. First, systems find ways to distinguish the funding of teaching and the funding of research. Second, they use the subsidiary research line of support more heavily, shifting funds from core support to research support so as to fund research selectively and competitively, thereby to reap the benefits of concentration and competition. As the institutional line becomes less generous, universities are forced to use the research line as an alternative source of funding.

Third, nongovernmental support increases, with tuition leading the way. In an outstanding overview of the general principles and mechanisms of higher education finance, J. R. Hough concluded that "one of the few clear trends that has emerged in patterns of funding has been for an increasing share of the total cost to be borne by students and their families."[19] When added to tuition, funds obtained from private fundraising, industry, and the selling of services make the third line the great diversifier of university revenues.

As seen in Part One, the American system is farthest along in these three developments. State-by-state differentiation of university, four-year college, and two-year college, together with private sector differentiation of research-first universities from service universities and liberal arts colleges, has firmly placed the majority of students and faculty in teaching-first institutions, with only a minority located in research-dominated environments. Then the national government, by means of a multitude of departments and agencies, has provided a broad research line of support that places clearly designated research dollars on top of what the state and private universities obtain by other means. Most important, the third route of support has been extensively and steadily enlarged. The leading private universities manage large investment portfolios to maximize income from endowments; they test the limits of student demand with tuition increases; they raise huge sums, for example, $100 million a year or more at 1990 prices, by means of annual intensely professional fund-raising from alumni and assorted well-wishers; they join with domestic and foreign firms in the pursuit of the returns of science and technology; and they manage each year to extract tens of millions of dollars from the federal government as charges for overhead costs on research grants and contracts flowing from federal agencies. They are modern "enterprises," multiproduct and multifunded. The leading American public universities, as we have seen, have similarly learned how to construct a diversified base that permits a local blending of support for research, teaching, and study. The support of their own states, long considered their institutional line of support, has now in many leading cases been reduced to a third or less of total income. Student fees, federal research grants, overhead charges on those grants, the sale of services, and extended private fund-raising diversify their income portfolio.

In lesser degree and in varied form, the other four countries were seen in Part One to be drifting toward a general pattern of diversified finance in their national systems in which second and third major lines of funding become more important for the universities that will remain research centered. Greater effort is made to differentiate financially between research-first universities and teaching-centered universities, implicitly if not explicitly, even in formally unified systems. Research is funded more selectively and competitively by means of the research council line. Universities are pushed "into the market," toward alternative sources of support (including regional and local government), while mainline support from a traditional single source is reduced as a share of total support. A financial marker of success on the income side is that a large share of total funds, for example, greater than 50 percent, is obtained by means of other than national governmental core support.

In sum: the unity of research, teaching, and study is adversely affected when traditional institutional funds become more segmented, earmarked for either teaching or research rather than allocated as general support. Funds become less blended at the source. In place of such integrated funding, research-first universities turn to a formula by which they receive a greater share of their support through selective and competitive funding in a research-focused line of support *and* pull in funds in a broad third stream that is not defined by a governmental patron. The broader funding base enhances their capacity to serve the faculty preference, deeply rooted in the Humboldtian ideology and its inherent rationality, to have teachers do research, to have researchers teach, and to have research-intended students brought together with research-minded personnel. Diversified funding becomes the funding key to the maintenance and enhancement of the research-teaching-study nexus. There are other ways of proceeding, as in the French pattern of knitting together CNRS laboratories and universities, but, as we see below, such ways are a distant second best.

FORMATIVE CONDITIONS IN THE UNIVERSITY

Nested within and closely related to the enabling conditions identified above are formative conditions at the level of specific institutions. What are the university bases for "centers of excellence" in research-guided advanced teaching and learning? Three features loom large. First is firm differentiation of an advanced tier, enhancing what can be termed the graduate school phenomenon. Second is the capacity of the university to self-fund research and research training according to its own desires, if need be to cross-subsidize from teaching to research and from preadvanced to advanced education. Third is competitive attainment of an institutional niche that in its scale and scope is strongly supportive of research and graduate training. In the best of all possible worlds (one not pursued here), the university is also led by a cohesive administration that symbolizes a unified identity, thereby helping to convert a loosely coupled assembly of diverse fields and interests into a *multi*versity if not a *uni*versity.

GRADUATE SCHOOL DIFFERENTIATION

At the institutional level, the most important favoring condition for effecting the unity principle is a formally constructed graduate or postgraduate tier. As seen in the U.S. analysis, the graduate school has been the structural heart of the capacity of American universities to place research foundations under teaching and advanced study.[20] It offers a fundamentally different orientation than that found in the undergraduate realm, where students typically are admitted to an undergraduate college rather than a department, there to partake of a certain amount of general education and then to choose whatever major they please. In contrast, earmarked as the place and time for specialization, the postbachelor's level is where the disciplines fully take over. Within its boundaries, faculties and departments are free to emphasize research to their heart's content. Graduate students are viewed as researchers-in-training and become invaluable research personnel. The graduate school sets rules for admission, retention, and degree attainment that provide a general framework for the departmental treatment of students. Varying by department but always present, there is a graduate curriculum, a critical feature of the basic units that is discussed below.

In the long-evolved American arrangement, professors typically desire to teach at the graduate level, for it is there that research, teaching, and study can clearly be fused. The resulting vigorous commitment of departments in the basic disciplines to their own graduate programs has become the backbone and the muscle of the graduate school phenomenon, an organizational feature that is much more important than the existence of a graduate school deanship or other offices in the central administration. Largely by virtue of the "luck" of its origins and evolution, the American vertical university, with its clear two tiers, has increasingly offered throughout the twentieth century a distinct and well-supported "home for science."[21] The organization framework has structurally favored the research-teaching-study nexus.

Universities in other major national systems, as we have seen, have historic patterns that are less directly supportive. In the German and

French systems, students have completed their general education in a longer and more effective secondary education and have entered the first major tier of university study to pursue a prolonged and specialized first degree. Ostensibly they all are already advanced. The postgraduate or most advanced level, as an organized sphere of activity, has been left relatively underdeveloped. Courses have been in short supply and students have not been immersed in a department-framed curriculum. The students who stay on become individual research students who informally or quasi-formally attach themselves as best they can to a professor or a research group, or they become employed as university personnel. Courses available to them are often mainly filled, as in Germany, by advanced first-tier students.

The English structure has heavily concentrated faculty attention on undergraduates, marginalizing the postbachelor students. In comparison to the campus residencies, seminars, tutorials, honors examination, and so on, that have supported a relatively intense undergraduate life, graduate work has had little or no organizational framework. In Japan, as we have seen, formal graduate schools are plentiful in number but woefully short of students. The Ph.D. is not the massive instrument of research training that it is in the United States. In Britain and Japan, as in Germany and France, the evolved organization of universities, in the context of the needs of mass higher education and modern science, is less structurally supportive of research and research training than in the United States. A home for science has had to be fashioned more within the commitments of the first tier or in ad hoc arrangements at the most advanced level.

As other nations have become interested in how to strengthen their most advanced work, essentially their doctoral programs, they have looked to the graduate school phenomenon in leading U.S. universities. The American graduate school stands out organizationally as a congenial place for disciplinary imperatives and the supportive structure that most undergirds institutional reputation based on research capability. Against constraining historic structures, other national systems are seeking to develop new arrangements that operate in a similar fashion.

SELF-FINANCE AND CROSS-SUBSIDIZATION

The capacity to effect cross-subsidies is basic to university self-control. In the American case, it contributes greatly to the vigor of the graduate level and the strength of its research foundations: teaching tends to subsidize research, and undergraduate education tends to subsidize the graduate level. Conceiving of universities in economic terms as "multiproduct nonprofit organizations," Estelle James has noted that "external actors, such as state legislators and private donors, have only limited influence over the behavior of [American] universities, because of the substantial opportunities for reallocation and cross-subsidization by internal actors in these educational institutions."[22] This institutional capability is a key difference between universities, public or private, and pure undergraduate institutions. James estimated that "graduate costs [U.S.] are at least three times as great as undergraduate costs, and the ratio doubles if research is treated as an input into graduate education."[23] Moreover, the relative cost per graduate student has been rising through time, yet "tuition charges are almost identical across levels, and graduate students are frequently given waivers of the nominal amount."[24]

Cross-subsidization highly favorable to graduate training and research comes about particularly through the most important, if largely hidden, subsidy of all: a heavy allocation of faculty time. This crucial feature is particularly difficult to capture in an even fashion in national figures on the academic segment of R&D expenditures. In general, however, in major U.S. universities, especially in the sciences, research commonly takes up a half or more of faculty time. Of the remaining time, largely devoted to teaching, half may be allocated to graduate courses. Hence the time allocated to research and graduate teaching together is many times greater than the time allocated to undergraduate teaching, giving rise to the 3:1 and 6:1 ratios identified by James. In the decades since World War II, the upward tilt has increased. All university activities have become more expensive, but research and graduate education have each and together risen more in cost than undergraduate instruction. Institutionally, principally among public universities, undergraduate education is a relatively low-cost operation.

Whatever one's view about the propriety of such cross-subsidization, it is virtually a genetic component of the American research university. The justifications are many. Noting that "undergraduate institutions can survive very well without graduate students, while graduate institutions cannot exist without a large undergraduate base," James has stressed that internal cross-subsidization is "an alternative funding mechanism to national government taxes [and direct government funding of the full cost of research and graduate training], avoiding many of the disincentive and informational problems inherent in taxes and central planning."[25] Cross-subsidization clearly promotes decision making at the university level that is more attuned than central decision making to local settings and different mixes of programs and fields. Critically, it promotes research and research training, the two activities that most enhance university reputation and cosmopolitan climate, general features that in turn attract undergraduates, despite the fact that the programs into which these students enter will include some large classes and some instruction by teaching assistants rather than professorial staff.

The fundamental contribution of cross-subsidization has not been lost on university administrators in the United States, although it is not their favorite topic for public discussion. David Gardner, president of the University of California between 1983 and 1992, while attempting to explain the dynamics of the American public research university to European observers, emphasized that individual American states will not directly subsidize research or graduate education at the level necessary for high productivity.[26] And, we might note, neither will the alumni and other gift givers, in the case of private universities. Popular appeal lies in undergraduate admissions and undergraduate student life. The best way to proceed in this context is to develop as many money streams as possible, mix them together locally, and then subsidize the high-cost ones that engage the interest of faculty, thereby tapping into the disiplinary dynamic and promoting critical means of institution building that revolve around faculty recruitment, retention, and productivity in research and research training.

Internal university funding is much affected by academic and institutional values that define the pursuit of what is variously called reputation, prestige, status, and stature.[27] Prestige is not an epiphenomenon, a gloss on practical matters of finance, teaching, and learning. It is also not merely a matter of attracting more research-minded faculty and research dollars. Standing often as the foremost consideration in institutional affairs, it directly underpins the undergraduate realm. In economic terms, "the higher the prestige of an institution, the greater its renown, and the larger the geographic market from which it can attract students. Similarly, the greater the prestige, the more inelastic is the demand for places within the institution, and the more easily tuition charges can be raised without a commensurate decline in student quality. As a result, institutions can trade off increased prestige—which is expensive and involves higher costs—for higher tuition, while still attracting students in sufficient numbers and of acceptable quality."[28]

The point is clear: to the extent that universities achieve diversified funding, especially via the third money stream of nongovernmental funding, they are positioned to internally roll funds toward research and the most research-centered level of instruction. To the extent that they are turned loose in this fashion to make their way, they become inclined to compete for reputation, the most valuable resource of all. And to the extent that expansion brought about by mass higher education gives them internally a large undergraduate base, they are better positioned to cross-subsidize. Hence this is ample reason to see the tendency toward cross-subsidization as a growing generic force in national systems of higher education generally. Viewing resource allocation in universities internationally, Ross Harrold has summarized the case:

> Research is of prime importance in academics' value systems.... University reward and status systems are premised on achievement in research. Yet the formulae by which universities are blockfunded are usually premised on the primacy of teaching activities: while there is typically an element supporting time for academic research, funding formulae are essentially enrollment driven. [University] academics must teach but they prefer to research. It could therefore be expected that the actual balance between research and teaching in the use of *the most expensive resource, the time of academics*, will differ from that assumed in the formulae used to allocate resources to and within academic departments. In short it is reasonable to expect that teaching activities will tend to subsidize research activities.[29]

Thus, whether in Germany, Britain, France, Japan, or elsewhere, to the extent that universities achieve a capacity to self-steer, by old-fashioned "leave-it-on-the-stump" block funding, or by modern diversification of funding sources, they will cross-subsidize in favor of research and advanced training. Funds shift toward the values of the academic staff. As academics become specialized, they prefer a combination of research and teaching to only teaching, with a tilt toward research. They also prize the research-centered advanced students who can become their academic and scientific descendants.

UNIVERSITY COMPETITIVENESS: NICHE, SCALE, AND SCOPE

The earlier discussion of the importance of competition as an enabling condition in a national system pointed to the centrality of research and scholarship in amassing a university's greatest single asset, a sterling reputation. While centralized national systems and state plans may formally assign reputation—an outstanding example is the prominent place given the University of Tokyo historically by the Japanese government—the more modern systems decentralize and differentiate their universities, the more reputation is competitively achieved. A search for advantage then underlies strategic decision. How can our institution, compared to others, best prosper? What are our acquired strengths and weaknesses, and shall we maximize strengths and cut away weaknesses or shall we attempt to bring our weaker programs up to par and exhibit strength across the board? Decentralization localizes such critical decisions in shaping institutional character.

The self-composing of a university niche in the national and international ecology of higher education increasingly has questions of scale that directly translate into economies of scope. The organizational constraint of graduate education in Britain and Japan observed in Part One pointed to the debilitating effects of relative smallness—the small size of departments when an English university is less than five thousand students, the cramped scale of primary base units when the chair in the Japanese university is permitted to have only a few master's and doctoral students and even the limited quotas go unfulfilled. Such scale sharply limits the range of specialties within a discipline that can be effectively covered: the strengthening of research-related graduate education then depends considerably on achieving larger organizational scale that permits broader substantive scope. Universities weakened by small size have only to look to strong institutions in their own country to see the increasing importance of greater scale and scope, let alone to American departments of fifty or more tenured faculty and perhaps thirty full professors that can cover in depth a half-dozen or more subfields.

Universities can overgrow themselves. The pre-1968 University of Paris, reportedly with 200,000 students, was an organizational monster that deserved to be broken up in the form of a dozen or so universities. Universities in Rome, Naples, and Mexico City that in the 1980s had students ostensibly enrolled and in attendance in numbers upward of 150,000, stretching perhaps to 300,000, were beyond all desirable limits of loose coupling. But many more universities are undergrown than oversized as they confront the competitive disadvantages of their size and scope. When a large number of American public universities operate in the range of 20,000 to 50,000 students and some leading private counterparts have enrollments of 15,000, with a critical mass of graduate students in a wide range of departments, they help set an international measure for minimal scale and scope. The relatively large undergraduate base in the U.S. public universities, we have seen, increases resources, based on student numbers and program coverage, that may be used for extensive cross-subsidization favoring research and graduate programs.

Comprehensive universities arguably support research and doctoral programs better than specialized universities that concentrate on a single professional field or a narrow set of disciplines. Under the principle of concentration, narrowly focused institutions are a tempting form of investment and commitment. Governments seek a focus in an area of national priority; some academics see a chance to position a university exclusively on the perspectives and interests of their own fields. But the specialized university reduces interaction across disciplines and specialties, while the university that encompasses a good share of the disciplines found presently in the sciences, the social sciences, and the humanities, along with a half-dozen or more professional areas such as engineering, education, business administration, architecture, law, and medicine, enhances the development of new streams of thought among as well as within the existing fields, for example, biochemistry, cognitive science, materials science, and environmental studies.

The comprehensive university is also inherently more cosmopolitan than its specialized counterparts, offering a culture that is richer in its diversity. A "technological university" always seems truncated; oddly assembled "universities" composed of two or three professional fields such as law, pharmacy, and pedagogy are widely seen as not true universities. Sharply delimited forms are generally not on the same plane of attractiveness and promise as the embracing comprehensive university. Even the most comprehensive universities now find their limits tested by expanding knowledge: increasingly all universities to some degree become substantively selective. But as an organizational form, the university is amazingly adaptive; it stretches horizontally by adding new fields side-by-side and vertically by adding more degree levels and tiers of training, especially ones positioned beyond the first major degree. The accumulation of fields widens the substantive base and increases the likelihood of interfield interaction. That interaction, on top of increasing specialization within the disciplines, gives rise to more advanced degrees in more fields, multiplying the sites where research activity and research training are the heart of the matter.

In short, the breadth of a university bears significantly on its relative capacity to generate growth in knowledge from its own research and teaching activities. Comprehensiveness is also an important ingredient in reputation. It also increases the possibilities of comingling funds, placing within one organization the funds for different disciplines, programs, and levels of instruction that otherwise would be separated in specialized institutions. And since the modern comprehensive university of substantial scale is too large, too deep, and too complex for anyone from the outside to grasp in detail, its breadth offers defense in depth against close top-down scrutiny, by government or other patrons, of the operating units in which research, teaching, and study are enacted.

ENACTING CONDITIONS IN THE BASIC UNIT

As we have seen, nations deeply advanced in higher education, here represented by the five leading national centers of learning in the Western world, possess in varying degree certain broad conditions in their university systems and individual universities that favor strong research foundations for teaching and advanced study. But whatever their nature, the macrocontexts only offer broad enabling and formative conditions: in themselves they do not finally tell us how university operations are actually carried out. For that we have to turn to the departments, chairs, institutes, faculties, subcolleges, and research clusters that in great profusion constitute "the factory floor" of higher education. Such basic units are the immediate nesting place for the nexus whose fate we seek to determine. While the large structures set frameworks, the basic units perform.

How do basic units most closely and effectively connect teaching and learning to research? What are the contemporary generic processes of research training? Those processes must necessarily incorporate and revolve around two forms of knowledge: tangible knowledge and tacit knowledge. Under modern conditions, each type of knowledge requires a particular carrying vehicle as its primary promoter. The two vehicles can be simply defined as the teaching group and the research group. The everyday fusion of these vehicles is "the institutional nexus," the modern organizational means for systematically blending research, teaching, and study.

TRANSMISSION OF TANGIBLE AND TACIT KNOWLEDGE

In setting forth tangible and intangible components of a "research–teaching nexus," Ruth Neumann, an Australian researcher, noted that the tangible component involves the transmission of "advanced knowledge and research skills," in the sense of materials that have been largely codified and even committed to text, while the intangible connection "imparts a questioning, critical attitude to knowledge as well as a positive attitude toward learning."[30] The intangible conveys subtle, predominantly invisible qualities, "an approach and attitude toward knowledge only gained through involvement in research."[31] Incapable of being formally defined and openly taught, the intangible is tacit, largely unspoken and silent in transmission.

Many opposite terms and descriptions that point to a distinction between the tangible and the tacit are found in the efforts of sociologists of science, and of scientists themselves, to identify what is involved in scientific "socialization."[32] The tangible aspects involve "knowledge of the literature," "specific substantive knowledge," and "information." The tacit is more subtle: "a wider orientation," "a style of qualitatively distinctive thought," and "a noncodified method of work" or "sense of how to do things." It involves "scientific taste," standards of actual performance, a better sense of the significant, a knack for finding what is important to look into. One scientist has attempted to capture the distinction in an analogy to music: the tangible is "'the words, the libretto"; the other, whatever we call it, is "the music." Tacit knowledge is sometimes referred to as "secret knowledge"; the actual practice of research is a store of such knowledge.[33] The broadest distinction is simply formal and informal socialization, a formula that connects the tangible-tacit distinction to basic sociological categories but offers little clarity for the analysis at hand.

Highly instructive is the extreme case of "the scientific elite" studied by Harriet Zuckerman by means of intensive interviews with over ninety Noble laureates.[34] When the future laureates were mere apprentices early in their careers, what did they learn from their masters, the great experts with whom they had closely worked? Zuckerman reported the following: "One point on which the laureates are largely agreed is that the least important aspect of their apprenticeship was the acquiring of substantive knowledge from their master. Some even reported that in the limited sense of information and knowledge of the scientific literature, apprentices, focused on one or another problem, sometimes 'knew more' than their masters."[35] What they got was something much more subtle. As reported by a laureate in chemistry,

> It's the contact: seeing how they operate, how they think, how they go about things. [Not the specific knowledge?] Not at all. It's learning a style of thinking, I guess. Certainly not the specific knowledge; at least not in the case of Lawrence. There were always people around who knew more than he did. It wasn't that. It was a method of work that really got things done.[36]

In composite, the laureates claimed that the principal benefit of their earlier study with a master was "a wider orientation that included standards of work and modes of thought." This was considerably more than what is ordinarily understood by "education" or "training": beyond specific knowledge and skills there was a transmission, essentially tacit, of norms and standards, values and attitudes.[37] It is the ineffable informal qualities of at-the-bench relationships that make them "essential in producing in young scientists a sense for a good question or a key problem, a style of doing research or theorizing, a critical stance, and a way of teaching their own intellectual progeny."[38] The tacit dimension involves a modeling effect that sometimes can occur in imaginative teaching in the lecture hall or lecture-oriented classroom but whose major force is found in intimate interactions within research groups and related mentor–apprentice relations.

Underreported, if not entirely missing, in such accounts, a common shortcoming when scholars discuss their early training, is how the scientists in this case learned the words, the libretto, before they learned, or while they learned, how to make the music. Required substantive knowledge in a discipline or major specialty steadily grows in breadth and depth. In the nineteenth-century German laboratory it could be picked up at the knee of the single master as he and his students moved from lecture hall to seminar table to laboratory. But no more. Across a discipline, or in many fields even across a major specialty, the master cannot possibly know enough. Thus while the transmission of tacit knowledge remains centered in specific research settings and the actual practice of research, transmission of tangible knowledge increasingly requires special supports of its own. We find those supports in settings of advanced didactic instruction staffed by a plurality of teachers. To train for research as well as to train by means of research, two kinds of groupings are required. The ultimate problem of the modern university in the performance of research tasks is how to sustain and interrelate these two types of groups.

THE ORGANIZATIONAL FUSION OF CARRYING VEHICLES

The idea of certain social systems serving as vehicles for carrying scientific knowledge, portrayed by Donald T. Campbell largely at the level of "the scientific community," may, as he pointed out, also be applied to individual disciplines and to single schools of thought within them.[39] The idea of "carrying vehicles" may also be readily applied to local *organizational* units, that is, departments and research groups. In his imaginative portrayal of a "cohesion-accuracy tradeoff," as a contradiction in academic organizations, Karl E. Weick discussed subunits of departments as "vehicles of knowledge" that directly reflect "the technology of research": even more than departments, "sub-units within departments such as research projects, research teams, co-investigators, or coherent specialties are all more plausible sites where the contradiction between [group] cohesion and [scientific] accuracy is felt more strongly."[40] From the side of "accuracy," such social systems as "teams, projects, and specialties are the vehicles within universities that register, preserve, and disseminate scientific knowledge." But then from the side of "cohesion," "if a social system, is to become a vehicle capable of improving our understanding of the world, it must first become a stable, enduring social system.... [It] must recruit new members, reward old members, publish results that are read.... Cohesion must be assured so that the vehicle persists long enough to gather and retain some knowledge."[41]

When we add the tangible-tacit distinction to the idea of basic units serving as carrying vehicles, we can fashion an organizational explanation of how research and teaching become integrated with student learning. In the concluding chapter of *Research Foundations*, life in a chemistry research group in an American university was used to illustrate how the group could be a productive and meaningful cluster of relationship and activity for professor, postdoctoral students, and graduate students alike.[42] Students caught up in such a group for four years or more, in the United States or elsewhere, are exposed to a flood of tacit knowledge as well as some codifiable information and technique. But that was not all: in the U.S. setting, the research group is typically not a stand-alone operation; instead it is nested within or closely related to a strong teaching group in the form of an encompassing department. In addition to having a distinct graduate curriculum, the department, not the research group, controls admission, assesses student progress, and awards degrees, with some oversight by the encompassing graduate school to ensure that universitywide requirements are met. From the beginning to the end of their graduate study, the students in such cases are in the hands of a department as well as participating in a research group. Returning to the music metaphor, in lectures and didactic seminars students learn the libretto before or during the time they learn the music. They may even learn some music while in the hands of the department, since, in the reported example of a chemistry department, the curriculum mandated short-term rotation of students through several laboratories.

Thus, more than has been generally recognized, the department per
se is primarily a teaching framework, one in which members of interior
research groups are involved. Notably, the heads of the research groups
are simultaneously part of the encompassing teaching staff. The resulting basic-unit organization is clearly two-sided, a structure of teaching
groups and research groups interfused with one another. The research-
teaching-study nexus is not forged at the level of the individual professor or student, or even in the master-apprentice pairing. It is organizationally determined by the systematic provision of two crosscutting
forms for grouping academics and students that in turn uphold teaching and research.

The formulation arrived at here extends prior conceptions of the social bases of scientific and scholarly knowledge. In an early striking contribution to the modern history and sociology of scientific knowledge,
Ludwik Fleck captured the relationship between a body of accredited
theoretical assumption and investigative technique, on the one side,
and a supporting group of practitioners, on the other, in the now-
classic concepts of "thought style" and "thought collective."[43] We can
now specify that a thought style has tangible and tacit components and
that these components are best transmitted by a combination of two
types of local collectivities. In the later anthropological formulation of
Becher, academia consists of cognitive "territories," the bundles of
knowledge of individual disciplines and specialties, that are possessed
and carried forward by academic "tribes," the members of related
fields.[44] We can now specify that the territories, whatever the academic
fields, always contain both tangible and tacit forms of knowledge and
that the supporting tribes increasingly contain teaching-centered and
research-centered subgroups.

The teaching group–research group distinction points to social for-
mations at the operating level that are increasingly characteristic of
strong research universities. Neither type of group alone can transmit
both tangible and tacit knowledge as well as the two groups combined. We need not argue over whether "the department" or "the research group" is *the* core unit of the modern university: both are increasingly required. For purposes of research accomplishment and
research training, the absence of either one is a major structural deficiency. Under modern conditions, the fusion of department and research group is where the marriage of higher education and science is
consummated.

AFFIRMATION OF THE NEXUS

It has long been clear that to effect a research-teaching-study nexus at the operating level of universities, research-centered groups are needed. Such groups were idealized in the great German university institutes, laboratories, and research-based seminars of the nineteenth and early twentieth century. At present, university academics in most nations commonly understand that actual participation in research activity, or in its "scholarly" counterpart in the humanities and certain social sciences, is the best form of teaching and study aimed at research training. Scientists and scholars speak glowingly of the days they spent in close interaction with their mentors and tell endless stories about the subtleties of learning that come about in the intense relationships of a research group. Modern historians and sociologists of science have traced the norms and practices of "the scientific community" and of "laboratory life," each as an entity in itself.[45] The essential nature of the research group is not in doubt: it is the primary carrying vehicle for the transmission of invaluable tacit knowledge.

But cross-national comparison points also to the growing importance of a university framework in which teaching groups are an essential component of advanced research training. To educate in a modern discipline, or even in a major disciplinary specialty, a plurality of teachers is required who teach systematized knowledge by means of courses and seminars. The academic department is now the strongest device for this task, effecting requirements on behalf of a whole field of study. It does what the single mentor, or singularly focused research group, cannot do; it provides a framework for the wholesale provision of tangible knowledge, a necessary resource not to be overlooked. Without it, as noted in national systems in which advanced students have little or no curriculum, the students are hard put to acquire disciplinary knowledge. For institutional purposes, the advanced students are "put back" in increasingly large classes populated by preadvanced students or are told to learn "the rest" on their own. In contrast, what a graduate school structure provides is an educational thrust, considerably student centered, that relates curriculum to research.

When other national systems attempt to move toward the American model of university organization, for example, in the Graduiertenkollegs in Germany, the écoles doctorales in France, and new graduate schools in Britain and Japan,[46] it is not broad scientific norms or laboratory life that is at issue. Front and center is the problem of relating research group activity to a structured curriculum organized and staffed by a larger and closely related teaching group. This combination constitutes strong local organization for the relating of study, teaching, and research to one another.

Such local enactment is promoted in the larger frameworks of national systems by competition among diverse and diversely funded universities. By stimulating local initiative, departmental and institutional competition becomes motor power for a rugged understructure that seemingly cannot be constructed by national plan or central direction. The state in itself cannot command adaptive departmental and institutional strength. It can, however, establish broad conditions of competitive achievement wherein some universities and basic units that largely self-steer are able to generate a virtuous cycle of strength begetting strength in research production and research training. The state can also encourage a "diversity of provision" for advanced education, a diversity that can keep pace "with the increasingly differentiated relations between knowledge and society."[47] The American case suggests, as broad structural lessons, that the needed diversity of provision flows from increases in scale and scope, enlarged decentralization of control, and extended institutional competition.

As we note the opposing tendencies of fragmenting forces and integrating conditions for the research-teaching-study nexus in various national systems, it becomes clearer why, despite all obstacles, integration often overcomes fragmentation. The nexus is a magnet for resources, power, and prestige. Nations continue to honor it, academics pursue it, and institutions seek to subsidize it. And it is not only in the nations that have the most advanced systems of higher education that commitment to academic research and the training of researchers is heightened. Developing societies also see the point. For example, Singapore: "Research is seen as absolutely vital, not only for the reputation and legitimization of Singapore's universities, but also indispensable for maintaining internationally acceptable high quality and standards.... In order to stimulate intellectual vitality within the academic departments, attractive postgraduate and research scholarships and fellowships have been offered by the universities through international competition. The intention is to attract the best talent irrespective of nationality."[48] Even more than in the most advanced systems, the universities in developing societies need a constant upgrading of the subject matter that is taught, especially in science and engineering but not limited to those fields, and "this upgrading takes place most effectively if at least some of the university teachers in each ... field are engaged in research, together covering a sufficiently wide range of subjects."[49] The elaboration of a department framework around research clusters is the way that the research groups are pulled together to cover the needed range of subjects.

But as an increasingly expensive relationship, the research-teaching-study nexus test the limits of scarce resources. Its application shrinks from whole system to subsector, from scatteration across all institutions of a modern system of higher education to concentration in one or two university sectors. Increasingly esoteric in substantive contents, the nexus also tests the limits of university education. Its application pulls back from all students to limited cadres of highly advanced students, from usage at all degree levels to concentration in advanced-degree programs, preeminently doctoral programs and postdoctoral appointments. Institutionally delimited, the nexus becomes virtually *the* basis for the differentiation of higher education among types of institutions and across degree levels. As such, it is the prime ingredient in the ranking of institutions and the hierarchy that results. Much sought after, it generates the tides of academic drift.

Governments and academic systems have fundamental interests in the promotion of a fruitful connection between research, teaching, and learning. They may debate the cogency of the unity principle and view the practicality of the nexus as problematic, but they cannot afford to surrender the basic idea. The enabling, formative, and enacting conditions of integration then become the basis for an agenda of strategic decision. And what finally counts most are the conditions of enactment in the interiors of universities. There, in the basic units, with ever-larger loadings of tangible and tacit knowledge, systematic instruction by a teaching group that offers a wider profile of the subject becomes a required activity alongside and fused with the role long played by research activity itself as a form of teaching and learning.

CHAPTER EIGHT

Places of Inquiry

Near the end of the twentieth century, little doubt remains that advanced nations move into a stage of development in which for individuals and organizations alike highly specialized and rapidly changing knowledge serves as a primary source of competence, intellectual energy, power, and wealth. Acquired mainly by means of organized study, this productive resource is rooted in training that develops problem-solving capabilities. Such schooling requires sustained investment in knowledge-creating capital: one or more sectors of society must develop substantial capacity to generate new knowledge and rapidly disseminate it. Only nations willing to serve as saving remnants for received wisdom and past virtue, and that alone, can ignore the modern need for a widening base of activities organized around inquiry, a base within which, in many forms, training for research continually expands.

As societies seek to develop an inquiring base, higher education is generally called to the fore. While much research is increasingly carried out in industry and other societal institutions, universities generally possess the best foundations and most effective methods for both long-run augmentation of the fund of knowledge and its distribution. Organized to develop and maintain operational communities of inquiry across many subjects, they are best positioned to train generations of inquiring minds in tandem with production of research results. Research universities constitute an important institutional pipeline to the future.

CENTRALITY OF INQUIRY IN THE UNIVERSITY COMPLEX

Universities are uncommonly organized around ongoing flows of knowledge that are encapsulated in disciplines, professions, and interdisciplinary fields.[1] Caught up in those flows and the interests of their supporting groups, modern universities are also uncommonly dominated by a research outlook. Esteemed contributions to knowledge become the highest achievements for faculty; research-based degrees, notably the doctorate, become high attainments for students. Universities make a particular wager with knowledge within which a scientific or rational pursuit of truth develops its own morality, one that leads some participants and constituent groups to a particular sense of responsibility embedded in the scientific ethic and the academic calling.[2] While subject to intensifying political and bureaucratic controls and confronted with deepening demands for mass instruction and occupational relevance, these enterprises place at their core a sphere of intellect in which theoretical knowledge is highly valued.

The location of universities on a foundation of knowledge and inquiry remains a poorly understood phenomenon. The subject has been avoided in perspectives that locate universities' center of gravity in the realm of student development in first-degree (undergraduate) programs. Such perspectives have dominated popular and academic thought in the United States and increasingly come to the fore in other countries as concern has risen about the quality and cost of mass higher education.[3] When observers and researchers concentrate on the admission, retention, and attainment of first-degree students, research activities typically are either ignored or viewed negatively as a distraction from teaching and learning. Teaching is seen as the central activity of academic staff, despite the clear evidence that in leading universities, and in other emulating universities and colleges caught in the tides of academic drift, research comes first in the reward systems of professors, basic units, and entire institutions—and, we can add, the academic profession generally. In the American case, the student-centered approach has fixated not only on undergraduates but also on the issue of liberal or general education, thereby overlooking the extensive work of the universities in advanced degree programs in letters and science fields and graduate professional schools, which together, as we have seen, account in major U.S. universities for over half of faculty time, *and* of total expenditures, *and*, in many leading private universities, even of students. Thus limited, the student perspective has been unable to grasp the diversity of tasks and complexity of organization that inhere in modern universities. Largely ignoring the central role of research activity and research training, analyses of student development have not sought to explain the three-way relationship between research, teaching, and learning.

A knowledge perspective stands in sharp contrast. It starts with the centrality of knowledge production, hence the primacy of inquiry, and pursues teaching and learning from that base. The institutional footholds of discovery are seen as foundation for virtually all else that goes on at advanced levels of university work in the basic disciplines and an increasing array of professional fields. At the same time, of course, a vast body of accumulated knowledge is at hand, available for instruction by teachers untouched by research activity. But even among those who purport to proffer the wisdom of the ages, and that alone, a restless spirit of critical analysis and revision typifies the academy. Embroiled in controversial interpretation, humanities professors treat revision of received doctrine as a scholarly form of discovery. In one form or another, social scientists become discovery oriented. Virtually without exception, academic fields seek to roll forward their modes of thinking and their bundles of knowledge. With inquiry as their focus, research universities increasingly look forward, not backward.

A perspective that emphasizes the development of knowledge must accommodate what at first glance is a contrary phenomenon: as a widening gamut of professions and semiprofessions develop specialized expertise, their recruits require more preparation and their established members more periodic retraining. More people then go on beyond the first major degree to take advanced vocational training that does not find its footing in intensive research activity. Graduate education in the United States, for example, as formulated by Geiger, has "two different faces. Study for the master's degree is largely oriented toward providing limited advanced knowledge of mostly practical fields. Business and education in fact account for half of all degrees. Doctoral study ... is distinguished by the eventual production of an original piece of scholarship."[4] In the United States or elsewhere, as we have seen, it can hardly be otherwise. Research-based doctoral work does not remain the only advanced activity, or even numerically the predominant one. Just as mass involvement in undergraduate (preadvanced) programs followed historically the development of mass secondary education, mass graduate education in time follows in train. Vocationally oriented graduate programs flower in bewildering complexity as new programs seek to mix the training needs of numerous outside occupational specialties with relevant disciplinary knowledge. As a common trend among advanced national systems, the directly vocational side of advanced work expands in size and proportion; the great expansion of business studies and management training in Britain and on the European continent is a strong case in point. In the American system, as noted, master's degrees and professional degrees together, by a ratio of ten to one, numerically dominate the research-based Ph.D.

With this growth in vocational advanced education, research and research training are seemingly pushed aside. But only in part. The attitude of critical inquiry, broadly construed, steadily infiltrates the vocational programs that seem tailored entirely for teaching. A taught master's, as in Britain, has the public face of a program that with little or no regard to research transmits the codified knowledge of a professional specialty: only formalisms of the lecture and the book are apparently needed. But teaching that is innocent of the research attitude does not wear well in advanced professional training and does not long endure. Themselves educated in universities, the teaching staffs are aware of the power and prestige of research. They may well have encountered the subtle ingredients of tangible knowledge and tacit attitude characteristic of programs based on strong research foundations. They will at least have become aware of the instructional value of gathering students in seminars and laboratory-like settings, places where students can grasp in a first approximation what inquiry is about and how knowledge percolates back from the frontiers of relevant specialties. Proof of this virtually inescapable infiltration is not hard to find: the research attitude spread a long time ago into medicine, law, engineering, and agriculture; it is also now thoroughly embedded in schools of management, education, architecture, social work, nursing, and librarianship.

In short, the inquiring attitude cannot be bottled up in certain areas of advanced education and kept entirely out of others. Barriers can be erected against its wholesale diffusion and adoption by such means as heavy teaching loads, research-absent funding, and low unit-cost support. But in advanced university education, the genie of inquiry is everywhere out of the bottle. While preparation for research work is research centered, preparation for professional practice is increasingly research informed. In one profession after another, we find a deepening need for research-sensitive practitioners: if you cannot understand and effectively evaluate "the literature," you cannot keep up. Such leavening by the research attitude, while concentrated on tangible doctrine and technique, may suggest to vocational students that the research process contains a realm of tacit learning. Minimally, professional-field students introduced to modes of inquiry are less likely to accept uncritically and passively the "truth" as propounded and handed down in lecture and book by the professional expert claiming closed mastery of an established body of thought and technique.

At the end of the twentieth century, it is not unreasonable for systems of higher education to attempt to educate a third or more of the traditional university age group as far as the first major degree. Among an increasing share of those who reach that level, there then emerges in most countries a competitive advantage to be gained by pursuing higher studies or returning for advanced degrees after some time at work. And, along the line, beginning in the upper years of first-degree programs, if not sooner, there is advantage in knowing what researchers are about, to grasp at least in a general way their thought processes and methods and to be able to communicate with those fully invested in research. Students in strong research environments gain access to special bodies of knowledge, including, as this study has emphasized, tacit as well as tangible elements. If other advanced students are kept entirely away from research environments, they are denied access not only to powerful bundles of knowledge but also to styles of thought and practices of inquiry that are valuable tools of problem solving.

Hence, in seeking to absorb a research attitude into their own midsts, it is not irrational or simply a matter of narrow self-interest that professional school faculties in effect ape the sciences or the social sciences or even certain scholarly approaches found in history, philosophy, and linguistics. Form the standpoint of widening access to knowledge, it is not irrational that nonuniversities should drift toward the research mentality of universities, even if their movement brings them only part of the way. As specialized knowledge becomes increasingly rarefied, continua of small differences in degree of research engagement, extending from research cores to practical peripheries, may serve to preserve contact among experts and between remote specialists and mainstream participants. Such linking contact is substantially weakened when sharp lines are drawn between types of institutions in an effort to keep research entirely out of vocational or undergraduate programs and to thereby confine half or more of postsecondary institutions to a posture of "teaching only." The struggle for access of the general citizenry to the knowledge of experts is aided by limited access in higher education of advanced students in professional fields, as well as preadvanced students who will go no further than the first major degree, to the thought styles of the academic tribes that most firmly possess the tools of the inquiring trade.

THE INEVITABILITY OF COMPLEXITY AND CONTRADICTION

From amid the many conditions of fragmentation and integration of the research-teaching-study nexus set forth in chapters 6 and 7, several trends that dominate, in turn, the research system, the higher education system, and the funding system come together to create a swell of complex and contradictory relations in the joined world of science and university. Foremost is the enormous driving force of the specialization imperative that characterizes the research system internationally and virtually all academic disciplines individually. The steady decomposing of disciplines into specialties, and then of specialties into still more specialties, operates across universities as an uncontrollable self-amplifying phenomenon. Disciplinary subdivision is a powerful pressure for departmental substructuring. Even when existing specialties are recombined in a new interdisciplinary field, as in cognitive science and environmental studies, the ironic result is a new specialty that in the bloom of success becomes a program, a type of degree, and a unit of organization. Departments, faculty, and students come under unrelenting pressure to attend to ever more specific specialties, with advanced levels of instruction specifically in the line of fire. Disciplinary steerage is widespread and intense, a penetrating mode of influence whose magnitude and depth distinguishes universities from other types of organizations such as business firms and governmental bureaucracies. A relentless sophistication of the university's primary commodity is inescapable.

Second, the university complex is inescapably elaborated and diversified. Planners, administrators, and faculty in many countries, as we have seen, often seek to define and then to fund universities as similar and equal. Formal categories are even used to declare all higher education institutions to be universities and part of a single unified system: in the 1970s and 1980s, such nominal equality has been newly evident in systems that stretch from Sweden to Australia. But no matter how fervent the desire, similarity and parity are not the long-lasting result. Instead institutional dissimilarity and inequality grow as systems struggle to differentiate large clienteles, contain the insatiable appetite of research budgets, and control overall costs. Central to the division of labor that emerges is the extent of research investment in different institutions and the consequent balance of effort between research-based advanced education, on the one side, and preadvanced instruction and codified vocational programs, on the other. Institutions then increasingly range widely along continua that stretch from extremely research dominated to fully teaching devoted, from top- to bottom-heavy in the weight of program and degree levels that range from postdoctoral work to the two-year degree.

In short, diversity, not uniformity, is the master trend. The need to concentrate and hence to differentially distribute financial resources *and* personnel *and* equipment *and* students grows ever stronger as higher education systems grow in population size and in coverage of cognitive territories. The institutional division of labor can no more be stopped, let alone reversed, than the division of labor in society. Hence the thought that all institutions of higher education can be equal becomes a species of utopianism. If differentiation is not effected among institutions, it will take place within them, producing ever more polyglot universities that call for heroic internal management to simply maintain peaceful relations among disparate factions and somehow insert a capacity for spontaneous change.

Third, the funding system moves in the direction of a diversity of sources for the individual university, with single-source support replaced by multiple governmental and nongovernmental channels. Central and provincial (state) governments everywhere have made clear that they will not offer full institutional support for ever-expandable mass higher education and especially for an increasingly intensified research enterprise. Greater pluralism in funding sources and channels is then inescapable: more central mission agencies, research councils, provincial and local public agencies, business firms, private foundations, professional associations, and individual benefactors and contributors. Such diversification has replaced lump-sum funding as the best guarantor of university autonomy; many partial dependencies offer better protection than full dependency on a single patron. University self-steerage comes to depend on fund-raising capabilities that stretch from lobbying numerous central ministries to manipulating student tuition and fees to competing for research grants to recovering costs on hospital services to convincing wealthy supporters that they should specify the university as a beneficiary in their wills. Funding diversification elaborates the business side of university affairs, encouraging the deployment of midmanagement staff in the form of development officers, public relations experts, and administrators in charge of auxiliary services.

The trends of knowledge specialization, university differentiation, and diversified funding lead inexorably to greater complexity and contradiction in the operation of individual universities and the university complex as a whole. Modern academic knowledge itself cannot be other than confused and confusing: in Peter Scott's terms, the academy's chief commodity "has become diffuse, opaque, incoherent, centrifugal."[5] Mass systems, quasi-universal in tendency, move in the direction of any person, any study, any research, any service. Despite widespread effort among officials, administrators, and academics to simplify and clarify, purposes multiply and become more ambiguous. Pushed and pulled in many directions, universities are less and less likely to be characterized by the tight linkage of unitary organization and more by the loose coupling characteristic of federations. Inherently centrifugal along its base of operations, the comprehensive university is a very complicated and generally loosely joined organism. The thrust of complexity is to turn universities into multiversities and then into conglomerates.

With deepening complexity, universities become unhappily more problematic. The institution that has three, five, or ten times the funds, staff, and students that it had a quarter-or a half-century ago is not simply the old institution written large. Transactions seemingly grow geometrically, along with much greater internal division and many more external ties. Operations become an impenetrable maze; bureaucracy grows, collegial clusters diverge. Critically, university operations become much more difficult for outsiders to perceive and understand. Old images of unifying central values and institutional simplicity no longer apply to the fast-changing reality of opaque complexity. Embedded incoherence promotes a sense of ongoing "crisis."

Much strain in modern research universities necessarily follows from the contradictory and confusing thrusts of the three primary efforts frequently noted in this study: education for the professions, or specialized vocational training more broadly; general or liberal higher education, where learning may be seen as an end in itself; and research and research training, the area of university operation on which this study has concentrated.[6] As we have seen, the university complex of each nation tends to tilt in one direction or another among these efforts, exhibiting strengths that beget weaknesses. Critically, each task becomes more varied with the passage of time. Research and professional education clearly become more diversified. As Ben-David has argued persuasively, general education must also take many forms: "Since general education has to cater to the largest variety of students, it can be successful only if there are different programs and constant change and experimentation."[7] Variety within and among universities is needed which is adaptive to the particular needs of different student publics; in particular, introductory levels of higher education are pulled in opposite directions. Clienteles coming from other than strict secondary schools, with attendant need for "remediation" or at least new approaches in teaching, pull the early years of university work toward a helping or developmental orientation that has long been more characteristic of secondary education, while the need to align preadvanced with advanced programs together with the specialized inclinations of academic staff pull teaching toward the focused study characteristic of the advanced levels. Indeed, in line with the latter bent, a liberal education arguably should incorporate an attitude of critical inquiry best acquired in specialized study, a strength of the British commitment to the specialized undergraduate degree.

If the main commodity of higher education—knowledge—becomes more diffuse, opaque, incoherent, and centrifugal and basic educational tasks more complicated and contradictory, then the struggle of various interest groups within universities and between them and external groups is bound to widen and intensify. As overarching values recede as the basis for trust and integration, the political struggle of faction against faction for resources and rewards is emboldened. In response, to contain conflict and provide some minimal clarity of purpose, the coordination of organizational structures and cultures takes on heightened importance. It is no simple matter in the mass university to commit effort in three or more major directions that are not mutually supportive; to fashion acceptable channels that constrain the interest group struggle; to provide accountability among basic units strongly impelled to self-steer; and to assert symbolic ties that bind the many parts into a whole.

The problem of responding to inevitable complexity and contradiction is not one of philosophical reconciliation of ideas. It is overwhelmingly a problem of organization, of structuring and restructuring of the university and the university complex within which the relationship of research activities to teaching and learning is always in issue. In one fashion or another, deliberately or unconsciously, the nexus highlighted in this study is organizationally sorted out.

THE ESSENTIAL COMPATIBILITY OF RESEARCH AND TEACHING

The way that universities have been transformed into places of inquiry during the last century and a half has shown that Humboldt's perceptions were acute: research and teaching can be integrated and made to serve each other. Research itself can be a highly efficient and effective form of teaching; when it also becomes a mode of learning, it can serve as the integrative vehicle for an intimate fusing of teaching and study. The resulting three-way nexus is the great operational secret of the well-ordered university laboratory in a scientific field and of the teaching-research seminar in the humanities and social sciences in which professors and students pursue a similar approach to research or a common set of research problems.

Once the possibilities and outcomes of a fruitful connection between research activities and the activities of advanced teaching and learning are grasped, the core strain in modern universities takes on a different light. In the standard view, the main conflict in faculty tasks lies between teaching and research. But the critical fault line actually runs between preadvanced instruction that presents codified knowledge and may operate at some distance from research and advanced teaching and advanced teaching closely linked to research. In American terms, the fault line is between undergraduate teaching, especially that devoted to the first two years of study, and graduate teaching, especially that found in doctoral programs. The first is not far from secondary school teaching; in contrast, the second often contains elements of at-the-bench interaction between expert and neophyte and a form of learning by doing that is found in research institutes inside and outside the university.

As systems of higher education both shift from elite to mass participation and incorporate ever more sophisticated knowledge, an incompatibility thesis seemingly acquires greater public acceptance and stronger voice in the academy. In the American system, it has for some time been voiced frequently and with much vigor. When professors in universities are not in the undergraduate classroom, they are viewed as having run off somewhere to do research, not recognizing that they also teach graduate students and do research in their company. The time

devoted to individual advanced students, especially on doctoral dissertations, is not counted as teaching time. The escape-from-teaching belief
was also strengthened in American circles during the 1980s by especially contentious battles over the curricular content of general education, fixated on the "canon" located primarily in a few literature and
history courses, that managed to radically downplay the importance of
the sciences in modern general education as well as to ignore advanced
programs. The call for more attention to teaching and less to research
that periodically enlivens the American scene has become in effect a
call for diversion of commitment and energy from advanced to preadvanced levels of instruction. Research is viewed as a wrongheaded and
dysfunctional distraction. The motto for reform becomes less research,
more attention to undergraduate teaching and general education.

As higher education systems differentiate into a range of research-
oriented and teaching-centered institutions, the incompatibility thesis
also finds comfort in aggregate statistics about what most faculty do
and think. Summary numbers lump together diverse settings and become a sum of opposite stories. For example, during the 1980s, conclu-
sions from national surveys in the diverse American setting were drawn
that relatively few faculty members actively engage in research, that
those who do publish research results are coerced to do so by institutional pressures—"publish or perish"—and that most faculty members
prefer to concentrate their energies on teaching rather than on research.
But when the global figures are disaggregated, the appropriate conclusion about whether American academics find teaching and research to
be compatible or incompatible is that outside of institutional settings
where they are expected to teach only undergraduates and to be in the
classroom twelve or fifteen or eighteen hours a week, they combine
teaching and research in the apportioning of their time and do so by
personal preference. How much and how they do so is heavily condi-
tioned by institutional locale. Notably, faculty in the best undergraduate-centered liberal arts colleges in the United States reported research
involvement, viewing it as necessary for effective undergraduate teaching in both the short run and the long run and essential for their personal development, standing, and identity as productive academics.[8] Such
academics know something that outsiders rarely see: research and
teaching are compatible, even in undergraduate programs and even
when defined in terms that largely leave out the close fusing of the two
in graduate forms of research-based teaching and study.

The zest for research widely found in both universities and liberal arts colleges in the American system is in many ways even more wide-spread in other leading national systems of higher education that, coming later to mass higher education, have not gone as far in separating teaching-dominated institutions. From Finland to Australia, and across the other major university systems reviewed here, the assumption has remained strong within and outside the national system that a large share of professors, if not all, should be engaged in research as much as a third or a half of the time. The research commitment is viewed as normal, rational, and preferable. But official preferences change when costs get in the way and greatly expanded instruction of beginning and intermediate students comes to the fore. Then the views of normalcy and rationality shift somewhat from research activity for all staff to its concentration in certain institutions and virtual elimination in others. The view that research and teaching are incompatible and ought to be separated then serves two practical and pressing demands: it helps to legitimate cost-cutting measures in line with the edict that "we cannot afford to support research in all universities and colleges"; it is also used to protect preadvanced programs—"we need to have more academics spend more of their time teaching the beginning students"—which also serves to contain costs.

But the case remains strong that even for preadvanced programs, from the entry year onward, student participation in a research environment can be a highly appropriate form of teaching and learning. Regardless of its specific nature, a research project involves a process of framing questions, developing reliable methods to find answers, and then weighing the relevance of the answers and the significance of the questions. Not only is student research activity a scholarly process for defining questions and finding answers but it is clearly also a way of inducing critical thinking and developing inquiring minds. Notably, it can be an active mode of learning in which the instructor provides a frame and an attitude but does not offer answers to be written down, memorized, and given back. Even when resources and setting do not permit an actual plunging of preadvanced students into projects, small or large, instructors who bring a research attitude into their teaching are likely to exhibit key features of the processes of inquiry. Good pedagogical reasons abound why academics, when told they must only teach, resist a flight from research.

The commandment to do research most fully takes over at advanced levels of university instruction in the basic disciplines. The nexus on which we have concentrated then becomes central. Our inquiry has identified essential conditions for its strong expression, for a full integration of advanced teaching and study with research perspectives and methods and with the learning that is bottled up within the working knowledge of academic disciplines. As concluded in chapter 7, what is finally most critical is the particular construction of on-the-ground local contexts in which faculty and students interact. The optimal setting can be likened to a double helix; it is composed of intertwined strands of teaching and research, institutionally expressed as a teaching group and a research group. The setting for students then takes the shape of a binary group. In a blended arrangement, their life of study extends simultaneously, or in a defined sequence of course work and dissertation, into a teaching setting that is intensively research oriented and into a research setting that is infused with instruction. The binary group is an anchor to the wind that holds the university against the tides of research drift and teaching drift. It counters the specific interests of government and industry that would otherwise place research in one isolated setting and teaching in another—and leave students to find their way to these different locations and to somehow bring them together.

When disciplines were new and simply composed, as was the case in many fields during the nineteenth century, the research group alone could possibly encompass all necessary teaching. Even a single mentor could hold in his or her mind and impart directly and indirectly to research apprentices the existing small sum of tangible disciplinary knowledge, along with the tacit knowledge that the research group unconsciously conveys. But when disciplines have become epistemologically complex, as in most fields in the late twentieth century, the single strand is not enough to flesh out the research-teaching-study nexus. In response, universities tend to develop the capacity to sustain a teaching strand and interweave it with the operational modes of research groups. That is the core of the graduate school phenomenon.

As the teaching group and the research group combine into a binary group, they become the chartered molecule in the university organism for a modern fusion of teaching and learning with intensified research. When well interrelated, these twin strands serve as a focal point of paired bases whereby science is strongly expressed in the educational work of higher education and, in turn, higher education is operationally expressed in the work of science. The binary group is the centerpiece of the infrastructure by which modern universities are best made into places of inquiry.

Notes

INTRODUCTION

1. Ben-David, *Centers of Learning*, 94.
2. For Germany (Federal Republic of Germany), a research group headed by Claudius Gellert; for France, Guy Neave and Richard Edelstein; for Britain, Tony Becher, Maurice Kogan, and Mary Henkel; for the United States, Patricia Gumport; and for Japan, a cluster of researchers led by Morikazu Ushiogi. See Clark, ed., *Research Foundations*.
3. The nexus terminology has been adapted from Ruth Theresia Rosa Neumann's study in Australia of "the research-teaching nexus." Neumann, "Study of the Research Role." See also Lindsay and Neumann, *Challenge for Research in Higher Education*, esp. 37–44 and 65–69. I have extended the concept to three elements, to include the element of "study."
4. Earlier efforts to delineate a much-needed "knowledge perspective" may be found in Clark, *Higher Education System*, and Clark, *Academic Life*.

CHAPTER 1.   THE FEDERAL REPUBLIC OF GERMANY

1. Humboldt, "On the Spirit and the Organizational Framework of Intellectual Institutions in Berlin," 243. On the historical context of the 1809–1810 memorandum drafted by Humboldt and the principles contained in it, see Turner, "University Reformers and Professorial Scholarship"; McClelland, *State, Society, and University*; Muir, "Historical Development of the Teacher-Researcher Ideal"; Rothblatt, "Idea of the Idea of a University"; Bertilsson, "From University to Comprehensive Higher Education"; Gellert, "German Model of Research and Advanced Education."
2. Ben-David, *Centers of Learning*, 22.
3. Rothblatt, "Idea of the Idea of a University," 11–12.

4. Bertilsson, "From University to Comprehensive Higher Education," 2.

5. Muir, "Historical Development of the Teacher-Researcher Ideal," 31–32.

6. Ibid., 38.

7. Ibid., 37. See also McClelland, *State, Society, and University*, 200–203.

8. McClelland, *State, Society, and University*, 200.

9. Ibid., 202.

10. Muir, "Historical Development of the Teacher-Researcher Ideal," 42.

11. Ibid., 39.

12. Holmes, "Complementarity of Teaching and Research," 164.

13. Ibid., 122. As a basic source, see also Fruton, *Contrasts in Scientific Style*, chap. 2, "The Liebig Research Group in Giessen."

14. Holmes, "Complementarity of Teaching and Research," 121.

15. Ibid., 127.

16. Ibid., 162–163.

17. Morrell, "Science in the Universities," 51–52.

18. Olesko, *Physics as a Calling*, vii–viii (foreword by L. Pearce Williams).

19. Ibid., 1.

20. Ibid., 5, 9.

21. Ibid., 15, 17.

22. McClelland, *State, Society, and University*, 279.

23. Ringer, *Education and Society*, 291.

24. Mommsen, "Academic Profession," 65.

25. McClelland, *State, Society, and University*, 279.

26. Olesko, *Physics as a Calling*, 41–42, 46.

27. Ben-David, *Scientist's Role in Society*, 122–123; Ben-David and Zloczower, "Universities and Academic Systems," 47–62; Ben-David, *Centers of Learning*, 97–103.

28. McClelland, *State, Society, and University*, 187–188.

29. Ibid., 280, 281, 282.

30. Ibid., 204, 205, 212.

31. Ibid., 239–242.

32. Ibid., 247–255.

33. For the classic statement of this shift, see Trow, "Problems in the Transition."

34. McClelland, *State, Society, and University*, 259–261.

35. Ibid., 263–264.

36. Beyerchen, "Stimulation of Excellence," 144.

37. Ibid., 152.

38. Ibid., 160.

39. On the founding and early development of the Kaiser Wilhelm Society, see particularly Johnson, *Kaiser's Chemists*. See also McClelland, *State, Society, and University*.

40. Ben-David, *Scientist's Role in Society*, 132.

41. McClelland, *State, Society, and University*, 301–304.

42. Johnson, *Kaiser's Chemists*, 19, 18.

43. Ibid., 18.

44. Ibid., 107–121.

45. Turner, *Two Germanies Since 1945*, 7.

46. See particularly Hoch, "Reception of Central European Refugee Physicists"; Hughes, *Sea Change*; Fermi, *Illustrious Immigrants*; Coser, *Refugee Scholars in America*.

47. Peisert and Framhein, *Systems of Higher Education*, 29.

48. Turner, *Two Germanies Since 1945*; Hearden, *Education in the Two Germanies*.

49. Mommsen, "Academic Profession," 68.

50. Ringer, *Education and Society*, 292.

51. Van de Graaff, "Federal Republic of Germany," 19.

52. Ibid., 20–22.

53. Ibid., 27.

54. Mommsen, "Academic Profession," 81.

55. Block, "Higher Education," 15.

56. Frackmann, "Resistance to Change," 188.

57. Kehm and Teichler, "Federal Republic of Germany," 241–247; Gellert, "German Model of Research and Advanced Education," 16–18.

58. Block, "Higher Education," 27; Frackmann, "Resistance to Change," 189.

59. Kehm and Teichler, "Federal Republic of Germany," 244–245, 253–255; Gellert, "German Model of Research and Advanced Education," 16; Frackmann, 189.

60. Teichler, *First Years of Study*, 28–29.

61. Gellert, "German Model of Research and Advanced Education," 20; Kehm and Teichler, "Federal Republic of Germany," 245–246, 257–258.

62. Teichler, *First Years of Study*, 38-39.

63. Teichler, "Federal Republic of Germany," 46–50.

64. Kehm and Teichler, "Federal Republic of Germany," 258; Gellert, "German Model of Research and Advanced Education," 32–33.

65. Teichler, *First Years of Study*, 96; Gellert, "Conditions of Research Training," 59–62.

66. Massow, *Organization and Promotion of Science*, 23.

67. Block, "Higher Education," 11–12.

68. Huber, "Field of Uncertainty," 302. Emphasis in original.

69. Gellert, "Conditions of Research Training," 56.

70. Ibid., 56–57.

71. Ibid., 47–59.

72. Huber, "Field of Uncertainty," 302.

73. Gellert, "Conditions of Research Training," 61.

74. Massow, *Organization and Promotion of Science*, 32–34; Seibold, "Funding of Research in Germany," 24–25.

75. Massow, *Organization and Promotion of Science*, 34–43; Seibold, "Funding of Research in Germany," 25–27; Gellert, "German Model of Research and Advanced Education," 22–32.

76. Seibold, "Funding of Research in Germany," 22.

77. Massow, *Organization and Promotion of Science*, 57–60.

78. Huber, "Field of Uncertainty," 298.

79. Ibid., 304.

80. Kehm and Teichler, "Federal Republic of Germany," 246–247.

81. In a famous metaphor that connected ideas and interests, Max Weber likened ideas to switchmen that set the tracks along which interests propel action. But primary influence can readily flow in the opposite form: interests can be the primary determinant, setting the tracks and propelling action, while ideas are selectively adopted which help to motivate and especially to legitimate. On the Weberian formulation, see Gerth and Mills, *From Max Weber*, 61–65, and Bendix, *Max Weber*, 68–69.

82. Article 5, par. 3, Basic Law, as reported in Massow, *Organization and Promotion of Science*, 15. On constitutional provisions, also Peisert and Framhein, *Systems of Higher Education*, 29–30, 40–45.

83. Gellert, "German Model of Research and Advanced Education," 22.

84. Jungnickel and McCormmach, *Intellectual Mastery of Nature*, xvii.

CHAPTER 2.   GREAT BRITAIN

1. E.g., Scott, *Crisis of the University*; Becher, *British Higher Education*; Stewart, *Higher Education in Postwar Britain*: Carswell, *Government and the Universities*; Halsey, *Decline of Donnish Dominion*.

2. Perkin, "Historical Perspective," 28.

3. Ibid., 16.

4. Perkin, "Academic Profession," 16.

5. Ibid., 18.

6. Ibid., 18. See also Rothblatt, *Revolution of the Dons*.

7. Perkin, "Historical Perspective," 36–37.

8. Ibid., 37.

9. Heyck, "Idea of a University," 205.

10. Ibid., 207.

11. Stewart, *Higher Education in Postwar Britain*, 275.

12. Halsey and Trow, *British Academics*, 60. See also Jones, *Origins of Civic Universities*.

13. Halsey and Trow, *British Academics*, 63.

14. Ibid., 63.

15. Eustace and Moodie, "CNAA," 20.

16. Knight, on the terms and conditions of service of academic staff, *Times Higher Education Supplement* (*THES*), no. 505, July 9, 1982, 12. See also, Becher and Kogan, *Process and Structure*, 33.

17. Knight, *THES*, no. 505, July 9, 1982, 12.

18. Perkin, "Academic Profession," 36.

19. Becher, Embling, and Kogan, *Systems of Higher Education*, 74.

20. Berdahl, "Coordinating Structures," 85.

21. Ibid., 89.

22. Crosland (Secretary of State for Education, January 1965 to August 1967), in Kogan, *Politics of Education*, 196.

23. Berdahl, "Coordinating Structures," 93.

24. Ibid., 97.

25. Perkin, "Academic Profession," 42; Stewart, *Higher Education in Post-war Britain*, 224–225.

26. Shattock, "UGC and Standards," 47.

27. Carswell, *Government and the Universities*, 159.

28. *Committee on Higher Education Report* (Robbins Report).

29. Shattock, "UGC and Standards," 49.

30. Neave, "Elite and Mass Higher Education," esp. 348–349. See also Kogan, "Implementing Expenditure Cuts."

31. Neave, "Elite and Mass Higher Education," 358.

32. Ibid., 361.

33. Ibid., 348–349.

34. Ibid., 358.

35. Farrant, "Central Control of the University Sector," 42.

36. Heyck, "Idea of a University," 215.

37. Ibid.

38. Becher, "Graduate Education in Britain," 134–135.

39. Henkel and Kogan, "Research Training and Graduate Education."

40. All three statements reported in Committee of Vice-Chancellors and Principals (CVCP), *State of the Universities*, inside front cover.

41. *THES*, editorial, February 28, 1992.

42. Eustace, "United Kingdom," 767. On the many sources of institutional similarity in the British university system, see also Trow, "Academic Standards and Mass Higher Education."

43. CVCP, *State of the Universities*, 5–6.

44. Williams, *University Responses to Research Selectivity*, iii.

45. Henkel and Kogan, "Research Training and Graduate Education," passim.

46. Ibid., 73.

47. Ibid., 73–76; Halsey, *Decline of Donnish Dominion*, 178–180.

48. Henkel and Kogan, Research Training and Graduate Education," 79.

49. Ibid., 76.

50. Eustace, "United Kingdom," 768–769.

51. CVCP, *State of the Universities*, 11.

52. "English Relies on Army of Temps," *THES*, February 28, 1992.

53. Benjamin, "Overladen with Honours," 18.

54. Henkel and Kogan, "Research Training and Graduate Education," 105; Henkel and Kogan, unpublished related data, 1988.

55. Simpson, *How the Ph.D. Came to Britain*; Hirsh, "Postgraduate Training of Researchers"; Rudd, *Highest Education*; Henkel and Kogan, "Research Training and Graduate Education," 86.

56. Hirsh, "Postgraduate Training of Researchers," 190.

57. Johnson, "National Styles in Economic Research," 70.

58. Williams and Blackstone, *Response to Adversity*, 41–42.

59. Ibid., 44.

60. Ibid., 42–43.

61. Becher, "Graduate Education in Britain"; Becher, *Academic Tribes and Territories*.

62. Becher, "Graduate Education in Britain," 120.
63. Ibid., 132.
64. Ibid., 120.
65. Ibid., 127.
66. Ibid.
67. Ibid., 134–135.
68. Ibid., 116, 150.
69. Becher and Henkel, "Micro-study: Economics in Britain," 10. Unpublished background report.
70. "External Examiner Crisis," THES, March 6, 1992.
71. Becher, "Graduate Education in Britain," 139–140.
72. Ibid., 137–138.
73. Ben-David, Centers of Learning, 105–106.
74. Benjamin, "Overladen with Honours," 18.
75. Scott, "Anachronistic Elites," THES editorial, early 1992.
76. Hogan, "Graduate Schools," 20.
77. Ince, "Science Mandarins Back Elite Schools," 18.

CHAPTER 3.   FRANCE

1. Sabine, "The Two Democratic Traditions." See also Gilpin, France in the Age of the Scientific State, esp. 79, and Hoffman, "Paradoxes of the French Political Community," esp. 8–12.
2. Shinn, "Specialized Institutions," 1225.
3. Palmer, Improvement of Humanity, 306–315; see also Palmer, "University Idea" and School of the French Revolution.
4. Geiger, Private Sectors in Higher Education, 110.
5. Shinn, "How French Universities Became What They Are," 160.
6. Ibid.
7. Ibid.
8. Ibid.
9. Ibid., 160–161.
10. Ibid., 161–163.
11. Geiger, "Reform and Restraint in Higher Education"; Weisz, Emergence of Modern Universities in France.
12. On the French profile of authority in the coordination of higher education, one shared with a number of other European systems and contrasting with British and especially American structures, see Clark, Higher Education System, chap. 4.
13. Shinn, "How French Universities Became What They Are," 162; see also Neave and Rhoades, "Academic Estate in Western Europe," 218.
14. Neave and Rhoades, "Academic Estate in Western Europe," 220–225.
15. Goldberg, "University System in France," 35–37.
16. Ibid., 40.
17. Ibid., 44–45.
18. Cazenave, "Financing of Institutions," 1369.
19. Van de Graaff and Furth, "France," 52.

20. Bienaymé, *Systems of Higher Education*, 18.

21. Van de Graaff and Furth, "France," 60–61.

22. Ibid., 62.

23. Neave, "France," 10.

24. Ibid., 11.

25. Crozier, *The Bureaucratic Phenomenon* (1964), *The Stalled Society* (1970), *Actors and Systems* (1977), *Strategies for Change* (1979).

26. Crozier, *The Stalled Society*, v.

27. Ibid., vi.

28. Crozier, *Strategies for Change*, 26.

29. Ibid., 107; see also Shinn, "Specialized Institutions."

30. Suleiman, *Elites in French Society*, 281.

31. Friedberg and Musselin, "Academic Profession in France," 97.

32. Durand-Prinborgne, "France," 218.

33. Friedberg and Musselin, "Academic Profession in France," 107.

34. Bernstein, *Fragile Glory*, 226.

35. Ibid., 263, 269.

36. Ibid., 269.

37. Neave and Edelstein, "Research Training System in France," 203–204; see also Durand-Prinborgne, "France," 221–222.

38. Neave and Edelstein, "Research Training System in France," 197.

39. Ibid., 196–197.

40. Ibid., 198.

41. Neave, "Séparation de Corps," 179.

42. Ibid., 160–161.

43. Ibid., 161.

44. Friedberg and Musselin, "Academic Profession in France," 105.

45. Neave, "Séparation de Corps," 171–173.

46. Ibid., 173.

47. Neave and Edelstein, "Research Training System in France," 200.

48. Ibid., 218.

49. Terry Clark, *Prophets and Patrons*, passim.

50. Rontopoulou and Lamoure, "French University Education," 43.

51. International Consultative Committee, "Postgraduate Research Training Today," 16–17.

52. Ibid., 23. Emphasis added.

53. Ashford, *Policy and Politics in France*, 125, 314.

54. Guin, "Reawakening of Higher Education in France," 144–145.

55. Ibid., 127.

56. Ibid., 128.

57. Neave, "On Meat and Poissons," 8–9.

CHAPTER 4. THE UNITED STATES

1. On the transition from one age to the other, see Hofstadter and Metzger, *Development of Academic Freedom*; Storr, *Beginning of the Future*; Veysey, *Emergence of the American University*.

2. Storr, *Beginning of the Future*, 38.

3. Hofstadter and Metzger, *Development of Academic Freedom*; Storr, *Beginning of the Future*; Veysey, *Emergence of the American University*; Oleson and Voss, *Organization of Knowledge*; Berelson, *Graduate Education*; Jencks and Riesman, *Academic Revolution*; Metzger, "Academic Profession"; Geiger, *To Advance Knowledge*.

4. William James, "The Ph.D. Octopus."

5. In particular, see Geiger, *To Advance Knowledge*. Also, Berelson, *Graduate Education*; Storr, *Beginning of the Future*.

6. Geiger, *To Advance Knowledge*.

7. Storr, *Beginning of the Future*, 64.

8. Berelson, *Graduate Education*, 11.

9. Rowland, "A Plea for Pure Science" (an 1883 address). At the least, as put by Richard J. Storr, institutions had been "founded in numbers that were monstrously large by British and continental standards." Storr, *Beginning of the Future*, 31.

10. Storr, *Beginning of the Future*, 31.

11. Ibid., 23–35.

12. Metzger, "Academic Profession," 145–146; Brubacher and Rudy, *Higher Education in Transition*, 373–375.

13. Storr, *Beginning of the Future*, 41–44; Berelson, *Graduate Education*, 9–11.

14. Storr, *Beginning of the Future*, 20–21.

15. Berelson, *Graduate Education*, 10–11.

16. Geiger, *To Advance Knowledge*, 18–19; Berelson, *Graduate Education*, 16–20.

17. Spurr, *Academic Degree Structures*, 118–119.

18. Storr, *Beginning of the Future*, 44.

19. Geiger, *To Advance Knowledge*, 59–61.

20. Ibid., 61–64.

21. Ibid., 87.

22. Ibid., 77–93.

23. Ibid., passim.

24. Ibid., 161.

25. Karl and Katz, "American Private Philanthropic Foundation," 266.

26. Geiger, *To Advance Knowledge*, 167–171.

27. Ibid., 172.

28. Storr, *Beginning of the Future*, 61.

29. Cheit and Lobman, *Foundations and Higher Education*, 3–5.

30. Berelson, *Graduate Education*, 24–25.

31. Ibid., 25; Trow, "Transition from Elite to Mass Higher Education."

32. Berelson, *Graduate Education*, 25.

33. Ibid., 25–27.

34. Geiger, "Historical Development," 12.

35. Ibid., 14.

36. Ibid., 14.

37. Ibid., 15.

38. Ibid., 16.

39. Ibid., 19.

40. Smith and Karlesky, *State of Academic Science*.

41. Geiger, "Historical Development," 22.

42. National Science Foundation, "Science Resources Studies Highlights," August 25, 1989, 2.

43. Geiger, "Historical Development," 22.

44. National Science Foundation, "Science Resources Studies Highlights," 1.

45. Ibid.

46. Clark, *Academic Life*, 69–81.

47. U.S. Congress, Office of Technology Assessment (OTA), *Educating Scientists and Engineers*, 79.

48. Organisation for Economic Co-Operation and Development (OECD), *Main Science and Technology Indicators*, table 2, p. 16.

49. National Science Board, *Science and Engineering Indicators—1991*, 91–93.

50. See Irvine and Martin, "International Comparisons," 387–388.

51. Institute for Scientific Information (ISI), "Latest Citation Statistics," Sept. 1992, 8.

52. ISI, "Chemistry That Counts," 1–2, 7–8; "Electrical Engineering Nifty 50," 7.

53. Portes, "Economics in Europe."

54. Rosovsky, *The University*, 29–36.

55. On the growth of master's degrees, see Glazer, *The Master's Degree*, and Conrad, Haworth, and Millar, *A Silent Success*.

56. Carnegie Foundation, *Classification of Institutions*, 1–9.

57. Ibid., 7. Emphasis added.

58. Ibid., table 6, p. 6.

59. Gumport, "Graduate Education and Research Imperatives," 277–285.

60. Ibid., 278.

61. Ibid., 280.

62. Ibid., 282.

63. Ibid., 283.

64. Ibid., 265.

65. Ibid., 266.

66. Ibid., 268.

67. Clark, *Research Foundations*, 372–376.

68. Estelle James, "Cross-Subsidization in Higher Education."

69. Freeland, *Academia's Golden Age*, 149.

70. Rosenzweig, "Graduate Education and Its Patrons," 7–8.

71. See Bowen and Rudenstine, *In Pursuit of the Ph.D.*

72. For an illuminating discussion of disciplinary and bureaucratic control, see Elzinga, "Research, Bureaucracy."

73. On state dependency leading to institutional isomorphism, see DiMaggio and Powell, "Iron Cage Revisited"; and Hackett, "Science as a Vocation."

CHAPTER 5. JAPAN

1. Ushiogi, "Graduate Education and Research Organization," 299–300. For other overviews of the origin and development of modern higher education in Japan, see Nagai, *Higher Education in Japan*; Amano, "Continuity and Change" and *Education and Examination in Modern Japan*; Kitamura, "Mass Higher Education."

2. Ushiogi, "Graduate Education and Research Organization," 300.

3. Bartholomew, *Formation of Science in Japan*, 108.

4. Ibid., 71.

5. Ibid., 71.

6. Ibid., 73.

7. Dore and Sako, *How the Japanese Learn to Work*, 25.

8. Ushiogi, "Graduate Education and Research Organization," 301–305.

9. Ibid., 311.

10. For a particularly illuminating discussion of the origin, development, and fate of American-imposed "liberal education" in the Japanese system, see Kimball, "Japanese Liberal Education."

11. Ushiogi, "Graduate Education and Research Organization," 306.

12. Ministry of Education, Science and Culture (Japan), *Statistical Abstract*, 1988, 122; Ushiogi, "Graduate Education and Research Organization," 311.

13. Kawashima and Maruyama, "Education of Advanced Students in Japan," 338.

14. Umakoshi, "Korean Higher Education," 66.

15. Geiger, *Private Sectors in Higher Education*; Levy, *Higher Education and the State*.

16. Ministry of Education, Science and Culture, *Statistical Abstract*, 1988, 64–66.

17. Ushiogi, "Graduate Education and Research Organization," 311–312.

18. Ibid., 317–320.

19. Campbell, "Japanese Budget *Baransu*."

20. *Science*, "News and Commentary," March 10, 1989, 1285–1287.

21. *Nature*, "Opinion: Tokyo's Basic Reform," March 9, 1989, 100.

22. Ibid.

23. Merton, "The Matthew Effect in Science"; Trow, "Analysis of Status."

24. Kawashima and Maruyama, "Education of Advanced Students in Japan," passim.

25. Ibid., 334–335.

26. Ministry of Education, Science and Culture, *Statistical Abstract*, 1989, 90–91.

27. Bartholomew, *Formation of Science in Japan*, 51–52.

28. Allen, *Japanese Economy*, 86.

29. Ibid., 94.

30. Ibid., 190.

31. Ibid., 95.

32. National Science Foundation, *Science and Engineering* (quoted by Richard C. Atkinson in *Chronicle of Higher Education*, March 2, 1988).

33. Allen, *Japanese Economy*, 95.

34. Koh, *Japan's Administrative Elite*, 75–76; see also Kubota, *Higher Civil Servants in Postwar Japan*, 58–91.

35. Allen, *Japanese Economy*, 95.

36. Ibid., 95.

37. Dore and Sako, *How the Japanese Learn to Work*, 7, 53.

38. Ibid., quoting Kinmouth, 54.

39. Ibid., 51–52.

40. Ibid., 53.

41. Rohlen, *Japan's High Schools*, 89. Emphasis added.

42. Ibid., 90.

43. Ibid., 88–89.

44. Ibid., 90.

45. Allen, *Japanese Economy*, 100.

46. Narin and Frame, "Growth of Japanese Science and Technology," 601.

47. *THES*, July 29, 1988, 11.

48. Narin and Frame, "Growth of Japanese Science and Technology," 601.

49. Ibid., 602.

50. Ibid., 602–604; quotation, 604.

51. Ministry of Education, Science and Culture, *Statistical Abstract*, 1988, 122.

52. National Research Council (U.S.), *Learning the R&D System*, 3.

53. Ministry of Education, Science and Culture, *Statistical Abstract*, 1988, 122.

54. Ibid., 122.

55. Beauchamp and Rubinger, *Education in Japan*, 149.

56. National Research Council (U.S.), *Working Environment for Research*, 18–19.

CHAPTER 6.   FORCES OF FRAGMENTATION

1. Clark, *Research Foundations of Graduate Education*, Conclusion.

2. ISI has constructed an elaborate Science Indicators Database that is internationally available for ready reference. As of 1989, the database tracked more than "8,200 currently active specialty areas in science." See ISI's newsletter, *Science Watch*. For particularly insightful analyses of national scientific performance and "research forecasting," see Irvine and Martin, *Foresight in Science*, and Irvine, Martin, and Isard, *Investing in the Future*.

3. The concept of reactive growth, in contrast to substantive growth, is developed in Metzger, "Academic Profession." Metzger defined reactive growth as growth that follows from increase in student numbers, that is, the push of pressures on the input side of the higher education system. I have extended the concept to include reaction to increase in labor market connections, the demands of training that pull on the output side of the system.

4. Kerr, "Critical Age," esp. 188–189.

5. OECD, *Future of University Research*, 44–46.

6. OECD, *Post-Graduate Education in the 1980s*, 14–18.

7. Ibid., 8. Emphasis added.

8. The concept of academic drift, referring to convergent institutional movement, was first set forth by John Pratt and Tyrell Burgess in an early study of the British polytechnic sector. See their *Polytechnics*.

9. See also the concluding chapter in Clark, *Research Foundations of Graduate Education*.

10. OECD, *Future of University Research*, 76–77.

11. Irvine, Martin, and Isard, *Investing in the Future*, 15.

CHAPTER 7.   CONDITIONS OF INTEGRATION

1. Ben-David, *Centers of Learning*, 14.

2. Kehm and Teichler, "Federal Republic of Germany," 248.

3. Ben-David and Zloczower, "Universities and Academic Systems." See also Ben-David. "Universities and the Growth of Science," and his *Scientist's Role in Society*.

4. Kerr, "New Race," 10.

5. Palmer, "University Idea," 14.

6. Ibid., 16.

7. Ibid., 14.

8. Ibid., 17. Emphasis added.

9. Neave, "On Preparing for Markets"; see also Neave, "On Visions of the Market Place."

10. Kerr, "New Race," 10.

11. Weber, *From Max Weber*, 61–65.

12. OECD, *Future of University Research*; see also Moses, "Teaching, Research and Scholarship."

13. Neumann, "Study of the Research Role."

14. Taxell, "Higher Education System," 3–4.

15. Jensen, "Research and Teaching," 17.

16. Rosenzweig, "Grant Financing: PI Salaries."

17. Harrold, "Resource Allocation," 1469.

18. Ball, "Merging of the PCFC and the UFC," 120; see also, OECD, *Financing Higher Education*.

19. Hough, "Finance," 1353.

20. See also the two-volume work by Roger Geiger on the development of the American research university, *To Advance Knowledge* and *Research and Relevant Knowledge*; Gumport's two chapters in *Research Foundations*, "Graduate Education and Organized Research" and "Graduate Education and Research Imperatives"; Smith, *State of Graduate Education*; Berelson, *Graduate Education in the United States*; Wolfle, *Home of Science*.

21. Wolfle, *Home of Science*.

22. James, "Cross-Subsidization in Higher Education," 238; see also, James, "Decision Processes and Priorities."

23. James, "Cross-Subsidization in Higher Education," 238.

24. Ibid., 248.

25. Ibid., 252.

26. Clark, "Is California the Model for OECD Futures?"

27. Harrold, "Resource Allocation," 1472.

28. Garvin, *Economics of University Behavior*, 15.

29. Harrold, "Resource Allocation," 1472. Emphasis added.

30. Neumann, "Study of the Research Role," 215.

31. Ibid., 174.

32. Zuckerman, *Scientific Elite*, 122–132.

33. Kanigel, *Apprentice to Genius*, 237.

34. Zuckerman, *Scientific Elite*.

35. Ibid., 122.

36. Ibid.

37. Ibid., 123.

38. Cole, *Fair Science*, 132.

39. Campbell, "Tribal Model."

40. Weick, "Contradictions in a Community of Scholars," 256–257.

41. Ibid., 259.

42. Clark, *Research Foundations of Graduate Education*, chap. 11, 372–376.

43. Fleck, *Genesis and Development*, passim.

44. Becher, *Academic Tribes and Territories*, passim.

45. E.g., Hagstrom, *Scientific Community*; Crane, *Invisible Colleges*; Latour and Woolgar, *Laboratory Life*.

46. In the 1987 OECD report, "Post-Graduate Education in the 1980s," the authors (Blume and Amsterdamska) pointed out that among the many OECD nations "the tendency today is toward an increasingly 'professionalised' system of doctoral training, based more or less on the system obtaining in the United States" (78).

47. OECD, "Post-Graduate Education in the 1980s," 80.

48. Selvaratnam, *Innovations in Higher Education*, 42, 46–47.

49. Thulstrup, *Improving the Quality of Research*, 10.

CHAPTER 8.   PLACES OF INQUIRY

1. An earlier formulation of the perspective developed here, stressing knowledge as the common commodity of higher education, may be found in Clark, *Higher Education System*, chap. 1, "Knowledge," and passim.

2. For an illuminating discussion of actual and possible moral effects of the scientific calling and its "wager with knowledge," see Scaff, *Fleeing the Iron Cage*, 112–120.

3. The student development line of research became a veritable academic industry in the United States, apace diffuse public and academic concerns about the many confusing effects of undergraduate programs. A review and synthesis of the American literature on student development in the undergraduate years published in 1970 identified 1,500 studies carried out up to that time. A second

encompassing review published in 1991 found an additional 2,600 studies. At the same time, graduate programs and their effects on students have gone virtually unobserved and unreported. See Feldman and Newcomb, *Impact of College on Students*, and Pascarella and Terenzini, *How College Affects Students*.

4. Geiger, "Introduction, Section II: The Institutional Fabric," 1034.

5. Scott, "Knowledge's Outer Shape, Inner Life," *THES*, August 16, 1991, 12.

6. See particularly, Ben-David, *Centers of Learning*.

7. Ibid., 91.

8. See Clark, *Academic Life*, 73–89.

Bibliography

Allen, G. C. *The Japanese Economy*. New York: St. Martin's Press, 1981.

Amano, Ikuo. "Continuity and Change in the Structure of Japanese Higher Education." In *Changes in the Japanese University: A Comparative Perspective*, edited by William K. Cummings, Ikuo Amano, and Kazuyuki Kitamura, 10–39. New York: Praeger, 1979.

———. *Education and Examination in Modern Japan* (Shiken no Shakai-shi). Translated by William K. Cummings and Fumiko Cummings. Tokyo: University of Tokyo Press, 1990.

Ashford, Douglas E. *Policy and Politics in France: Living with Uncertainty*. Philadelphia: Temple University Press, 1982.

Ball, Christopher. "The Merging of the PCFC and the UFC: Probable, Desirable, or Inevitable?" *Higher Education Quarterly* 45, no. 2 (1991): 117–124.

Bartholomew, James R. *The Formation of Science in Japan: Building a Research Tradition*. New Haven: Yale University Press, 1989.

Beauchamp, Edward R., and Richard Rubinger. *Education in Japan: A Source Book*. New York: Garland Publishing, 1989.

Becher, Tony. *Academic Tribes and Territories: Intellectual Enquiry and the Cultures of Disciplines*. Milton Keynes, U.K.: Society for Research into Higher Education and Open University Press, 1989.

———. "Graduate Education in Britain: The View from the Ground." In *The Research Foundations of Graduate Education: Germany, Britain, France, United States, Japan*, edited by Burton R. Clark, 115–153. Berkeley, Los Angeles, and Oxford: University of California Press, 1993.

———(ed.). *British Higher Education*. London: Allen and Unwin, 1987.

Becher, Tony, Jack Embling, and Maurice Kogan. *Systems of Higher Education: United Kingdom*. New York: International Council for Educational Development, 1977.

Becher, Tony, and Maurice Kogan. *Process and Structure in Higher Education.* London: Heinemann, 1980.

Ben-David, Joseph. "The Universities and the Growth of Science in Germany and the United States." *Minerva* 7 (1968): 1–35.

———.*The Scientist's Role in Society: A Comparative Study.* Englewood Cliffs, N.J.: Prentice-Hall, 1971.

———. *Centers of Learning: Britain, France, Germany, United States.* New York: McGraw-Hill, 1977.

Ben-David, Joseph, and Abraham Zloczower. "Universities and Academic Systems in Modern Societies." *European Journal of Sociology* 3 (1962): 45–84.

Bendix, Reinhard. *Max Weber: An Intellectual Portrait.* Garden City, N.Y.: Doubleday, 1960.

Benjamin, T. Brooke. "Overladen with Honours." *Times Higher Education Supplement,* January 17, 1992, 18.

Berdahl, Robert. "Coordinating Structures: The UGC and US State Co-ordinating Agencies." In *The Structure of Governance of Higher Education,* edited by Michael Shattock, 68–106. At the University, Guildford, Surrey: Society for Research into Higher Education, 1983.

Berelson, Bernard. *Graduate Education in the United States.* New York: McGraw-Hill, 1960.

Bernstein, Richard. *Fragile Glory: A Portrait of France and the French.* New York: Alfred A. Knopf, 1990.

Bertilsson, Margareta. "From University to Comprehensive Higher Education: On the Widening Gap between '*Lehre und Leben.*'" Stockholm: Studies of Higher Education and Research, Council for Studies of Higher Education, no. 1, 1991.

Beyerchen, Alan. "On the Stimulation of Excellence in Wilhelmian Science." In *Another Germany: A Reconsideration of the Imperial Era,* edited by Jack R. Dukes and Joachim Remak, 139–168. Boulder, Colo.: Westview Press, 1988.

Bienaymé, Alain. *Systems of Higher Education: France.* New York: International Council for Educational Development, 1978.

Block, Hans-Jürgen. "Higher Education in the Federal Republic of Germany: Facts, Trends, and Policies." Unpublished paper, 1989.

———. "The University System in Transition: Possibilities and Limitations of Universities in the 'Steady-State.'" In *The Research System in Transition,* edited by S. E. Cozzens et al, 35–50. Dordrecht: Kluwer Academic Publishers, 1990.

Bowen, William G., and Neil L. Rudenstine. *In Pursuit of the Ph.D.* Princeton: Princeton University Press, 1992.

Brubacher, John S., and Willis Rudy. *Higher Education in Transition: A History of American Colleges and Universities, 1636–1968.* New York: Harper and Row, 1968.

Campbell, Donald T. "A Tribal Model of the Social System Vehicle Carrying Scientific Knowledge." *Knowledge* 1, no. 2 (1979): 181–201.

Campbell, John Creighton. "Japanese Budget *Baransu.*" In *Modern Japanese Organization and Decision-Making,* edited by Ezra F. Vogel, 71–100. Berkeley, Los Angeles, and London: University of California Press, 1975.

Carnegie Foundation for the Advancement of Teaching. *A Classification of Institutions of Higher Education: 1987 Edition*. Princeton: Princeton University Press, 1987.

Carrier, Denis, and Frans A. van Vught. "Government and Curriculum Innovation in France." In *Governmental Strategies and Innovation in Higher Education*, edited by Frans A. van Vught, 143–167. London: Jessica Kingsley Publishers, 1989.

Carswell, John. *Government and the Universities in Britain: Programme and Performance 1960–1980*. Cambridge: Cambridge University Press, 1985.

Cazenave, P. "Financing of Institutions." In *The Encyclopedia of Higher Education*, edited by Burton R. Clark and Guy Neave. Vol. 2, *Analytical Perspectives*, 1367–1376. Oxford: Pergamon Press, 1992.

Cheit, Earl F., and Theodore E. Lobman. *Foundations and Higher Education: Grant Making from Golden Years through Steady State*. Berkeley: Carnegie Council on Policy Studies in Higher Education, 1979.

Clark, Burton R. *The Higher Education System: Academic Organization in Cross-National Perspective*. Berkeley, Los Angeles, and London: University of California Press, 1983.

———. *The Academic Life: Small Worlds, Different Worlds*. Princeton: Carnegie Foundation for the Advancement of Teaching and Princeton University Press, 1987.

———. "Is California the Model for OECD Futures?" In *The OECD, the Master Plan, and the California Dream*, edited by Sheldon Rothblatt, 61–77. Berkeley: Center for Studies in Higher Education, University of California, Berkeley, 1992.

———, ed. *The Research Foundations of Graduate Education: Germany, Britain, France, United States, Japan*. Berkeley, Los Angeles, and London: University of California Press, 1993.

Clark, Terry Nichols. *Prophets and Patrons: The French University and the Emergence of the Social Sciences*. Cambridge: Harvard University Press, 1973.

Cole, Jonathan R. *Fair Science: Women in the Scientific Community*. New York: Free Press, 1979.

Committee of Vice-Chancellors and Principals (CVCP). *The State of the Universities*. London: CVCP, 1991.

Committee on Higher Education Report (Robbins Report). Cmnd. 2154, H.M.S.O. 1963.

Conrad, Clifton F., Jennifer Grant Haworth, and Susan Bolyard Millar. *A Silent Success: Master's Education in the United States*. Baltimore: Johns Hopkins University Press, 1993.

Coser, Lewis A. *Refugee Scholars in America: Their Impact and Their Experiences*. New Haven: Yale University Press, 1984.

Crane, Diana. *Invisible Colleges: Diffusion of Knowledge in Scientific Communities*. Chicago: University of Chicago Press, 1972.

Crosland, Anthony. In Edward Boyle and Anthony Crosland, *The Politics of*

Education, edited by Maurice Kogan. Harmondsworth, Middlesex, England: Penguin Books, 1971.

Crozier, Michel. *The Bureaucratic Phenomenon*. Chicago: University of Chicago Press, 1964.

———. *The Stalled Society*. New York: Viking Press, 1973.

———. *Strategies for Change: The Future of French Society*. Cambridge: MIT Press, 1982.

Crozier, Michel, and Erhard Friedberg. *Actors and Systems: The Politics of Collective Action*. Chicago: University of Chicago Press, 1980.

DiMaggio, Paul J., and Walter W. Powell. "The Iron Cage Revisited: Institutional Isomorphism and Collective Rationality in Organizational Fields." *American Sociological Review* 48 (April 1985): 147–160.

Dore, Ronald P., and Mari Sako. *How the Japanese Learn to Work*. London: Routledge, 1989.

Durand-Prinborgne, C. "France." In *The Encyclopedia of Higher Education*, edited by Burton R. Clark and Guy Neave. Vol. 1. *National Systems of Higher Education*, 217–224. Oxford: Pergamon Press, 1992.

Elzinga, Aant. "Research, Bureaucracy, and the Drift of Epistemic Criteria." In *The University Research System: The Public Policies of the Home of Scientists*, edited by Björn Wittrock and Aant Elzinga, 191–220. Stockholm: Almquist & Wiksell International, 1985.

Eustace, Rowland. "United Kingdom." In *The Encyclopedia of Higher Education*, edited by Burton R. Clark and Guy Neave. Vol. 1. *National Systems of Higher Education*, 760–777. Oxford: Pergamon Press, 1992.

Eustace, Rowland, and Graeme C. Moodie. "CNAA: Case for the Preservation." *Times Higher Education Supplement*, March 6, 1992.

Farrant, John H. "Central Control of the University Sector." In *British Higher Education*, edited by Tony Becher, 29–52. London: Allen & Unwin, 1987.

Feldman, Kenneth A., and Theodore M. Newcomb. *The Impact of College on Students*. Vol. 1. *An Analysis of Four Decades of Research*. San Francisco: Jossey-Bass, 1970.

Fermi, Laura. *Illustrious Immigrants*. 2d ed. Chicago: University of Chicago Press, 1971.

Fleck, Ludwik. *Genesis and Development of a Scientific Fact*. Chicago: University of Chicago Press, 1979. (Originally published in German, 1935.)

Frackmann, Edgar. "Resistance to Change or No Need for Change? The Survival of German Higher Education in the 1990s." *European Journal of Education* 25, no. 2 (1990): 187–202.

Freeland, Richard M. *Academia's Golden Age: Universities in Massachusetts 1945–1990*. New York: Oxford University Press, 1992.

Friedberg, Erhard, and Christine Musselin. "The Academic Profession in France." In *The Academic Profession: National, Disciplinary, and Institutional Settings*, edited by Burton R. Clark, 93–122. Berkeley, Los Angeles, and London: University of California Press, 1987.

Fruton, Joseph S. *Contrasts in Scientific Style: Research Groups in the Chemical and Biochemical Sciences*. Philadelphia: American Philosophical Society, 1990.

Garvin, David A. *The Economics of University Behavior*. New York: Academic Press, 1980.

Geiger, Roger L. "Reform and Restraint in Higher Education: The French Experience, 1865–1914." Working Paper no. 2, Higher Education Research Group, Yale University, October 1975.

————. *Private Sectors in Higher Education: Structure, Function, and Change in Eight Countries*. Ann Arbor: University of Michigan Press, 1986.

————. *To Advance Knowledge: The Growth of American Research Universities, 1900–1940*. New York: Oxford University Press, 1986.

————. "Historical Development of the American Research University." Paper presented at the annual meeting of the American Association for the Advancement of Science, San Francisco, January 16, 1989.

————. "Introduction, Section II: The Institutional Fabric of the Higher Education System." In *The Encyclopedia of Higher Education*, edited by Burton R. Clark and Guy Neave. Vol. 2. *Analytical Perspectives*, 1031–1047. Oxford: Pergamon Press, 1992.

————. *Research and Relevant Knowledge: American Research Universities Since World War II*. Oxford: Oxford University Press, 1993.

Gellert, Claudius. "The German Model of Research and Advanced Education." In *The Research Foundations of Graduate Education: Germany, France, Britain, United States, Japan*, edited by Burton R. Clark, 5–44. Berkeley, Los Angeles, and London: University of California Press, 1993.

————. "The Conditions of Research Training in Contemporary German Universities." In *The Research Foundations of Graduate Education: Germany, France, Britain, United States, Japan*, edited by Burton R. Clark, 45–66. Berkeley, Los Angeles, and London: University of California Press, 1993.

"German Universities Bursting at the Seams." *Science*, vol. 243, March 17, 1989, 1427.

Gerth, H. H., and C. Wright Mills, eds. *From Max Weber: Essays in Sociology*. New York: Oxford University Press, 1946.

Gilpin, Robert. *France in the Age of the Scientific State*. Princeton: Princeton University Press, 1968.

Glazer, Judith S. *The Master's Degree: Tradition, Diversity, Innovation*. ASHE-ERIC Higher Education Research Report no. 6, 1986. Washington, D.C.: Association for the Study of Higher Education, 1986.

Goldberg, Pierre. "The University System in France." In *Funding Higher Education: A Six-Nation Analysis*, edited by Lyman A. Glenny, 25–51. New York: Praeger, 1979.

Guin, Jacques. "The Reawakening of Higher Education in France." *European Journal of Education* 25, no. 2 (1990): 123–145.

Gumport, Patricia J. "Graduate Education and Organized Research in the United States." In *The Research Foundations of Graduate Education: Germany, Britain, France, United States, Japan*, edited by Burton R. Clark, 225–259. Berkeley, Los Angeles, and London: University of California Press, 1993.

————. "Graduate Education and Research Imperatives: Views from American Campuses." In *The Research Foundations of Graduate Education: Ger-*

many, Britain, France, United States, Japan, edited by Burton R. Clark, 261–293. Berkeley, Los Angeles, and London: University of California Press, 1993.

Hackett, Edward J. "Science as a Vocation in the 1990s." *Journal of Higher Education* 61, no. 3 (1990): 241–279.

Hackman, Judith Dozier. "Power and Centrality in the Allocation of Resources in Colleges and Universities." *Administrative Science Quarterly* 30 (1985): 61, 77.

Hagstrom, Warren. *The Scientific Community*. New York: Basic Books, 1965.

Halsey, A. H. *Decline of Donnish Dominion: The British Academic Professions in the Twentieth Century*. Oxford: Clarendon Press, 1992.

Halsey, A. H., and M. A. Trow. *The British Academics*. Cambridge: Harvard University Press, 1971.

Harrold, R. "Resource Allocation." In *The Encyclopedia of Higher Education*, edited by Burton R. Clark and Guy Neave. 2: 1464–1476. Oxford: Pergamon Press, 1992.

Hearnden, Arthur. *Education in the Two Germanies*. Boulder, Colo.: Westview Press, 1976.

Henkel, Mary, and Maurice Kogan. "Research Training and Graduate Education: The British Macro Structure." In *The Research Foundations of Graduate Education: Germany, Britain, France, United States, Japan*, edited by Burton R. Clark, 71–114. Berkeley, Los Angeles, and London: University of California Press, 1993.

Heyck, Thomas William. "The Idea of a University in Britain, 1870–1970." *History of European Ideas* 8, no. 2 (1987): 205–219.

Hirsh, Wendy. "Postgraduate Training of Researchers." In *The Future of Research*, edited by Geoffrey Oldham, 190–209. At the University, Guildford, Surrey: Society for Research into Higher Education, 1982.

Hoch, Paul K. "The Reception of Central European Refugee Physicists of the 1930s: U.S.S.R., U.K., U.S.A." *Annals of Science*, vol. 40, 1983, 217–246.

Hoffman, Stanley. "Paradoxes of the French Political Community." In *In Search of France*, edited by Stanley Hoffman, 1–117. Cambridge: Harvard University Press, 1963.

Hofstadter, Richard, and Walter P. Metzger. *The Development of Academic Freedom in the United States*. New York: Columbia University Press, 1955.

Hogan, J. V. "Graduate Schools: The Organisation of Graduate Education." ESRC Policy Document. Warwick: Center for Educational Development Appraisal and Research, University of Warwick, 1993. Occasional Paper.

Holmes, Frederic L. "The Complementarity of Teaching and Research in Liebig's Laboratory." In *Science in Germany: The Intersection of Institutional and Intellectual Issues*, edited by Kathryn M. Olesko, 121–164. Philadelphia: History of Science Society, 1989. *Osiris*, vol. 3.

Hough, J. R. "Finance." In *The Encyclopedia of Higher Education*, edited by Burton R. Clark and Guy Neave. 2: 1353–1358. Oxford: Pergamon Press, 1992.

Huber, Ludwig. "A Field of Uncertainty: Postgraduate Studies in the Federal

Republic of Germany." *European Journal of Education* 21, no. 3 (1986): 287–305.

Hüfner, Klaus. "Differentiation and Competition in Higher Education: Recent Trends in the Federal Republic of Germany." *European Journal of Education* 22, no. 22 (1987): 133–143.

Hughes, H. Stuart. *The Sea Change: The Migration of Social Thought, 1930–65.* New York: Harper & Row, 1975.

Humboldt, Wilhelm von. "On the Spirit and the Organizational Framework of Intellectual Institutions in Berlin." Translated by Edward Shils. *Minerva* 8 (1970): 242–250.

Ince, Martin. "Science Mandarins Back Elite Schools," *Times Higher Education Supplement*, 1992.

Institute for Scientific Information (ISI). "The Electrical Engineering Nifty 50: Top 25 Universities and Top 25 Industrial Firms Ranked by Citation Impact." *Science Watch* 2, no. 9 (October 1991): 1–8.

———. "Chemistry That Counts: The Frontrunners in Four Fields." *Science Watch* 3, no. 3 (April 1992): 1–8.

———. "Latest Citation Statistics Show U.S. Science Still Strong." *Science Watch* 3, no. 7 (Sept. 1992): 1–8.

International Consultative Committee on New Organizational Forms of Graduate Research Training. "Postgraduate Research Training Today: Emerging Structures for a Changing Europe." Ministry of Education and Science, The Netherlands, 1992.

Irvine, John, and Ben R. Martin. *Foresight in Science: Picking the Winners.* London: Frances Pinter, 1984.

———. "International Comparisons of Scientific Performance Revisited." *Scientometrics* 15, nos. 5/6 (1989): 369–392.

Irvine, John, Ben R. Martin, and Phoebe A. Isard. *Investing in the Future: An International Comparison of Government Funding of Academic and Related Research.* Aldershot, Hants., England: Edward Elgar, 1990.

James, Estelle. "Cross–Subsidization in Higher Education: Does It Pervert Private Choice and Public Policy?" In *Private Education: Studies in Choice and Public Policy*, edited by Daniel C. Levy, 237–257. New York: Oxford, 1986.

———. "Decision Processes and Priorities in Higher Education." In *The Economics of American Universities*, edited by Stephen A. Holmack and Eileen L. Collins, 77–106. Albany: State University of New York Press, 1990.

James, William. "The Ph.D. Octopus." In James, *Memoirs and Studies*. London: Longmans, Green, 1912.

Jencks, Christopher, and David Riesman. *The Academic Revolution.* Garden City, N.Y.: Doubleday, 1968.

Jensen, Jens-Jorgen. "Research and Teaching in the Universities of Denmark: Does Such an Interplay Really Exist?" *Higher Education* 17 (1988): 17–26.

Joas, Hans. "The Federal Republic of Germany: University and Career Opportunities for Young Scientists." *Higher Education Policy* 3, no. 1 (1990): 41–45.

Johnson, Harry G. "National Styles in Economic Research: The United States, The United Kingdom, Canada and Various European Countries." *Daedalus* (Spring 1973): 65–74.

Johnson, Jeffrey Allan. *The Kaiser's Chemists: Science and Modernization in Imperial Germany*. Chapel Hill: University of North Carolina Press, 1990.

Jones, David R. *The Origins of Civic Universities: Manchester, Leeds, & Liverpool*. London: Routledge, 1988.

Jungnickel, Christa, and Russell McCormmach. *Intellectual Mastery of Nature: Theoretical Physics from Ohm to Einstein*. Vol. 1. *The Torch of Mathematics 1800–1870*. Chicago: University of Chicago Press, 1986.

Kanigel, Robert. *Apprentice to Genius: The Making of a Scientific Dynasty*. New York: Macmillan, 1986.

Karl, Barry D., and Stanley N. Katz. "The American Private Philanthropic Foundation and the Public Sphere 1890–1930." *Minerva* 19 (1981): 236–270.

Kawashima, Tatsuo, and Fumihiro Maruyama. "The Education of Advanced Students in Japan: Engineering, Physics, Economics, and History." In *The Research Foundations of Graduate Education: Germany, Britain, France, United States, Japan*, edited by Burton R. Clark, 326–353. Berkeley, Los Angeles, and London: University of California Press, 1993.

Kehm, B., and U. Teichler. "Federal Republic of Germany." In *Encyclopedia of Higher Education*, edited by Burton R. Clark and Guy Neave. Vol. I. *National Systems of Higher Education*, 240–260. Oxford: Pergamon, 1992.

Kerr, Clark. "A Critical Age in the University World: Accumulated Heritage versus Modern Imperatives." *European Journal of Education* 22, no. 2 (1987): 183–193.

———. "The New Race to be Harvard or Berkeley or Stanford." *Change* (May/June 1991): 8–15.

Kimball, Bruce A. "Japanese Liberal Education: A Case Study in Its National Context." *Teachers College Record* 83, no. 2 (1981): 245–261.

Kitamura, Kazuyuki. "Mass Higher Education." In *Changes in the Japanese University: A Comparative Perspective*, edited by William K. Cummings, Ikuo Amano, and Kazuyaki Kitamura, 64–82. New York: Praeger, 1979.

Kogan, Maurice. "Implementing Expenditure Cuts in British Higher Education." Paper presented at the International Conference on Studies of Higher Education and Research Organisation, Dalerö, Sweden, 1983.

Kogan, Maurice, with E. Boyle and A. Crosland. *The Politics of Education*. Harmondsworth (U.K.): Penguin, 1971.

Koh, B. C. *Japan's Administrative Elite*. Berkeley, Los Angeles, and London: University of California Press, 1989.

Kubota, Akira. *Higher Civil Servants in Postwar Japan: Their Social Origins, Educational Backgrounds, and Career Patterns*. Princeton: Princeton University Press, 1969.

Latour, Bruno, and Steve Woolgar. *Laboratory Life: The Social Construction of Scientific Facts*. Beverly Hills, Calif.: Sage Publications, 1979.

Levy, Daniel C. *Higher Education and the State in Latin America: Private Challenges to Public Dominance*. Chicago: University of Chicago Press, 1986.

Lindsay, Alan W., and Ruth T. Neumann. *The Challenge for Research in Higher Education: Harmonizing Excellence and Utility.* ASHE-ERIC Higher Education Report no. 8. Washington, D.C.: Association for the Study of Higher Education, 1988.

Lundgren, Peter. "Differentiation in German Higher Education." In *The Transformation of Higher Learning 1860–1930: Expansion, Differentiation, Social Opening, and Professionalization in England, Germany, Russia, and the United States,* edited by Konrad H. Jarausch, 149–179. Chicago: University of Chicago Press, 1983.

McClelland, Charles E. *State, Society, and University in Germany 1700–1914.* Cambridge: Cambridge University Press, 1980.

Massow, Valentin V. *Organization and Promotion of Science in the Federal Republic of Germany.* Bonn: Inter Nationes, 1986.

Merton, Robert K. "The Matthew Effect in Science." In Robert K. Merton, *The Sociology of Science,* 439–459. Chicago: University of Chicago Press, 1972.

Metzger, Walter P. "The Academic Profession in the United States." In *The Academic Profession: National, Disciplinary, and Institutional Settings,* edited by Burton R. Clark, 123–208. Berkeley, Los Angeles, and London: University of California Press, 1987.

Ministry of Education, Science and Culture (Japan). *Statistical Abstract of Education, Science and Culture.* 1988 ed. Tokyo, 1988.

———. *Statistical Abstract of Education, Science and Culture.* 1989 ed. Tokyo, 1989.

Mommsen, Wolfgang J. "The Academic Profession in the Federal Republic of Germany." In *The Academic Profession: National, Disciplinary, and Institutional Settings,* edited by Burton R. Clark, 60–92. Berkeley, Los Angeles, and London: University of California Press, 1987.

Morrell, J. B. "Science in the Universities: Some Reconsiderations." In *Solomon's House Revisited: The Organization and Institutionalization of Science,* edited by Tore Frängsmyr, 51–64. Canton, Mass.: Watson Publishing International, 1990. (Science History Publications, U.S.A.)

Moses, Ingrid. "Teaching, Research and Scholarship in Different Disciplines." *Higher Education* 19 (1990): 351–375.

Muir, William R. "The Historical Development of the Teacher–Researcher Ideal in Germany and the U.S.A." Paper presented at the Annual Meeting of the Association for the Study of Higher Education, San Diego, Calif. February 1987.

Nagai, Michio. *Higher Education in Japan: Its Take-Off and Crash.* Translated by Jerry Dusenbury. Tokyo: University of Tokyo Press, 1971.

Narin, Francis, and J. Davidson Frame. "The Growth of Japanese Science and Technology." *Science* 245 (August 11, 1989): 600–604.

National Research Council (U.S.). *Learning the R&D System: University Research in Japan and the United States.* Washington, D.C.: National Academy Press, 1989.

———. *The Working Environment for Research in U.S. and Japanese Universities: Contrasts and Commonalities.* Washington, D.C.: National Academy Press, 1989.

National Science Board (U.S.). *Science and Engineering Indicators—1991*. Washington, D.C.: U.S. Government Printing Office, 1991. (NSB 91–1.)

National Science Foundation (U.S.). *Science and Engineering Education for the 1980s and Beyond* Washington, D.C.: NSF, 1981.

———. "Science Resources Studies Highlights." August 25, 1989. Washington, D.C.: NSF, 1989.

Nature. "Opinion: Tokyo's Brave Reform." Vol. 338, March 9, 1989, 100.

Neave, Guy. "Elite and Mass Higher Education in Britain: A Regressive Model?" *Comparative Education Review* 29, no. 3 (1985): 347–361.

———. "France." In *The School and the University: An International Perspective,* edited by Burton R. Clark, 10–44. Berkeley, Los Angeles, and London: University of California Press, 1985.

———. "On Preparing for Markets." *European Journal of Education* 25, no. 2 (1990): 114–116.

———. "On Visions of the Market Place." *Higher Education Quarterly* 45, no. 1 (1991): 25–40.

———. "Séparation de Corps: The Training of Advanced Students and the Organization of Research in France." In *The Research Foundations of Graduate Education: Germany, Britain, France, United States, Japan,* edited by Burton R. Clark, 159–191. Berkeley, Los Angeles, and London: University of California Press, 1993.

———. "On Meat and Poissons: Exceptionalism and Similarity in the French Research Training System." Unpublished paper, 1992.

———. "Utilitarianism by Increment: Disciplinary Differences and Higher Education Reform in France." Unpublished paper.

Neave, Guy, and Richard Edelstein. "The Research Training System in France: A Microstudy of Three Academic Disciplines." In *The Research Foundations of Graduate Education: Germany, Britain, France, United States, Japan,* edited by Burton R. Clark, 192–220. Berkeley, Los Angeles, and London: University of California Press, 1993.

Neave, Guy, and Gary Rhoades. "The Academic Estate in Western Europe." In *The Academic Profession: National, Disciplinary and Institutional Settings,* edited by Burton R. Clark, 211–270. Berkeley, Los Angeles, and London: University of California Press, 1987.

Neumann, Ruth Theresia Rosa. "A Study of the Research Role within Academic Work." Ph.D. dissertation, Macquarie University, 1990.

Olesko, Kathryn M. *Physics as a Calling: Discipline and Practice in the Königsberg Seminar for Physics.* Ithaca: Cornell University Press, 1991.

Oleson, Alexandra, and John Voss, eds. *The Organization of Knowledge in Modern America, 1860–1920.* Baltimore: Johns Hopkins University Press, 1979.

Organisation for Economic Co-operation and Development (OECD). *The Future of University Research.* Paris: OECD, 1981.

———. *Post-Graduate Education in the 1980s.* Paris: OECD, 1987.

———. *Universities Under Scrutiny.* Paris: OECD, 1987.

———. *Financing Higher Education.* Paris: OECD, 1990.

———. *Main Science and Technology Indicators: 1992 (2).* Paris: OECD, 1992.

Palmer, R. R. "The University Idea in the Revolutionary Era." In *The Consortium on Revolutionary Europe, 1750–1850*. 1972 Proceedings, edited by Lee Kennett, 1–17. Gainesville: University of Florida Press, 1972.

———. *The School of the French Revolution*. Princeton: Princeton University Press, 1975.

———. *The Improvement of Humanity: Education and the French Revolution*. Princeton: Princeton University Press, 1985.

Pascarella, Ernest T., and Patrick T. Terenzini. *How College Affects Students: Findings and Insights from Twenty Years of Research*. San Francisco: Jossey-Bass, 1991.

Peisert, Hansgert, and Gerhild Framhein. *Systems of Higher Education: Federal Republic of Germany*. New York: International Council for Educational Development, 1978.

Perkin, Harold. "The Historical Perspective." In *Perspectives on Higher Education: Eight Disciplinary and Comparative Views*, edited by Burton R. Clark, 17–55. Berkeley, Los Angeles, and London: University of California Press, 1984.

———. "The Academic Profession in the United Kingdom." In *The Academic Profession: National, Disciplinary, & Institutional Settings*, edited by Burton R. Clark, 13–59. Berkeley, Los Angeles, and London: University of California Press, 1987.

Portes, Richard. "Economics in Europe." *European Economic Review* 31 (1987): 1329–1340.

Pratt, John, and Tyrell Burgess. *Polytechnics: A Report*. London: Pitman, 1974.

Ringer, Fritz K. *Education and Society in Modern Europe*. Bloomington: Indiana University Press, 1979.

Rohlen, Thomas P. *Japan's High Schools*. Berkeley, Los Angeles, and London: University of California Press, 1983.

Rontopoulou, Jeanne Lamoure, and Jean Lamoure. "French University Education: A Brief Overview, 1984–1987." *European Journal of Education* 23, nos. 1/2 (1988): 37–45.

Rosenzweig, Robert M. "Graduate Education and Its Patrons." Keynote Address, 28th Annual Meeting, and Occasional Paper. Washington, D.C.: Council of Graduate Schools, 1988.

———. "Grant Financing: PI Salaries." *Science* 247 (March 23, 1990): "Letters."

Rosovsky, Henry. *The University: An Owner's Manual*. New York: W. W. Norton, 1990.

Rothblatt, Sheldon. *The Revolution of the Dons: Cambridge and Society in Victorian England*. Cambridge: Cambridge University Press, 1981. (First published by Faber & Faber and Basic Books, 1968.)

———. "The Idea of the Idea of a University and Its Antithesis." Bundoora, Australia: Seminar on the Sociology of Culture, La Trobe University, 1989.

Rowland, Henry A. "A Plea for Pure Science" (an 1883 address to the American Association for the Advancement of Science). In *The Physical Papers of Henry Augustus Rowland*, 593–619. Baltimore: Johns Hopkins University Press, 1902.

Rudd, E. *The Highest Education*. London: Routledge and Kegan Paul, 1975.

Saline, George H. "The Two Democratic Traditions." *Philosophical Review* 61 (October 1952): 451–474.

Scaff, Lawrence A. *Fleeing the Iron Cage: Culture, Politics, and Modernity in the Thought of Max Weber.* Berkeley, Los Angeles, and London: University of California Press, 1989.

Science. "News and Comment: Japan Faces Big Task in Improving Basic Science," vol. 243, March 10, 1989, 1285–1287.

Scott, Peter. *The Crisis of the University.* London: Croom Helm, 1984.

———. "Knowledge's Outer Shape, Inner Life." *Times Higher Education Supplement* (August 16, 1991): 12.

———. "Anachronistic Elites." *Times Higher Education Supplement,* 1992.

Seibold, E. "Funding of Research in Germany." *Science and Public Affairs* 4 (1989): 21–30.

Selvaratnam, Viswanathan. *Innovations in Higher Education: Singapore at the Competitive Edge.* Washington, D.C.: World Bank, March 10, 1992. (Background paper, Education and Employment Division, Population and Human Resources Department.)

Shattock, M. L. "The UGC and Standards," In *Standards and Criteria in Higher Education,* edited by Graeme Moodie, 46–64. At the University, Guildford, Surrey: Society for Research into Higher Education, 1986.

Shinn, T. "How French Universities Became What They Are." *Minerva* XXIII, no. 1 (Spring 1985), 159–165.

———."Specialized Institutions: *Grandes Ecoles.*" In *The Encyclopedia of Higher Education,* edited by Burton R. Clark and Guy Neave. Vol. 2, *Analytical Perspectives,* 1225–1229. Oxford: Pergamon Press, 1992.

Simpson, Renate. *How the Ph.D. Came to Britain: A Century of Struggle for Postgraduate Education.* At the University, Guildford, Surrey: Society for Research into Higher Education, 1983.

Smith, Bruce L. R., ed. *The State of Graduate Education.* Washington, D.C.: Brookings Institution, 1985.

Smith, Bruce L. R., and Joseph J. Karlesky. *The State of Academic Science: The Universities in the Nation's Research Effort.* New York: Change Magazine Press, 1977.

Smith, Robert J. *The École Normale Supérieure and the Third Republic.* Albany: State University of New York Press, 1982.

Spurr, Stephen H. *Academic Degree Structures: Innovative Approaches.* New York: McGraw-Hill, 1970.

Squires, Geoffrey. *First Degree: The Undergraduate Curriculum.* Buckingham: Society for Research into Higher Education, 1990.

Stewart, W. A. C. *Higher Education in Postwar Britain.* London: Macmillan, 1989.

Storr, Richard J. *The Beginning of the Future: A Historical Approach to Graduate Education in the Arts and Science.* New York: McGraw-Hill, 1973.

Suleiman, Ezra N. *Elites in French Society: The Politics of Survival.* Princeton: Princeton University Press, 1978.

Taxell, Christoffer. "Higher Education System and Higher Education Policy in Finland." Paper presented at conference "Policy Change in Higher Education," Univiersity of Turku, Turku, Finland, June 1990.

Teichler, Ulrich. "The Federal Republic of Germany." In *The School and the University: An International Perspective*, edited by Burton R. Clark, 45–76. Berkeley, Los Angeles, and London: University of California Press, 1985.

———. *Changing Patterns of the Higher Education System: The Experience of Three Decades*. London: Jessica Kingsley Publishers, 1988.

———. *The First Years of Study at Fachhochschulen and Universities in the Federal Republic of Germany*. Kassel: Wissenschaftliches Zentrum für Berufs- und Hochschulforschung der Gesamthochschule, 1990.

Times Higher Education Supplement, July 29, 1988.

Thulstrup, Eric W. *Improving the Quality of Research in Developing Country Universities*. Washington, D.C.: World Bank, January 11, 1992. (Background paper, Education and Employment Division, Population and Human Resources Department.)

Trow, Martin A. "Problems in the Transition from Elite to Mass Higher Education." In *Policies for Higher Education*, 51–101. Paris: OECD, 1974.

———. "The Analysis of Status." In *Perspectives on Higher Education: Eight Disciplinary and Comparative Views*, edited by Burton R. Clark, 132–164. Berkeley, Los Angeles, and London: University of California Press, 1984.

———. "Academic Standards and Mass Higher Education." *Higher Education Quaterly* 41, no. 3 (1987): 268–291.

Turner, Henry Ashby, Jr. *The Two Germanies Since 1945*. New Haven: Yale University Press, 1987.

Turner, R. Steven. "The Growth of Professorial Research in Prussia, 1818 to 1848—Causes and Consequences." *Historical Studies in the Physical Sciences*. 3 (1971): 137–182.

———. "University Reformers and Professorial Scholarship in Germany 1760–1806." In *The University in Society*. Vol. 2. *Europe, Scotland, and the United States from the 16th to the 20th Century*, edited by Lawrence Stone, 495–531. Princeton: Princeton University Press, 1974.

Umakoshi, Toru. "Korean Higher Education from a Japanese Perspective." In *Development of Higher Education in Korea and Japan*, 63–73. Seoul: Korean Council for University Education, 1985.

U.S. Congress, Office of Technology Assessment (OTA). *Educating Scientists and Engineers: Grade School to Grad School*. OTA-SET-377. Washington, D.C.: U.S. Government Printing Office, 1988.

Ushiogi, Morikazu. "Graduate Education and Research Organization in Japan." In *The Research Foundations of Graduate Education: Germany, Britain, France, United States, Japan*, edited by Burton R. Clark, 299–325. Berkeley, Los Angeles, and London: University of California Press, 1993.

Van de Graaff, John H. "Federal Republic of Germany." In *Academic Power: Patterns of Authority in Seven National Systems of Higher Education*, edited by John H. Van de Graaff, Burton R. Clark, Dorotea Furth, Dietrich Goldschmidt, and Donald F. Wheeler, 15–36. New York: Praeger, 1978.

Van de Graaff, John H., and Dorotea Furth. "France." In *Academic Power: Patterns of Authority in Seven National Systems of Higher Education*, edited by John H. Van de Graaff, Burton R. Clark, Dorotea Furth, Dietrich Goldschmidt, and Donald F. Wheeler, 49–66. New York: Praeger, 1978.

Veysey, Laurence R. *The Emergence of the American University*. Chicago: University of Chicago Press, 1965.

Weber, Max. *From Max Weber: Essays in Sociology*. Translated by H. H. Gerth and C. Wright Mills. New York: Oxford University Press, 1946.

Weick, Karl E. "Contradictions in a Community of Scholars: The Cohesion-Accuracy Tradeoff." *Review of Higher Education* 6, no. 4 (1983): 253–267.

Weisz, George. *The Emergence of Modern Universities in France, 1863–1914*. Princeton: Princeton University Press, 1982.

Williams, Bruce. *University Responses to Research Selectivity*. London: Center for Higher Education Studies, Institute of Education, University of London, 1991.

Williams, Gareth, and Tessa Blackstone. *Response to Adversity: Higher Education in a Harsh Climate*. SRHE Leverhulme 10. At the University, Guildford, Surrey: Society for Research into Higher Education, 1983.

Wolfle, Dael. *The Home of Science: The Role of the University*. New York: McGraw-Hill, 1972.

Zuckerman, Harriet. *Scientific Elite: Nobel Laureates in the United States*. New York: Free Press, 1977.

Index

Advisory Board for Research Councils (ABRC), 76, 88
Advisory Council on Science and Technology (ACOST), 76
Allen, G. C., 175
Althoff, Friedrich, 31
American Council of Learned Societies, 127
Amsterdamska, Olga, 199, 265 n.46
Ashby, Lord Eric, 63
Association of American Universities (AAU), 123, 152

Beauchamp, Edward R., 182
Becher, Tony, 81, 82, 83–84, 236
Ben-David, Joseph, 3, 86, 211, 215, 248
Berdahl, Robert, 63, 64
Berlin Doctrine of 1810, 22
Bernstein, Richard, 102
Bertilsson, Margareta, 22, 23
Bienaymé, Alain, 97–98
Bildung, 22, 25, 27, 29
Blackstone, Tessa, 79, 80
Block, Hans-Jürgen, 44
Blume, Stuart, 199, 265 n.46

Carnegie Commission Catalog Study, 148
Carnegie Foundation, classification of institutions, 139–141
Carnegie Institute of Washington, 125, 127
Cazanave, P., 96
CNRS (National Center for Scientific Research), 9, 89, 106–108, 112–114 passim

Colleges of Advanced Technology (CAT), 66
Committee of Vice-Chancellors and Principals (CVCP), 69
Council for National Academic Awards (CNAA), 62
Council of Graduate Schools (CSG), 123
Crozier, Michel, 100

Department of Education and Science (DES), 63, 64, 67, 75, 76
Dore, Ronald P., 162, 177, 178

Ecole national d'administration (Ena), 102–103
Ecole polytechnique, 103
Eustace, Rowland, 62, 70

Fachhochschule, 40, 41, 201, 214
Faculty salaries, state subsidy of, in United States, 135–136
Fascist period, 37, 38
Fleck, Ludwik, 236
Fragmenting forces in the higher education system, 189–210; governmental interests in teaching and research drift, 202–207; industry interests and its national variations, 207–210; negotiation of the research-teaching-study nexus, 209–210; research and teaching drift and their national variations, 193–202
Frame, J., Davidson, 180
Fraunhofer Society, 47
Friedberg, Erhard, 101
Furth, Dorothea, 97, 98–99

Gardner, David, 228
Garvin, David A., 228
Geiger, Roger, 92, 126, 242
Gellert, Claudius, 44–45, 46
German Research Society, 48
Gesamthochschulen, 41
Giessen, University of, 24–26, 27, 30
Goldberg, Pierre, 95
Graduate education in the United States: cross-subsidization of, 150, 152; departmental structure in, 122–124 passim, 146–155; disciplinary differences in, 144–146; extensive course work in, 147–149, 157–158; as the graduate department university system, 155–158; institutional differentiation in, 139–155, 225; student enrollment in, 150, 151
Grandes écoles, 9, 89, 91, 92, 100, 101, 102, 109–110, 204
Guin, Jacques, 112

Harrold, Ross, 229
Henkel, Mary, 74–75
Heyck, Thomas, 60
Higher education in Finland, 219
Higher education in the Federal Republic of Germany, 7–8, 19–55; academic competition in, 30–32, 49; disciplinary specialization in, 23–24, 26; diversification of an institute system, 46–50; doctoral training in, 43–44, 49–50; *fachhochschulen* in, 40, 41; Fascist period in, 37–38; fragmenting forces in, 37, 49, 189,195, 201, 206, 208; funding of, 47–49; graduate school differentiation in, 225–226; industry and national government involvement in, 31, 33–34, 51–52; as the institute system, 50–55; institutes (*see* Institute System [Germany]); institutional differentiation in, 40, 41, 201, 214; integrating factors in, 30, 214, 217, 219, 225–226; lines of change in, 55; mass enrollments in, 8, 32–33, 40–46, 52, 53, 189; nonuniversity research in, 34–35, 37, 46, 49, 51–52; philanthropy in, 36–37; politicization of, 41; research and teaching drift in, 37, 49, 195, 201, 206, 208; research university differentiation in, 214; single-tier structure of, 42, 43–44, 49, 53–54; student expansion in, 32–33, 52; system conditions in, 30–37; teaching-research laboratories and seminars in, 17, 24–30, 50–51, 52; twentieth-century issues in, 8, 37–50
Higher education in France, 9–10, 89–

115, 190; as the academy university, 92, 112–115; degrees in, 92, 103–104; differentiation of research universities in, 214, 217; doctoral studies in, 108–112; education ministers in, 94, 99; evolution of a nationalized system, 91–101, 106, 107; fragmenting forces in, 195, 201; governmental interests in, 204; graduate school differentiation in, 225–226; industry interests in, 208–209; integrating forces in, 214, 217–218; lines of centralization in, 95–97; mass enrollments in, 10, 101–104, 113–114, 190, 201, 230; modern complex of universities and research centers in, 101–112; Orientation Act of 1968, 98; primacy of CNRS in, 106–108; reforms in, 94, 98, 99, 104, 110, 111; research drift in, 195; research training in, 104; restructuring in, 104–106; teaching drift in, 201
Higher education in Great Britain, 9, 56–88; academic research in, 74–78, 85; binary principle in, 66, 67, 70, 201; as the collegiate university, 63, 68, 84–88; departmental structures in, 59, 79, 80, 81, 82–83, 87; differentiation of research universities in, 214; exclusive base of, 57–61, 84; fragmentation of, 195, 201, 204–205, 208; funding of, 60–61, 64–65, 70–78, 82; governmental interests in, 204–205; graduate school differentiation in, 226; industrial interests in, 208; integration of an academic research system in, 74–78, 214–218; nationalization of, 61–74, 85; nonuniversity sector in, 62, 66, 67, 70, 76, 85; polytechnics in, 66–67, 85, 201, 214; quality emphasis in, 56–57, 61, 69–70, 78–86; research and doctoral training in, 57, 61, 74–75, 78–85, 86, 88; research drift in, 195; small size of institutions in, 60, 61, 68, 81, 87, 230; teaching drift in, 201; teaching-research-study nexus in, 86–88
Higher education in Japan, 11–12, 159–185, 190, 191; as the applied university, 179–185; bureaucratic funding base of, 167–171, 184; chairs in, 167–170; constraints on graduate education in, 159–167, 170; differentiation of research universities in, 213–214; disciplinary differences in, 171–179; doctorates in, 159, 161, 163–167 passim, 171–172, 174–178 passim, 180–181; effect of small scale on, 230; foreign-study students in, 161–162, 182, 184; fragmenting forces in, 196,

200–201, 205–206; government interests in, 205–206; graduate enrollments in, 165–166, 184; industry connections to, 175–178, 181, 182–184, 185; integrating factors in, 213, 214; mass enrollments in, 166, 167, 200–201, 205, 226; master's degree in engineering and, 175–178, 180–181, 191; National Ministry of Education, 160, 163, 167–171, 178–179; private sectors of, 166–167; proliferation of graduate schools in, 167; reforms in, 182–185; research drift in, 196; teaching drift in, 200–201; technology vs. science in, 178–179

Higher education in Scotland, nineteenth-century professorial system in, 58–59

Higher education in the United States, 10–11, 116–187; competitiveness of, 218; cross-subsidy funding in, 226–228; differentiation of research universities in, 213; early two-tier arrangements in, 3, 120–122; emergence of the vertical university in, 118–124; first academic revolution in, 117–118, 124, 155; fragmenting forces in, 196, 200, 206, 208; as the graduate department university system, 155–188; graduate education in (see Graduate education in the United States); ideology of unity in, 220; industry sponsorship of, 132, 156; institutional embodiment of research in, 131–139; integrative funding of, 223; mass enrollments in, 128–129, 190, 200–201; national governmental funding in, 128–131, 152, 156; private patron funding in, 124–128; problems in, 152–155; research drift in, 196; second academic revolution in, 118; state funding of, 132–135; state research universities in, 133–134; teaching drift in, 206, 208; third academic revolution in, 118, 128–131; voluntary convergence and standardization in, 123–124

Holmes, Frederick L., 24–25

Huber, Ludwig, 44

Humboldtian doctrine, 1–4, 13, 15, 212, 219–222; formulation and founding fathers of, 19, 20, 50; institutional definition of, 21–37; operational tools of, 24–30; system conditions in, 30–37; vicissitudes of, 19–55

Industrial research and development (R&D), 13, 47, 207, 209; in Germany, 208; in Great Britain, 208; in Japan,

179–180, 208; in the United States, 135, 136–137, 208

Inquiry model of higher education systems, 14–15, 240–252; centrality of, 241–245; compatibility of teaching and research in, 249–252; complexity and contradictions of, 245–249

Institute for Scientific Information, 263 n.2

Institute System (Germany), 195; chair-institute relationship, 28–29, 39–40, 51; diversification of, 46–50; institute-minister link, 32; institute university concept, 50–55

Institutes of technology (IUT), 89, 113, 201

Integrating forces in the higher education system, 13–14, 192, 211–239; comprehensiveness, 231; cross-subsidization, 226–229; departments and research groups, 234–237; differentiation of research universities, 213–215; enabling conditions in national systems, 212–219; enacting conditions, 232–237; formative conditions, 224–232; funding, 220–224; graduate school differentiation, 225–226; ideology of unity, 219–220; reputation, 215–219, 228; research-teaching-study nexus, 12, 13, 237–239; tangible and tacit knowledge, 232–234; university competitiveness, 231

Irvine, John, 210, 263 n.2

Isard, Phoebe, 210, 263 n.2

James, Estelle, 227

Johns Hopkins University, 120, 121

Jungnickel, Christa, 54

Kaiser-Wilhelm-Gesellschaft, 34, 37, 46. See also Max-Planck Society for the Advancement of the Sciences

Kawashima, Tatsuo, 171, 173

Kerr, Clark, 215

Kinmouth, E. H., 177

Kogan, Maurice, 74–75

Königsberg Seminar, 127

Lehrfreiheit and Lernfreiheit, 21, 23, 26, 82

Leverhulme Study, 79

Liebig, Justice, 24–27 passim

McClelland, Charles E., 28, 30–31

McCormmach, Russell, 54

Martin, Ben R., 210, 263 n.2

Maruyama, Fumihuro, 171, 173

Max-Planck Society for the Advancement of the Sciences, 34, 46, 54, 195

Metzger, Walter, 263 n.3
Mommsen, Wolfgang J., 28
Moodie, Graeme, 62
Morrell, J. B., 26
Muir, William, 22
Musselin, Christine, 101

Narin, Francis, 180
National Advisory Board for Local Authority Higher Education (NAB), 67, 76
National Aeronautics and Space Administration (NASA), 130
National Institutes of Health (NIH), 129
National Research Council, 127
National Science Foundation (NSF), 129, 176
Neave, Guy, 99, 104, 106, 112
Neumann, Franz, 27
Neumann, Ruth, 232–233, 253 n.3
1976 Framework Law, 40

OECD (Organisation for Economic Co-operation and Development), 1987 report on postgraduate education, 199
Olesko, Kathryn, 26, 29
Orientation Act of 1968 (France), 98
Oxford and Cambridge, 56–61, 81, 84, 85, 87

Palmer, Robert, 93, 217
Perkin, Harold, 63
Philanthropy, role of, in research funding, 36–37, 48–49
Polytechnics, 201, 214. See also Institutes of technology

Redbrick universities, 59
R&D. See Industrial research and development (R&D)
Research drift, 193–197, 209–210; governmental and industrial interests in, 202–209
Research literature output, 137–139, 263 n.2
Robbins Report of 1963, 65, 79–80

Rockefeller Institute for Medical Research, 125–127
Rosenzweig, Robert, 152, 220
Rosovsky, Henry, 139
Rubinger, Richard B., 182
Ryūgakusei. See Higher education in Japan, foreign-study students in

Sako, Mari, 162, 177, 178
Scott, Peter, 87–88, 247
Shattock, Michael, 66
Shinn, T., 93, 94
Social Science Research Council, 127
Sorbonne. See University of Paris
Storr, Richard, 121
Student development research, 241–242, 265 n.3
Suleiman, Ezra N., 100

Teaching drift, 197–202, 209–210; governmental and industrial interests in, 202–209
Technische Hochschulen, 34
Turner, Henry, 37

University Funding Council (UFC), 62, 71, 76, 77
University Grants Committee (UGC), 61–67 passim, 74, 76, 77, 222
University of London, 59, 62, 88
University of Paris, 91, 98, 102, 105, 230
University of Sussex, 68
University of Tokyo, 160, 167, 178, 179
University of Warwick, 70, 88
Ushiogi, Morikazu, 163

Van de Graaff, John, 97, 98
Von Bismarck, Otto, 23, 30

Weber, Max, 256 n.81
Weick, Karl E., 235
Weimar Republic, 37–39 passim
Williams, Bruce, 74
Williams, Gareth, 79, 80
Wissenschaft, 22, 27, 29, 217

Zloczower, Abraham, 215
Zuckerman, Harriet, 233–234

Designer: U.C. Press Staff
Compositor: Asco Trade Typesetting Ltd.
Text: 10/13 Sabon
Display: Sabon
Printer & Binder: Edwards Brothers, Inc.